AND SPEAKING OF
SCORPIONS. . .

THE AUTOBIOGRAPHY OF
HERMAN "ZE GERMAN" RAREBELL

WITH

MICHAEL KRIKORIAN

ISBN: 1463601107
ISBN-13: 9781463601102

ABOUT THE AUTHORS

Herman Rarebell- Known and loved around the world as one of the original members of the greatest German rock band of all time, the Scorpions, as history shows, he was arguably the catalyst behind the band's string of successful albums in the late 1970's and 1980's. Along with his duties as the drummer for the legendary group during their "heyday", he also authored many of their biggest hits. AOR staples like "Rock You Like A Hurricane", "Make It Real", "Passion Rules the Game", "Bad Boys Running Wild", "Another Piece of Meat", "Dynamite", "He's a Woman... She's a Man" and "Blackout" to name but a few, all have a home on his résumé.

Herman's list of accomplishments beyond the band is also quite extensive. Upon departing in the mid-1990's, he went on to head up Monaco Records, which he co-owned with his good friend, His Highness Prince Albert of Monaco. He is currently still active in music playing with a variety of artists in the studio and on the road as well as producing new material with his own band Herman Ze German and Friends. His latest album is titled *Take It As It Comes*. (Available on his website www.hermanrarebell.com as well as most online outlets.)

Michael Krikorian- Michael is best known as the head of the Rock and Roll Remembers Foundation (www.rockandrollremembers.org) that was founded to aid those within the rock and roll community who fall on hard times. A long-time writer for various newspapers, magazines and on line outlets like his current column for Examiner.com where he is the San Francisco Rock Music Examiner, he is also known as the creative force behind the hilarious novelty music artist/CD, "Armen, the Armenian Deli Man". He currently has one other book on the market, *Tomorrow Will Be Yesterday-The Story of BASH*, which is the "true" story of a "fictional" rock and roll band from the 1970's. (The book and accompanying soundtrack music CD are both available on most online outlets.) Krikorianmichael@yahoo.com

DEDICATION

I dedicate this to all of you who are reading this dedication. My life has always been about entertaining you in the hopes of bringing you happiness and joy. And so within these pages you will find your book. It is meant as my personal thank you for your allowing me to forever be a part of your life.

FOREWORD

By: Dieter Dierks (The Sixth Scorpion)
Scorpions Producer 1975-1988

Having already read what you are about to read and having lived so much of that which is included within this book, I can say in all honesty, Herman should never quit his day job!

Seriously, though, those years now seem like they were part of some far-off wonderland to me. However, as I read the retrospective done by Herman within the pages of this book, I was given a wonderful gift of remembrances. I have had the honor of working with a lot of great artists from all around the world, and yet those years working with the Scorpions will forever remain some of the fondest memories I am sure I will ever have. Herman Rarebell was a big part of that.

More than just a drummer, Herman was an integral part in the development of that which eventually became known as the classic Scorpions sound. Music starts with the drummer. Not many people realize this. However, if you look at the "success" of the group, or, perhaps more appropriately, the lack thereof, prior to the arrival of Herman "Ze German" as well as that which has eluded them since his departure, I think you can see exactly how pivotal his role was within the band.

The stories told within these pages are more than just the overtly glamorized pulp fiction that is a staple of these sorts of memoirs. Though many will surely cast aside autobiographies like this as little more than just tawdry and garish accounts of unrestrained sexual behavior and over-indulgence in the drug inspired counter-culture of the day for purposes attracting attention, Herman doesn't stoop to that kind of sensationalized cliché. His preference is that of telling it like it really was, and he captures the true essence and spirit of the band as well as that of the now bygone era. Thankfully, he doesn't try to sugarcoat any of it, and, more importantly, he hasn't opted to take out any of his old spandex from its mothball-laced tomb. The latter would not be a pretty picture. And so, in the end, what you have is the all too true story of not only a man who openly admits to having had more than his share of ups and downs, but also one who is not afraid to speak his mind. He has been able to weather many storms and overcome his afflictions and addictions. He openly confesses to his weaknesses while making no attempt to justify his behavior. He pulls no punches in mercilessly lambasting himself and his choices. Rather than trying to find an appropriate scapegoat, he prefers to spend his life looking beyond yesterday to tomorrow. This is the part of the man that is so very refreshing and endearing. It is the reason, to this day, I still consider him a very good friend.

However, there is much more here than just Herman's story. Not to be overlooked or marginalized in the least is the story of an incredible group of musicians. The Scorpions was a band that wasn't supposed to be successful, and had no chance of "making it". They were cast aside and ridiculed as dreamers, even laughed at by those supposedly "in the know" when they said they wanted to go to America. But they were not deterred or even mildly intimidated. They believed in themselves, and together they rose to arguably unparalleled greatness in the world of rock and roll music. This is truly the definitive history of the Scorpions. That, in itself, is a story well worth the price of admission.

And not to be forgotten is the storyteller himself. Herman's lighthearted and at times self-deprecating sense of humor adds so much to this book that I am certain even those who may never have even heard of the Scorpions will find this piece of literature entertaining and fun.

I am so very proud to have been asked to write this brief prelude for this book, and even more honored that I am considered the "sixth Scorpion" because so much of the work I am given to do is forgotten the moment a band leaves the studio. I am not one who wishes to trumpet my own successes as so many others in my line of work will do, so as I read the wonderful things Herman had to say about me I was honestly touched quite deeply. As such, this is an honor to be sure, and I'm so very pleased to say to all of you this book is not a book about a man or even a band so much as it is an unabashed celebration life and living. To those of you who do not know Herman Rarebell I will say be ready for an introduction into the times and thoughts of one of the true gentlemen of this industry not to mention one of the great musicians of his generation.

Enjoy.
Dieter

DISCLAIMER  (Well, sort of...)

<u>Warning!</u>

The following is meant for entertainment purposes only!
Leave your troubles and worries outside the covers. There is nothing inside here
but fun. So please don't look for anything else!
Welcome to the world of the Scorpions!

Herman

P.S.- Unless otherwise noted, all puns are intended.

1
THE WIND OF CHANGE

The summer of 1989… Perhaps that seems like an odd place to start. Yet given the rite of passage that came as a result of our musical endeavors, and the immense opportunity placed at our doorstep by the controlling powers, such as they were, I am sure many of you will agree that it may well be the perfect place to begin our journey through the history of one of rock and roll's most improbable stories. I am proud to say I was part of it, and together over the next few hundred pages we'll relive the triumphs over adversity, the construction of a legacy and, thankfully, even the death of disco! The latter may be one of the greatest thrills any of us ever had! But as Jerry Garcia so lucidly wrote in the Grateful Dead classic, "Truckin'", "What a long, strange trip it's been…" Or more appropriately, what a long, strange trip it was. We truly defied the odds and did the impossible. We overcame the naysayers and the pundits, not to mention the persistent political obstacles and industry-wide roadblocks, to do what the so-called experts said would be out of the question. No one opened any doors for us when we knocked. We had to kick them down to get attention all by ourselves. We grew together. We fought like siblings. We shared the life of nomads. We did it not so much for ourselves but for you, our fans. Ultimately, no band can endure for as many years as we did if their motive is selfishly derived from anything other than the pleasure of the fans.

And so, appropriately, we begin at the outset of what would eventually become part of a new beginning for millions of people around the world. Having been raised in postwar West Germany as I was, the sense of yesteryear was undoubtedly never stronger than it was for those of us who were exposed to the omnipresent and omnipotent monument that was conceived, constructed and consecrated for the sole purpose of being the definitive symbol of oppression as well as a stark reminder of the difference between east and west, the "Berlin Wall". Recalling the words and thoughts of the former and quite popular U.S. President Ronald Reagan who referred to it as "The Evil Empire", you can only imagine how I felt as our plane began its descent into Sheremetyevo Airport on the outskirts of Moscow, U.S.S.R.

Though we had played within the borders of the Soviet Union the previous year in the city of Leningrad, which today is St. Petersburg, it seemed like it was part of a dream and had since blurred together with so many of our earlier destinations as well as those that came in between. It was still Russia, and yet it didn't seem the same to me. There was actually a bit of a "western" feel to the city, if you can believe that. We had never seen pictures of the Hermitage or St. Isaac's Cathedral or other significant historical landmarks within the city. As such, we really didn't specifically associate them with Russia. It was quite a contrast from the country's modern-day capital city that we had all seen time and again in newsreel footage as well as on television. And my feelings were actually warranted, as we would discover, because Moscow was quite a different city, to say the least — much more in line with our original expectations.

To be honest, the atmosphere on board the plane was pensive and a wee bit tense given the circumstances surrounding our belated arrival. We were all quite able to remember the reasons for the hastily contrived amendment to our schedule in 1988. We were booked to play in Moscow at that time, but we were prohibited from performing

2

there for what could only be termed "political reasons". Being only the second western hard rock group to perform in the Russian capital, the first being Uriah Heep, we were anxious to find out what awaited us. Would it be a replay of our shows to the north where the audiences were quite responsive and genuinely glad to see us? Or would there be the expected turmoil that altered the schedule on our aborted visit?

As I looked out the window at all that was below, so many thoughts came to mind. I wondered how it was that I was about to land in a place that had been for so many years locked behind a metaphoric shroud of steel. I also pondered the thoughts that must have been in the minds of at least a few of our fellow countrymen who most assuredly had to consider us traitors of one sort or another. That was justifiable even if unfair from our point of view. We weren't trying to make a statement. We weren't treasonously acting against our own people. We were simply trying to give something back to our fans that just happened to live inside the Soviet Union. Was that their fault? Were they all resolute in their hatred of the west and all that it stood for?

As the plane went in and out of the clouds on its final approach, I continually found myself looking anxiously for some familiar site like the Kremlin or Red Square. I did not realize at the time that both were more than 20 miles to the east of the airport runway. And so from my vantage point, as I looked below, I could only see what appeared to be a smattering of small homes not so different from those in my own country. How could it be, I thought, that people who not only represented the enemy for so many years but also dominated pairs figure skating with the help of the "puppet" judges from the "Eastern Block", could possibly live in a manner that was not so different from myself? Yes, it was 1989 and perestroika was in full bloom. Yet, it wasn't so many years earlier that the look of the Soviet landscape seemed so much more menacing and ominous. However, as I thought about it, I realized that our world, the one within which I lived, was not about politics but one of entertainment. Music was not a divisive element but one of unity. Though they could lock away the people, they could not lock up the airwaves.

As I said, we were hardly the first western musicians to "invade" Soviet sovereignty. Nor were we probably even the first group of Germans since the Third Reich "goose-stepped" toward the Volga. I'm sure there had to have been some polka bands "umpah, pahing" their way into the hearts (Though heartburn might be more appropriate...) of the faithful. We were but the latest and definitely the first rock band of any kind from West Germany. And yet as our plane came to rest on the tarmac and began to taxi toward the terminal, I looked around at the Cyrillic letters that graced every building and knew how Dorothy felt when she entered the Land of Oz. Though we saw the same thing in Leningrad, for some reason it just struck me as being quite different. I suddenly understood better the frustrations of those who are not literate in their own language as I saw words that should have meaning and did to those of the proper lineage. But to me, none of it meant a thing.

Certainly there are those of you out there right now reading this saying to yourself, "Aw, come on Herman, what is this crap? We want to read about all the babes on the road in '85. By 1989 you had already passed those years." Well to them I can say that which I'm certain most doctors utter countless times a day... "No, I'm sorry, I don't take American Express." No, that's not it. They leave that sort of thing to the good-looking broads working out front. Oops... Sorry... I slipped. I meant to say lovely young maidens manning the reception desk. I forgot. I'm writing in English. This means I'm forced to be politically correct since most of the English speaking, and for that matter, reading countries tend to subscribe to such hogwash. So I shouldn't make any sexist remarks. Well, actually, if I'm going to refrain from that, pretty much the rest of this book is going to be kind of boring since so much of what we were about as a band, or at least that which we were accused of whether or not it was true (I can tell you, it wasn't our goal.), "unintentionally" leaned quite heavily on the hedonistic foot pedal. Those of you who have seen our album covers or taken time to learn any of the lyrics to the majority of our songs will surely understand. (Honestly, we never really intended for our work to be considered or interpreted that way. However, it's always nice to be considered regardless of the framework for the consideration.) For those of you who haven't, I can only wonder why you're reading this book. I'm not complaining, mind you… Just curious.

I do want to say a few words here about political correctness, if I can, since the issue will come up time and again within this book. I think it's important to offer clarification of my personal position on this subject. Anyone familiar with the Scorpions is surely able to understand why I say this. I really am amazed at this concept, and how it has evolved over the past couple of decades – not really amazed so much as shocked. To me, it is nothing more than just another way of making money by hurting other people. People have obviously discovered there's money to be made by being "sensitive". I guess it's nothing more than a sign of the times. When I was young people used to say, "Sticks and stones may break my bones, but names will never hurt me…" (Okay, so they didn't say that exactly, but they did say the German equivalent.) Today, however, sticks and stones are far less offensive to people than words. There is no money in it! (Unless, of course, you manufacture sticks or stones…) This is offensive to me. (It's probably offensive to the sticks and stones people, too, since I'm certain many have been driven out of business by political correctness.) (By the way, I still play with sticks, of course, and I have at times in my life, been "stoned". But I don't think that's the same thing.)

Anyway, getting back to the point, if, in fact, I was actually trying to make a point prior to stepping up to my bully pulpit. I really didn't want to start spewing philosophies so early, but I just couldn't help it. The subject is one that I find quite personal for a variety of reasons. So getting my opinion out in the open early I feel is going to help you understand the rest of this book. I will tell right here and now, nothing within this book is written in an effort to hurt anyone. It's all meant for fun. So please, take it all in the spirit with which it is offered.

You have to admit, well, actually you don't have to, but I hope you will, I was fairly well-behaved for the first couple of pages. Bet you thought I was going to write a normal, dry, dull book about the events of my life within the Scorpions, huh? Well, I really can't do that to you. (I couldn't do that to anyone.) I mean how interesting would it be to read, "And then we went to Omaha, Nebraska. And then we played in Helsinki, Finland. And then we did a concert in Tokyo…" (Some routing, huh? Don't laugh. There are bookers who actually put schedules like that together. I suspect they also have very lucrative life insurance policies on each member of the band…) I think books like that are meant as sleep aids – a lot like the local penal code I'm sure. And in truth, such books really don't tell you much about who the person truly is. In fact, I don't think the penal code would tell you anything about me. So I prefer to be myself and have some fun while telling you the story of the band. I hope you don't mind.

Nevertheless, I was going to say to those of you who want me to immediately jump into the middle of the waterbed as so many books of this nature do, let me be doctor while you be patient. (I know, that was about as clever as an umbrella in a blizzard.) I promise, we will get to everything in due time. Okay so maybe this book isn't going to rival anything by Twain or Pushkin, but in the end, I think you're going to enjoy the ride we're on together because honestly it was a lot of fun and, yes, we will go through it all.

Oh, who is Pushkin, right? All right, so some of you might be wondering who the hell Twain is, as well. For the latter group, I am not sure I can help you. (Not sure anyone can.) But for those who are curious, perhaps as many as six of you, Alexander Pushkin was a 19th century Russian author and in the opinion of many literary scholars, the greatest of all Russian writers. So what is he doing in a book written by a German who is currently living in England? Well, aside from being renowned as one of the great philanderers of his time, behavior we often inadvertently emulated ourselves, he was a Russian, as I mentioned, and that's where we were in 1989. Remember?

Of course, as famous as he is within his own country, as legend has it, and as I understand it, even the great Pushkin may be dwarfed in repute by an alleged 20th Century Soviet diagnostician, Dr. Vladimir Ternyerhedenkov. (Remember, the Soviet Union developed their own version of history during the Cold War...) The story as I have heard it is, even though he never won any sort of award or acclaim for his accomplishment from his colleagues within the field of medicine or even that of those toiling within the halls of academia who to this day supposedly refer to his "discovery" as "an embarrassing fluke", nonetheless, there is nary a doctor on either side of the Atlantic that does not utilize the Ternyerhedenkov method for diagnosing hernia. I know my doctor does. So I can personally attest to this. And I doubt there is a patient anywhere in the world that doesn't hear the name Ternyerhedenkov during a physical examination.

At any rate, although the side notes might be more entertaining, let's get back to the story in order to allow me to meander in other directions. Now as history shows, certifiable history, by that time, the summer of 1989, the Scorpions had travelled just about around the world. (I'm sure right now there is someone reading that who has jumped on his computer to tally up the actual amount of the world we had covered by 1989 to see if I'm telling the truth. He's probably saying, "Hey, you didn't go to Antarctica!")(It's probably the same guy who is checking to find out who Dr. Ternyerhedenkov is...) However, on that trip there were still many new emotions spawned and sparked by the grandeur of the experience. We were in a place we'd only read about. A place that I personally never once ever thought I would visit let alone be welcomed into as a visiting celebrity. We were not political in the least, nor were our songs until that day. Though most of us grew up listening to and playing protest songs about the war in Viet Nam, even if we didn't know what all the words meant at the time, we were not inspired to do the same with our talents. I will admit that I personally have always been quite conscious of events within the world and all that goes on around me. But that's about as far as it has ever gone. And yet as innocent and naïve as we may have been as we disembarked and entered the small, unpretentious terminal that was the gateway to communism, we all felt something. There was definitely a "Wind of Change" in the air, and there was no denying that we were standing in the midst of history once again.

As I briefly mentioned, we were originally scheduled to play there in the spring of 1988 – late April through early May to be exact. But those dates were cancelled because of concerns over rioting and public drunkenness during the important holiday celebration on May 1, officially dubbed the holiday of labor. As I came to learn, Russians rarely needed a reason to drink vodka just as Germans don't need much inspiration to down a beer or two. Most would toast a crack in the sidewalk or put a crack in the sidewalk to toast. So on holidays, you can imagine the atmosphere was much more volatile. I suspect the local authorities at the time just didn't want to risk an onslaught of negative publicity should westerners experience or see anything that didn't paint their country in the best of colors. (As if we had never seen any drunks before. Hell, we all knew the British rock band UFO's bass player, Pete Way.) (Ha Ha!!! Take that you bloody Limey bastard!) (It's a good thing he's a friend... Or at least he was before that comment.)

And so it was that we returned in the summer of '89, only a handful of months before true history were to be made. No not history like a bunch of Germans with guitars playing music. (We were full of a lot of things but never so full of ourselves to make even the slightest comparison.) So even though it was but a few months down the road at the time, we had no idea what lay ahead for our fellow countrymen in the autumn as more than leaves would be falling. Sure there were rumblings. Scuttlebutt was what the media always lived for. We remembered listening to President Reagan once again, who, while standing at the foot of the Berlin barricade that separated east and west, made a strong statement to his Soviet counterpart on June 12, 1987, "Mr. Gorbachev, tear down this wall..." all the while thinking,

"Yeah sure... Who's he kidding? It will never happen." And yet, even though the miracle was just around the bend, we really had no idea that it would happen so soon, and the eventual reunification of our country would become a reality. Today, an entire generation of not only Germans but I suspect people around the world knows only about east and west separation inside our borders by reading the history books, although within our country, the date of November 9, 1989 is one that every German citizen knows as well as his own birthday. If they had just waited a couple of weeks, it would have coincided with my date of birth. I wish someone had consulted me. Yes, indeed, there truly was a wind of change in the air as we began our trip into the center of the once forbidden city to the east. Thank God Klaus Meine got the words written before too many changes took place. It could have ruined a great song!

Throughout the drive from the airport we all took note of how different and yet the same everything looked upon closer scrutiny. I think I could have been an architect in Russia at the time. There was a similarity to the simplistic structural design and construction that graced the streets upon which we rode. Every building seemed to have been erected for practicality more than aesthetics. There were, in places, rows and rows of uniformly built flats (apartments). Some stood as high as perhaps thirty floors in the air. And yet, there was no majesty to them – only practicality. That seemed to be the familiar theme. There was no sign of poverty; how could there be given the communist theory? But there was no sense of joy or happiness in the eyes of many we saw during those initial hours in the capital city, which did little to help curb our anxieties. It was, once again, a starkly different picture from the one we remembered seeing in Leningrad. We wouldn't see eyes like those again until much later when we faced a legion of adoring fans all wanting to hear us play. However, as we looked around at those who were in their much more natural environment, we had to wonder if the scenes we recalled from our previous trip itself weren't all an act staged for purposes of propaganda.

I wish to say something at this point in time to those who have not had the opportunity to travel in Eastern Europe and more specifically, Russia. In my opinion, some of the most beautiful women in the entire world live within the borders of the countries that at one time made up the former Soviet Union. I say "some of" because, as you will discover later, I have a favorite city when it comes to beautiful women – the most beautiful in the entire world (at least in my opinion). And I can tell you up front it's going to surprise the hell out of you!

Anyway, as we drew closer and closer to the city center, the buildings became less monotonous and more individual with even a western feel in some respects. It was as if there was a conscious paranoia within the politburo that they were being watched and had to put up a positive front for all the visiting dignitaries to insure there was never a less than glowing review of life in their "Union". If Moscow, the flagship and standard-bearer for the country, looked antiquated or archaic, it would surely mean a black eye for the propaganda machine.

As I mentioned, we really didn't know what to expect from the audiences even after our shows the previous year. We knew our ballads like "Still Loving You" and "Holiday" were very popular throughout Eastern Europe and often heard on the radio. But we wondered how it came across to what were predominantly non-English speaking listeners. Music had always been considered a universal language, but the reason we decided to forego singing songs in German and opted for the more complicated, at least from our perspective, English, was because rock and roll was English music. If we had any hope of scaling the heights beyond Hannover, West Germany, we knew it had to be in English. So how much of what we were about to share with our audiences was going to be about our music and how much would be just about the novelty of having western music and western musicians playing in their country?

As our time passed, we began to see a hunger in the eyes of the young people. Some hung on our every word and seemed to thirst for knowledge with those who did speak one of our languages, even a little, asking all sorts of questions and translating for those who didn't. Though we were guarded and shielded from a lot of spontaneous interaction, as was the Soviet custom, we still were able to exchange brief words with many of the locals, which helped dispel our own curiosities in many ways. As teenagers greeted us at our hotel, it was clear we were indeed a bit of a novelty to many even though the time when there were no magazines, music or movies from our part of the world invading the soils behind the "curtain" had long passed. Even the "Golden Arches" of McDonald's had found a home within walking distance of Lenin's Tomb which may, in fact, have had him resting much less peacefully.

Originally, we were scheduled to play five dates in Moscow in 1988 but that was changed in favor of our taking part in two much larger shows at Moscow Stadium in 1989 on August 12th and 13th. The concert was called the "Moscow Music Peace Festival". Yet, a look at the other acts made us wonder how peaceful it would be. With groups like Motley Crue and Ozzy Osbourne sharing the bill, we could only imagine whose definition of tranquility they were using. Actually, sharing the bill might not be the best way to describe it. That sounds much too pacific given the myriad of egos involved. Ozzy and Crue both seemed intent on being billed higher, and so that led to a bit of backstage bickering. Bon Jovi was in the same sort of position. Jon himself, who I spoke to, was steadfast in his desire to headline the shows even though, in truth, not that many people in Russia even knew who they were. I tried to explain this to him, but he'd have none of it, and as such the billing and playing order was followed and ultimately proved out what I suspected. At that point in time, in all modesty, the Scorpions were a much bigger act in that part of the world than Bon Jovi, and the audience's responses seemed to support that. But I tried. I really did try.

As we took the stage that summer, within a few verses of our opening song, "Blackout", there was no longer a thought about where we were playing only that we were playing for over 135,000 screaming fans that all seemed to know our music. The happiness and

11

joy returned to their eyes and told a story all by itself. To paraphrase my friend Justin Heyward of the Moody Blues, we were the epitome of being "the music to the story in their eyes". Surely, that was the most telling sign of the future events. But as I think back now, we didn't really take time to think about it then. For us, music was our world and our world had just grown by more than 250,000,000 people who we never even realized knew we existed. If I'm wrong about the Soviet population in 1989, please don't get upset with me. I'm a musician, not a census taker.

After the last show on August 13, we were taken to Gorky Park and a place the promoters called the Hard Rock Café I guess as some sort of an illustration as to how progressive the Soviet Union had become. It looked every bit the same as any of those sporting the name elsewhere. On the menu were hamburgers and the standard junk food fare that you can find in most of those establishments today along with the expected rock music memorabilia. It gives one "food" for thought, though, because all of this time I thought it was a Hard Rock Café aligned with those we had visited in other major cities. But as I was researching this book, I came to learn that that franchise had not reached Russian soil in 1989.

It was during a subsequent trip that we had the very great honor and pleasure of meeting with soon to be deposed Soviet Leader, Mikhail Gorbachev. His days, as well as those of the government he headed, were numbered though at that time he didn't admit it even if he knew it. Despite what others may have come to learn about Mr. Gorbachev, I found him to be a very likeable, dare I say, buoyant man, who I believe truly spoke from his heart. In my life, few politicians I've met or even heard speak, ever seemed to say what they really thought or even believed that which they were saying. But with Mr. Gorbachev, I have no doubt that he was a very sincere man. Having since come to learn so much more about how our world is run and those in charge of it, I respect him even more today. I would love to say I was able to communicate to Mr. Gorbachev the very real need to tear down the Berlin wall and convince him to indeed remove it, but

I'm not really going to sit here and say something so clearly bogus that anyone with half a brain would know is a lie. I prefer to save my lies for more important things like women!

One of the things that I found to be very engaging and surprising about Mr. Gorbachev was his sense of humor. The face of Russia and the Soviet Union always seemed so dark and eerie with men like Leonid Brezhnev and Nikita Khrushchev not to mention the portentous and threatening Joseph Stalin, stoically parading quite forebodingly before the western cameras. Mr. Gorbachev was nothing of that kind. For one thing, he actually seemed to know who we were and, I don't know if he was being honest about this, but even knew our music. He laughed and joked with us, which was quite contrary to what we expected. He even took time to explain to us what real "heavy metal" was. He said it was former Premier Khrushchev pounding his shoe on the table at the United Nations in 1960. He also explained that the Americans made their biggest mistake in 1964 when they let the Beatles in, as they were responsible for changing America. He related that it was analogous to his letting us come to Russia. I don't know if we were directly responsible for the downfall of communism and the Soviet Union, but it does make a good story, don't you think? I don't mind taking credit if he wishes to give it to us.

At the end of the day, our journeys east can be labeled successfully, we believe. We got paid. Not much... But we got paid. That's always a sign of success in our business. I know you're wondering how that could be but truthfully, some of the stories I could tell you and will tell you later, will surprise the heck out of you perhaps. Things like contracts don't always mean very much to some of those involved with promoting concerts.

As we spent more time with the people, we began to see a difference. Maybe we started to become accustomed to the more traditional Russian behavior, which is not to smile all the time and remain private. At least that was my impression. But no longer did they seem distant or cold. Perhaps, as I said, that was a result of our having spent time there getting to know a little about the culture and feeling more comfortable with the surroundings. Maybe politics can learn something from rock and roll. Having met many leaders through our travels as I have said, and having had the chance to see more of the world than I ever dreamed I would when growing up in West Germany, I will always be thankful to my mom and dad for allowing me to pound on those pots and pans so many years ago.

2
LITTLE HERMAN ZE GERMAN

I did not realize it until a friend of mine brought it to my attention, but I was born exactly 21 years after another icon, though be it an American one, on November 18, 1949. No, I wasn't born in 1970, nor do I really consider myself an icon. The icon about which I speak was "born" on November 18, 1928. I hope I won't have to explain everything to you throughout this book. It will wind up with a length rivaling that of "War and Peace" and, as everyone knows, no one ever gets through "War and Peace". Now tell me the truth, how many autobiographies about rock and roll musicians have you read that make reference to both Tolstoy and Pushkin within the first handful of pages? And they say rock and roll isn't educational. The "E" in Herman stands for education!

Anyway, I know I may be a bit presumptuous considering myself on an equal level with Mickey Mouse, with whom I share the common date of origin, and yet I suspect to some within this world, as it is with most who attain a level of celebrity, I undeservedly have been given a status of that nature. Those who do know me know that I am hardly one who wishes to trumpet my own accomplishments or myself. And so writing a book, as I am, is hardly in keeping with what was and I still believe is a very humble beginning and life. But I am not writing for me but for those who, like myself, have an interest

15

in people who perhaps had an impact or influence on their life. I don't know how much of an impact I had on anyone's life in particular though I do think it's safe to assume a lot of guys probably got laid while "Still Loving You" was on the radio.

Speaking of getting laid, I was born in the city of Lebach-Saarland, West Germany. (How was that for a segue? I know it's weak, but heck, I couldn't resist.) Technically, the region is on the cusp of the French border and the often-disputed Alsace/Lorraine territory therein not to mention that marvel of French engineering (Though futility may be the more appropriate term.), the "Maginot Line". (Well, there goes the French market for distribution of this book... Oh well.) At the time of my birth, the region was under French control though young children like myself never really even realized it. Being an only child, I was, in truth, a bit spoiled even though by today's standards, I hardly think anyone would have that same opinion.

My family lived not in Lebach but in Huettersdorf, which is about six kilometers from Lebach. My father, Hermann Erbel, was in the field of law enforcement. In other words, euphemisms aside, he worked as a policeman. Being that we were not, per say, a musical family (Unlike some of you may think, policemen only sing in *West Side Story*.), my mother Kaetharina (Kaethe) and father were understandably a bit surprised at my inclination to make noise at a young age. Not really so surprised that a five year old would make noise but more by the approach I took to it which was that of pounding on pots and pans with spoons. They were quite tolerant given the fact that they did wonder whose side of the family was responsible for it. But I am thankful they didn't chastise me too harshly for my hobby.

My father worked as a policeman, as I said, despite the fact that in West Germany there were no donut shops to be found. (I don't think there were any in East Germany either.) Come to think of it, there were no donuts either. Maybe that was the problem. I envy children in the U.S. today whose fathers work in law enforcement. I know this isn't the healthiest thing in the world, but I'm not exactly a diet guru. And no, I'm not promoting obesity. I am just stating a fact that anyone who has ever eaten a donut will agree with. Anyway, we lived what could be considered a very normal West German life circa the early 1950's. (Okay, so what is normal if we are all supposedly different? The concept of "normalcy" is one that is and rightfully should be debated endlessly.) However, sadly yet cordially, my parents divorced in 1957. In spite of the appearance of dysfunction externally, unlike too many couples today, there was none of the squabbling (Normally over money...)(I think the divisiveness caused by greed can be universally considered "normal".) that so destroys relationships between parents and children, and I'm very thankful for that.

After the breakup, my mother and I chose (Actually, it was my mother who made the choice.) to move back to the place of my birth, Lebach-Saarland. Probably the reason had more to do with the fact that that was where my mother's parents lived than the quality of the schools or the depth of the roster of the local football team. They had extra room, and so that is who we lived with and where we stayed until I was 14. In other words, we lived with my grandparents for all the obvious reasons. At least they were obvious to us. When I was 14, my mom was able to secure a job at the Deutche Bahn railway station as a telephone operator, so we moved to the city of Saarbrucken where the legend of Herman Ze German began.

I know there are those of you who are wondering why I'm wasting so much time with this. Well, this is the story of my life, and, honestly, you didn't think I was just created by some mad scientist for the express purpose of playing the drums, did you? And yet, the impatience of those waiting to read all about the sex, drugs and general debauchery, not to mention rock and roll, may never be fully rewarded. But wait... I just put some sex in. As I said, I wasn't just created. I had to have gone through the normal birthing process. And I've already talked about people getting laid. I think that's pretty significant. Okay, so that's not what most of you have in mind. But still, you will have to wait a little and indulge me in the interim because, in all sincerity, who I am today has a lot to do with who I was then. I think it is the same for most people in this world. What you learn as a child and how you are raised will forever influence your life whether you realize it or not. My mother and father allowing me to pound on the pots and pans in the kitchen when I was five gave me encouragement to not only try the patience of everyone around me and make noise in front of much larger audiences but also to learn more about the rhythm and syncopation that seemed to be a part of my soul. However, if they were to have been asked, I am sure at that point they probably thought I simply had a hankering to make noise. Perhaps they would have even preferred it.

Initially, I suspect my parents figured it was a phase I was going through as a child. Some children play with boxes. Others play with rocks. Some climb on the every piece of furniture in the house. Me? I played with pots and pans, which come to think of it, should have concerned my parents more than it did. I am more than certain they didn't hope to have a short order cook in the family. Maybe that was the reason my mother bought me some brushes to use on the pots. Then again, as I think back, maybe the brushes were for cleaning not creating the legendary sound that has made me so famous today. Perhaps I was being groomed and encouraged to work in a kitchen and didn't even realize it. She may have feared that I might start using sausages rather than spoons. Nevertheless, whatever the reason may have been, if either had been the case, it's quite possible you'd be reading a cookbook today rather than an autobiography.

My grandfather on my father's side was the first to see the handwriting on the wall, I think. After he yelled at me for misspelling a couple words I wrote there, he told my mother she needed to essentially "nip the drums in the bud" because he didn't want some lowlife, scumbag musician messing up his family. In his opinion we already had one sap on the family tree, though he wouldn't name names. Perhaps he would have been happier had I chosen to pursue a culinary career. At least that would have been honest work. He was a very considerate grandfather, always thinking of others and their eardrums.

Anyway, seriously, he knew that music was infectious, though I don't know why. He wanted to keep it out of my blood. He held a very high profile, public position, as he was the commissar of the police (As if that was honest work…) and had a reputation to think about. He told my mom to get it out of my system and focus me on more important things like… Well, actually, I can't think of anything more important than being the best-darned drummer in the entire universe. But I'm sure grandpa had a whole list of preferable, not to mention, acceptable occupations. Then again, I don't know for sure, but I do wonder how often those studying to be bankers or accountants get to spend the night with ten adoring groupies. Maybe I'll ask mine someday. I have to laugh as I think about this. Can you imagine what an accounting groupie would be like? "Oh, come on Herman baby, do it to me one more time… Do it to me like no one else can! Balance my check book!"

At any rate, I suspect the conversation around the Erbel home… That's right the Erbel home. I guess I should explain this to you. Our family name was, in fact, Erbel. It wasn't until I moved to England in the early 1970's that it was altered sort of by circumstance. For some reason, people in the United Kingdom had difficulty pronouncing Erbel and kept calling me Rarebell. To this day, I can't explain it nor do I understand it. But they had that problem, and so from that time forward I was called Herman Rarebell.

I know that story was about as interesting as watching paint dry. Hey, I wonder if my grandfather would have been happier if I had become one of those? Herman Erbel, the official paint drier watcher! It sounds quite prestigious, don't you think? And imagine what my autobiography would have been like then! Okay, so some of you are thinking probably about as tedious as this book. Look, I'm the writer. I'm the only one allowed to make obnoxious comments about me.

Well, anyway, as I was saying, I suspect the discussion amongst our small family was much the same as it is around most homes. When they finished talking about how tough it was to make a living, and how there was nothing good in the newspaper anymore, and how

I was surely going to put someone's eye out with a drum stick, they finally got around to discussing my future and me. I think if someone were to have asked them, they would have said that they figured the drums would be a hobby and probably out of my system long before I reached age six. And so they were encouraging of my banging, as I have said, or at least not discouraging of it. Unlike I think too many parents today, they wanted to let their son enjoy himself.

You know... Well, actually, you can't know since I haven't written it. If you did know it, you would be a mind reader and wouldn't need to read this book because you would already know what it says. But that's all beside the point. What I wanted to say is that one thing that I am disappointed in is my own life as a parent. I have a daughter, Leah, who is now 21. She is studying in Glasgow, Scotland to be a speech therapist and wants to work with the disabled. (Hey, maybe she can teach the people in the UK to pronounce Erbel.) I love her dearly. I am not disappointed in the least with her. My disappointment is in my own life's priorities while she was growing up. I was absent far too much but given my occupation, it couldn't be helped. However, for those of you who are reading this, please know that if you live a nomadic life and have options that perhaps would allow you to remain at home more, you will regret not taking that path. Sure, being on the road with a rock band is wonderful for the young. It appears quite glamorous on the outside. But it's also very lonely in many ways. Very empty. And for a marriage, it normally chimes a death knell. It's impossible to turn your head forever as most rock and roll wives claim they do. Money can be a salve for the open wounds only so long. And for children, even though it's probably fun to have a famous father, they cannot replace him and all the money in the world won't buy back those years. As for my daughter's choice in a future mate, I will encourage her to marry anyone she wants. I don't wish to dissuade her from loving someone based solely on his occupational pursuit. So I will be happy with anyone she marries so long as he's a businessman.

All of that was simply a side note to the thought I wanted to share with you, however. Take it for whatever it's worth but from my perspective, I believe one of the gravest disservices any parent can do to a child is that of direction. I see it so often. Parents who orchestrate their child's life from the day he's born to the day he gets married. The child's life is seemingly checkered with preordained decisions. The structure for children has become so great that it has taken away their opportunity for creative individuality. Within my life, my parents allowing me to bang on those pots and pans as they did and their encouragement of my drumming whether intentional or not, was quite important to my personal development and individuality. They didn't tell me to put down the pot because I had to go and play Little League baseball. (To this day I haven't really put down the pot. But that's another story all together.) Okay so forget the fact that there was no baseball in Germany at the time. They didn't make me go and play football, which for those of you in America is your game soccer. Yes, I know you think everything was invented in America. That's why I call it your game. Don't get me wrong. I love America and Americans. I loved them every chance I got. But that, too, is another story for later. Actually, it's several stories for later. I'm only up to age five. Anyway, as one parent to another, since I suspect most of you reading this are parents, please allow your children to be themselves and encourage every activity they undertake, even undertaking if they are so morbidly inclined, especially if they take up activities of their own accord. Like water, they will find their own level one day. Allow them the chance to find it for themselves. I will forever give thanks to my parents for their support and understanding. They always had the best kitchenware. Even then, I guess, I knew quality!

So now we'll fast forward a bit. Heck, even in the New Testament they sort of jump from birth, after making a very brief stop at around age 12, to age 30… Please don't take this out of context. I'm not comparing myself to Jesus Christ or comparing this book to the Bible. Just using it as a point of reference. There are far too many people who look for problems rather than simply allowing life to be lived. They need to understand that being overly sensitive leads to very little good.

Be that as it may, let us move forward to the early 1960's. I was twelve years old and fell in love for the first time. No, this isn't going to be one of those stories. My virginity was still quite safe. In fact, don't tell my wife, but when I fell in love, it might have been the only time I ever truly was in love. Sorry, honey. No slight to you in the least. I was at a wedding and couldn't take my eyes off her. The most beautiful girl in the entire world... A glitter white, Trixxon drum kit that shined and gleamed and attracted my undivided attention throughout the reception to the frustration of many preteen girls who were also in attendance. While most of them were focused on frivolous things like the wedding dress and the cake, and the flowers, and all the other typical female things, the drummer captivated me. On second thought, that might be misleading. Please understand, some of my best friends are gay, so I don't mean this as a negative. In fact, I live in the "gayest" city in England, Brighton. And honestly, I can't really remember completely what the drummer looked like, but I am quite certain he wasn't my type. Anyway, in truth as a player, he probably was no Gene Krupa; and yet to a young, impressionable child in 1962, he was every bit his peer. During the course of the reception I was able to get behind the set for a few minutes, and even though my parents probably didn't realize it, the most important thing in my life from that day forward was hardly that which I was being taught at school or football or even girls. My life was all about music. As I think about it, it's a shame my focus has changed. Sorry again, honey.

After that reception, I began scrimping and saving every penny I got for my own set of drums. I knew I had to have one, and it took me several months to save up the money. At five Deutsche Marks per week allowance that my mother gave me, when I was 13 I eventually got my first set. It was very basic consisting of only a bass, a snare and one cymbal. There was no high-hat or tom-tom. But for me, it was the Holy Grail. My family quickly started to miss my hanging in the kitchen. There was no garage to banish me to. So they were stuck having to listen to me pound away in a small room inside the house. I'll be completely honest with you, although the drums are in my opinion the most beautiful of all instruments, there is much to be said about the guitar or even the tuba when it comes to learning. While at least those instruments can be known even to beginners to make a melodic sound, drums never sound like very much to those who are not in the fraternity until put together with an ensemble.

On the educational front, I will honestly admit I was never confused with Einstein in the classroom. However, even though my grades were never that great (From what I understand, neither were Einstein's.), somehow my parents' perhaps sadistic sense of ironic logic deduced that I should attend the school of economics which at the time was perceived to be the most challenging of all educational institutions in West Germany. I realize this sounds a lot like a guy who is being beaten senselessly by the #148th ranked heavyweight boxer arrogantly challenging the champion of the world! But heck, if you're going to have someone beat the hell out of you, you may as well have it done by the best! And so with that train of thought firmly in place, that of my educational needs not that of someone beating the hell out of me, off I went to the school of hard knocks, I mean economics!

It was during this time, the time at the new school, that my first school band came into existence, and I quickly got an advanced, first-hand education in economics. The Mastermen, as we called ourselves, was simply a group of guys I went to school with; a group surely to get into the, ah hem, "Rock and Roll Hall of Fame" before the Scorpions... Don't get me started with that. I'll vent on that subject a little later.

Anyway, the Mastermen was nothing more than just a bunch of us kids playing the songs we heard on records or the radio like it is, I suspect, everywhere in the world. So why "The Mastermen"? Well, that was the brainstorm of one of the fathers. He wanted us to be like all the popular groups of the day. He got us all some flowered shirts, so that we'd match to go along with the idea that we were "Mastermen". You know, even today as I think about that, I don't quite understand the concept. And then when you consider that was only a handful of years after the end of the Nazi regime and the concept of a "master race", it might not have been the most diplomatic name for a band. But we were playing music, and that was what mattered. Well, that, and the assorted fringe benefits.

As I am sure many of you are aware, a lot of young people get into bands to meet girls. I was no different, really. I recognized that very early on and wanted to take advantage of what the opportunity afforded me. We played just about every weekend somewhere and made what was the equivalent of about 150 Euros. At that time, that was a lot of money! And when you have money for things like soda or ice cream when others guys don't, you attract the attention of girls. Funny how that works, huh? I guess that's sort of a natural instinct with the female gender as well. (Please, ladies, don't get upset with me. I only said that because guys like to read that sort of thing.) It was quite an advantage to say the least. Not only did we attract girls because we were in the band, but we also attracted them because we could take them places that the other guys could not.

I had my first real girlfriend, (i.e., we had sex…) I think, during those years though I suspect she always felt as if she was little more than just second banana to my drums. Can't say that I blame her really because she was. She wasn't able to earn me 150 Euros on a weekend. In fact, from what I remember, she may have cost me more than that. This was a lesson they weren't teaching at the school of economics. But honestly, even at that age, I was 15, I remember trying to put on a show for the girls, and how they would seem more attracted to me than even the other members of the group! I suspect it was the result of the nature of percussion itself. It's quite physical, verging on animalistic perhaps. Singing and/or playing a guitar is much less so. And so there seemed to be an attraction to some girls who loved the idea of the syncopated power and aggression of a drummer. Or maybe it was just the fact that I was by far the best looking guy in the group! Who am I to say otherwise?

Honestly, what I remember most about those years in the Mastermen is the fact that it was truly one of the best times of my life. I'm not kidding. I know there are those of you who will ask, "How can that be..." given all that has happened within my life? But let me tell you, the memories of youth can never be supplanted, nor should they be. Going to school, sort of, and playing on weekends... I thought I was in heaven – at least until I was out on tour and surrounded by groupies. But I happily traded that in for a lovely wife and home life. (As you read that, was there a lightning strike anywhere?)

3
FINDING MY WAY

It was around that time, the mid-1960's, a little-known group of guys from Liverpool, England, was suddenly everywhere surrounded by droves of screaming girls called, interestingly enough, the Beatles. No, of course, the girls weren't called the Beatles. I meant the band was called the Beatles. Now in all candor, not being the very imaginative sort, I thought they were named after a bug. My grasp of English at that point was not exactly on a par with that of Winston Churchill. To be honest, it's not so great right now. Probably about as good as Arnold Schwarzenegger's, but I think I can pronounce California better than he can though I don't think that really matters. (Hey, you know, as I think about this, maybe we should have been called the "Scorepions"! You know, "score" like a musical piece? I guess no one was that creative in the band when they came up with the name.)(Actually given our on road reputation, "score" might have been appropriate for describing our off-stage antics.) What matters is the impression the Beatles made on a hormonal teenager in Saarland who had finally and begrudgingly come to realize that the drums did have their limitations with regard to matters of "amore". I tried to cuddle closely with them on several occasions, but in all honesty, it just wasn't the same as the soft, supple body of a teenage lassie. However, there was much less upkeep – a new head from time to time, maybe some polish…

I will admit that I was fascinated by the playing of Ringo Starr not only because the girls screamed and seemed to love him but also because of his steady, solid, simplistic rhythm that seemed so perfectly in tune with what the others in the band were doing. I began to take note of what he and many other drummers of that era did and came to appreciate and understand the importance of percussion to the establishment of an identity for a band. That sounds so impressive doesn't it? Truthfully, I just liked to listen to and copy the way they played. The rest is for those of you who are going to scrutinize this book for literary reasons. I have to make sure I put in enough adjectives, adverbs and metaphoric inferences to keep you happy as well.

At any rate, like most musicians, I had a great many artists whom I looked up to. (No, not because they were taller.) Some of my earliest influences were not only Ringo but also Charlie Watts of the Rolling Stones and Peter York of the Spenser Davis Group. At no time, however, did I dare imagine I would ever meet any of these luminaries of the Mylar or even be classified within their peer group by some who may have had more than their share of Heineken. But the hours I spent listening to their records and copying their licks the best I could are, as I said, some of the happiest times I remember.

Kids today will never share that same joy I fear. With everything available online and on DVD, young performers don't have to practice their craft and develop their ear. They can simply watch their favorites via one form of media or another whenever they like or buy an instructional video produced by one of them showing all of their tricks. It's so difficult to explain to a young drummer or any musician, for that matter, how priceless the development of their ear is. Being able to hear music allows a musician the ability to pick up anything and translate it directly to his own work in a manner far different from watching and learning from someone else. When you play "Satisfaction" or "She Loves You" a thousand times along with the record, you not only learn what the drummer on the song was doing but what he could have done that might even have been better.

This is how you develop your own style. I don't try to play like Ringo or the Who's Keith Moon or Led Zeppelin's John Bonham. I try to play like Herman Rarebell.

By age 17, the Mastermen had run their course, and I wanted to turn professional. I decided to start my own band RS Rindfleisch where I picked all the musicians. In a short time, we began working the circuit. The circuit, of course, was a series of nightclubs and bars in and around the general area where I lived. After having come to see me at one of our club engagements and, of course, wisely consulting with my mother, my father told me if I was serious about music I should at least have the proper background and training. And so he thought it would be a good idea if I enrolled at the Saarbrucken Music Academy. There, he surmised, I would get training not only in drums and percussion but also receive the appropriate classical foundation as well as learning other "real" instruments like piano. It all sounded good to me. I wasn't about to argue. Hell, at that point I would have contracted jaundice if knew it would get me out of that damned school of economics.

Taking time to think back about it now, there may have been another reason for their suggestion/recommendation. It may well have been just to get me out of the house with my drums. Can't say that I blame them, given the fact that the drums aren't for everyone. What one has to remember is that up until the 1900's there was no such thing as a drum kit. There were drums in bands, of course. Every polka was played with the support of a bass drum, a snare and cymbals. However, a separate person played each. I can't imagine sitting all day long playing a steady drone as had to be the case with a bass drum player. But I guess there are those who can't imagine playing in a band named after an arachnid either.

As I entered the music academy, I continued playing in RS Rindfleisch. I know there are those who'll wonder why I didn't consider playing for 150 Euros a weekend, as I did with the Mastermen, as professional? Well, the difference, at least by our definition, was the type of bookings we were playing. Rather than playing exclusively on weekends, we were playing seven nights a week at nightclubs and other assorted sleazy establishments. These were steady gigs that would run one month or more at a time.

RS Rindfleisch lasted only a short period of time and morphed into a band with the cute little name Fuggs Blues. It was important to mention the spelling because some people confused the name with a similar sounding word that, of course, I never use myself. Anyway, Fuggs Blues' gigs, as I said, were mostly playing in clubs, and we covered everything on the radio. Songs like "It's All Over Now" and "The Last Time" by the Stones and, of course, Beatles' songs like "She Loves You" and whatever else was popular all had a place on our playlist. We tried our best to play everything exactly like our British idols. Remember, at that time there was no German band for anyone to emulate. That day wouldn't come for many years. Rock and roll was English music at least in terms of the language.

As Fuggs Blues grew in popularity, we had at least six fans, you can, of course, imagine that our bookings became much bigger engagements than just local clubs. Eventually, we secured several one-month stints at U.S. Military clubs including ones in Frankfurt, Schweinfurt and Nuremberg, playing four sets each night. These in particular stand out in my mind not for reasons which some of you might imagine, but because they were truly tales of two clubs. First one has to remember that was during the time of the Viet Nam war, and so soldiers were coming and going constantly, and the bases were harbors of activity. As I think about it today, I'm sure many of the soldiers I met during those days never returned from battle. It is a sobering reality when you think how fragile life can be. But even beyond that, those military base gigs were very interesting for us because for the first 10 days or two weeks of each month the clubs would be packed. You couldn't find a seat even if you said you knew Richard Nixon personally. (What people tend to forget is that President Nixon was quite popular in the late 1960's and early 1970's everywhere except Hanoi and Moscow.) So during the first part of the month we played to lively audiences filled not only with beer and sausage, but money. However, by the middle of the month, most of the extra cash was gone as was our audience, and so we played the remainder of the 30 days for some very cordial, though quite quiet, tables and chairs. It wasn't so bad for us as I'm sure it was for the occasional comedian booked as part of the entertainment. Furniture is not very responsive to one-liners – like most critics, I'd say. Of course, critics are considered sweethearts compared to some of the lizard-like creatures that call themselves agents. (Please forgive me for the comparison. I don't want to offend any reptiles.)

As some of you can imagine, and even if you can't, I'm going to ask that you try to, at that time, West Germany was a very conservative country, and even though rock and roll was popular in cities like Hamburg, which, of course, became the legendary launching pad for the Beatles at the Star Club, the look, styles and sounds were not so readily accepted by the masses. I was fortunate that my mother worked at the train station, as she was able to get us free train tickets to and from Hamburg. We used them to go and see whatever rock and roll bands were there. I remember seeing bands like the Yardbirds, Spooky Tooth, Remo Four, and a German group called the Rattles. This gave us an advantage over other young musicians who were in the same position as we were. I suspect it was similar to the early 1950's in America, as there were very few radio stations or clubs within the country that featured rock music. So our exposure was, at times, limited to what, if any, radio reception we could get from the BBC or American Armed Forces Radio. As you can imagine, seeing bands live performing songs we played as well (Don't confuse this thought. We never thought we played the songs as well as they did... I simply meant we played their songs, too... But then again... No, that would be presumptuous even if it might have been true.) and having the chance to watch how they "worked a crowd", gave us an opportunity to really grow and develop as players and performers above and beyond that of other bands.

You know along that line, I think there are several very important things that young people today miss out on as a result of the way the industry has changed. As I mentioned already, the availability of video products has taken away the development of musical ears. I also have noticed that musicians no longer seem as interested in playing live, or just jamming with friends for hours and hours. With the availability of software programs that can give anyone a complete home recording studio for a few hundred dollars, playing no longer matters so much as recording songs. You musicians focus on recording or making videos because that's how you get "discovered". Well from me to all of you who may be dreaming of one day being in a band like the Scorpions, there is no substitute for playing. Whether you play in someone's basement or garage, or you play at a party for friends or in front of an audience at school, the more you play the sharper you will become, and the much more savvy you will appear to have when or if you ever get a chance to step up and play before 100,000 people in a stadium. Whether you play for five people or five thousand, the performance should never change!

Being a drummer, I can tell you there are great differences in the ways drummers present themselves. I was captivated Keith Moon to say the least. He knew how to perform with a veracity and ferociousness that was unlike any I had ever seen. The power he brought to the sound of the Who attracted me to them greatly. And then adding to that his propensity for the destruction of his entire kit at the close of each night's show, well, I can honestly say that was all about presentation and performance. Though he was a bit "over the top", it still got my mind thinking about ways to make sure I was noticed, and how to avoid being stigmatically type-cast as just a drummer in a band. Arguably, it is safe to say that I don't think the Who ever fully recovered from the loss of Keith Moon in 1977. He was an integral part of the band's makeup and sound. The same can be said about John Bonham's role in Led Zeppelin. Both Moon and Bonham were, in my opinion, irreplaceable.

Anyway, getting back to the story, as you may well have figured out, in conservative West Germany in the late 1960's, we, as musicians, got a lot of interesting looks from people. We had to look and play the part of being rock stars whether we were or not, if we were going to convince our audience that we were credible. So with our "beat" hairstyles, "Beatle" boots and "mod", polyester attire, we did attract a lot of attention. Of course, in a lot of ways, I suspect it helped us with the girls because they were much more attracted to us than they were to guys wearing ties and sport coats and studying nuclear fission in school. (They probably figured we needed help with our fashion sense so it may have been a sympathy thing.) Okay so for the most part, those guys today probably are much more successful than most of the guys I knew and played music with. But at the time, we didn't measure success in terms of Dollars or Deutche Marks. We looked at success by the quality of the girls we'd meet and date. Everyone wanted to date the best looking girl. And so playing music and looking a little different with, of course, the aforementioned money in our pockets, gave us a tremendous advantage. And you can't really blame the girls. Why would they want to be with a guy who would consider a big evening one where he spends most of the time explaining the complexities and intricacies of "trickledown" economics? All right, so that probably wasn't exactly the case because I think that term came into fashion a few years later in the U.S., n'est pas? Never really being very interested in such things, even though I did attend the school of economics (You see what sort of impression that made on me.), I don't really know what the intellectuals discussed while out with girls. But whatever it was, it sure seemed to make us musicians more popular. I thank God that they drew such a clear contrast for the ladies. Maybe the next time I talk to my accountant I'll think differently about him and thank him for having contributed so much to my maturation.

Even though you may find this impossible to believe given all that I've already said to the contrary, I didn't get into music for the girls. However I adapted quickly. Okay, so who the heck am I kidding? I saw the way the girls reacted to the Beatles and Stones and thought immediately, "That's for me!" Anyone who says otherwise is lying. It was a wonderful byproduct of the industry, and yet it did have its drawbacks after a certain point. Just as was so aptly put in the very popular American movie, "Rocky", women truly do "weaken legs". But even at such a low level as we truly were, though at the time we thought we were doing very well, the girls were there lending to the illusion we were perpetrating for the sake of our egos. However, as I said, I do hope my daughter will be more interested in a businessman than a musician.

As you may recall, in the late 1960's, music went through a tremendous amount of change. At least rock music did. Dean Martin and Frank Sinatra didn't really change very much which is understandable. However, in popular rock and roll, very few artists were able to overcome the changes that were taking place. By 1967, all but gone was the "doo-wop" I grew up with. It was replaced by music with a much harder edge. Groups like the Yardbirds and Cream and later on Led Zeppelin, Deep Purple and Black Sabbath began to develop a style of music that really attracted my complete attention. As a group playing at the military bases, our sets began to include harder edged rock as well.

At this time, my influences began to lean heavily in that direction as well. Mitch Mitchell, for example, who played with the Jimi Hendrix Experience, was one of those as was John Bonham of Zeppelin. The minute I heard Led Zeppelin, I knew what kind of music I wanted to play. I wanted to be in a band like that and play hard rock.

4
THE BRITISH INVASION

As I've come to learn, geography isn't something stressed in every country especially as it applies to the rock and roll genre and landscape. But at the time and even today, Germany was hardly the country to be discovered in as a musician or to become part of a hard rock act. All right, since you already know how the story turns out, perhaps you don't believe that. It's not everyone who can travel 500-1000 kilometers to a completely different country only to wind up meeting with and joining a group of guys from his homeland. You have to admit that took a special sort of talent!

You know, there is kind of a disadvantage in writing a story like this. Unlike a novel, in this book I am telling you more of an inside story about a story you may already know bits and pieces about. There is very little suspense in some aspects. You already know where I wind up and what songs are going to be worldwide hits. Some of you may even know my shoe size. Don't know why. But I have found that there are those who seem to enjoy collecting data about those in the world's spotlight that, at times, can verge on meaningless trivia. But knowing what will happen in the story does take a little of the mystery out of it as you read. It has to. Then again, if you wanted mystery, you'd be reading Agatha Christie. But as I mentioned already, I suspect the reason many of you are reading this, and I hope there are many, not few, is to find out more about what went on backstage while you were watching us on stage at the Los Angeles Forum, Madison Square Garden or Hammersmith Odeon.

Anyway, continuing with the actual story, though the time spent at the Saarbrucken Music Academy was a tremendous part of my education, one I would not surrender for anything, classical music and drumming were hardly synonymous. There was no future in such playing unless you wanted to play bass or timpani in the Berlin Philharmonic. I guess if I had, I would have eventually played with the Scorpions though it would have been about 30 years later. (Some of you who lost interest in the band after I left, that's probably about three of you, might not know they recorded an album of some of our biggest hits with the Berlin Philharmonic titled, *Moment of Glory*.) Of course, I may well have been the catalyst that launched their career. (I'm having a lot of trouble buying all of this so just ignore it.) However, there is an actual argument to be made along that line on my behalf. I won't make it. Not yet anyway. But there is one. I personally love *In Trance* and *Virgin Killer* not to mention *Lonesome Crow* and *Fly to the Rainbow*. They were great albums. But sometimes within the framework of a band there is a chemistry that can't be explained – a combination of exacting elements that seem to mesh together perfectly. I think you can see that if you trace the history of a lot of bands. To me, as I already mentioned, the Who never sounded like the Who after their *Who Are You* album which, coincidentally, was the last one Keith Moon played on. And Ted Nugent, whom we toured with in America quite often because we shared the same management, Leber/Krebs, never seemed to attain the same level of success with any album after *Double Live Gonzo* which was the last that featured the original support personnel of bass player Rob de la Grange, singer Derek St. Holmes and probably the most important man behind Ted, drummer/producer Cliff Davies. I think you all know similar bands and comparable stories or at least have opinions along that line. Perhaps you idolized one at one time or another but then lost interest as the names and sound changed. There is just something special, magical if you will, that cannot be explained when it comes to creativity and music. Once you find it, you know it. In a great many ways, it's a lot like love.

By the autumn of 1971 I had finally recognized that I wasn't going to go much higher in music if I stayed in Germany. I figured out after four semesters in the music school that the only future I had would be as part of an orchestra working at a television or radio station or perhaps, as I said, a philharmonic in some city. I was a bit slow, so it took me longer than perhaps it would have others. As a result of that revelation, I decided it was time to venture out of Germany to seek my fame and fortune in my quest for stardom. Rock music, at least the kind I was interested in playing, seemed to be based in London at the time. And so with what I thought was my vast knowledge of English (I knew the lyrics to just about every song by Freddie and the Dreamers... Both of them... Okay so there were a few more. It's a joke for crying out loud. Don't knit-pick! The point is I knew very little English even though I thought I knew a lot. Okay?), I headed off to London.

I packed my bags and left Saarbrucken bound for the Magic Kingdom. No, that's not right. Wrong kingdom. I wouldn't visit Disneyland for a few more years. I packed and left for the United Kingdom figuring I would go over there and immediately step into playing with one of the top groups. After all, I had been the drummer in the Mastermen, RS Rindfleisch and Fuggs Blues! With a prestigious résumé like that, how could I have expected anything less? England was waiting for me. I was sure of it! I really believed that stuff if you can believe that! I told you, I wasn't the brightest light on the theater marquee. I was sure I'd be a hot property in England right up until I stepped off the boat in Dover and immediately noticed there were no signs at the gate saying "Welcome Herman!", nor was there anyone laying palm leaves to pave my pathway into the city. There was a jackass, of course... Me... I guess that was my first hint. No, not that I was a jackass. I already knew that. I meant the first clue that maybe it would take me a week or two to become part of Uriah Heep. Little

36

did I know, like I said, that I went all that way to England to become part of a German band from Hannover, of all places. It didn't get its nickname "Hangover" for nothing.

It wasn't too long after I arrived that I discovered I wasn't alone. Actually, I knew rather quickly I wasn't alone as London was a big city. I didn't mean physically alone. Anyway, being that London was second, at least in my opinion, to Los Angeles and New York for rock and roll… No, that would make it third, huh? Math was never my long suit either. Perhaps you've started to recognize this. Keep in mind, I was the same guy whose parents sent him to the school of economics. You know the more I think about it, since I'm writing my story I'll keep London second. In fact, it might well have been first. You do your own scoring. At any rate, being a musical crossroads as it was, there were musicians from everywhere on the continent. Sweden, Italy, France, Belgium, Holland, Denmark… Well you get the picture. I don't think I need to do a complete roll call. We were all there trying to accomplish the same thing – nailing birds (British girls). I mean, we all wanted to "make" the British music "scene". It was a scene not a business so much in those days. I learned that very early on. I had to act "groovy" to try and fit in. I already had the wardrobe, so I thought, though one look at me immediately screamed "foreigner" to the locals. But my mind was convinced that I was able to fit in, and so all that was left was mastering the beat lingo as quickly as possible! Perhaps had I tried to learn English, I would have been more successful.

Keep in mind, as I was just off the boat from Germany and as I said I knew next to no English though I thought I knew a lot (That, as it seems is the case in many large cities, qualified me to be a taxi driver, which was one of my first jobs there.), my first order of business was finding a place to live. I didn't have many friends there as you can surely understand since Al Gore had not yet invented the Internet… Nor had the people who really did invent it. From my days playing clubs in my homeland I did know a couple Go Go dancers named Monique and Jane who lived there. In case you aren't familiar with the term Go Go dancers, they weren't part of the entourage and stage

37

act for the somewhat famous all-girl rock band from Los Angeles. Go Go dancers would be most closely equated to strippers today though a bit more tame to say the least. Most actually wore clothes. I didn't really know where Jane lived, but Monique I knew was married to an English musician and told me, "When you come to England, you can stay with us until you find a job." So with visions of a "ménage a trios" dancing merrily in my head, I went to see Monique. However, when I arrived, she was fighting with her husband, so the fantasy of a sordid and seamy sexual liaison was quickly dashed. Also eliminated was the possibility of my just bunking there for a couple days to get settled into life in the UK.

Obviously, I needed a place in quite short order. With such a tight time frame and a less than Donald Trump-like bank account, I was only able to find a small "bedsit" (A one-room flat with a bed.) in Notting Hill Gate, London. It cost me six pounds a week. It had no bathroom inside the room. Six people shared the one on the floor. Thankfully, it was all men, so we could share it quite easily. Didn't even have to think about putting the seat down.

After getting the room, I went to the Victoria train station where I had left my luggage and drums. As I'm sure you can imagine, in a small apartment I couldn't very well practice without taking some steps to at least show some consideration to the others on the floor. Granted, the kit pretty much filled whatever extra space I had in my "executive suite", but I like to think positively, and so it's better I call it that in order to properly establish my level of confidence. For practice, however, I had to cover the drumheads with rubber to muffle the sound. This allowed me to keep sharp while not keeping everyone awake and annoyed. I was already an invading German, and so they weren't all that happy with me in the first place. The number of times I had to relive the "Battle of Britain" should have put me in line for the Iron Cross.

London circa 1971 was quite different than I expected. The Beatles were gone, as was Cream. The Yardbirds had successfully transitioned from fowl to dirigible. (For those of you who don't remember, the

Yarbirds evolved into Led Zeppelin. In fact, as some of you may not know, the first version of the Zeppelin classic "Dazed and Confused" was recorded and released by them on their *Live Yardbirds featuring Jimmy Page* album, though at that point the title of the song was simply "I'm Confused".) I was truly just one of seemingly thousands of aspiring musicians wandering the streets and trying to find work. Thankfully, I had some training. I was an illustrious alumnus of the prestigious Saarbrucken Music Academy! (Let me know when you're finished laughing... No one in London had heard of it either.) The years spent at the Saarbrucken Academy did, however, give me a tremendous leg-up over a lot of the other guys, and I was eventually able to find work as a session player. I could learn parts quickly and played very fast, which saved a lot of time. Studio musicians earn their pay by saving money. Producers love us for that very reason. Not as often as they love aspiring young female singers on their makeshift casting chesterfields. Or are they davenports? Not that it matters. Call it whatever you want, couch, sofa, love seat... It's all the same. But what matters is very few of them save producer's money, and session players tend to have longer careers than most female singers. The good ones, studio musicians, not flooz, I mean bimb, I mean female singers, can get parts completed in less time than the original performing artists, and as such, rather than paying for 12 hours of studio time, they might be able to get the same work done in four. The average female singer wouldn't even have her makeup done in four hours. (You know, I'm not making many friends here, huh?)

I realize I may be sharing a trade secret, but it's okay. I think the average "fan" would be surprised at how many albums are not actually recorded by the musicians that make up a band. Often, producers will hire studio session players to record the music and then teach the songs back to the band. The reason is completely financial. Recording time is expensive as are cross-country or, in some cases, cross-continent flights to parachute in a band for a couple hours of work in the studio. Most producers, if the truth be told, don't want to waste time with bands in the studio when they can get the same thing done in so much less time. (This doesn't even begin to address the actual ability, or perhaps more appropriately, inability many musicians and bands have to "focus" long enough to address the task of working in the studio. You can figure out your own interpretation for the term "focus".) The band is always the band on the road, and they do write their own music and sing most all of the parts and, of course, play the majority of instrumental solos on the albums. But as I said, for reasons of expedience, the rhythm guitar, the bass or even the drums quite often will be played by someone who is a hired-hand.

Also, and fairly, on the other side, bands are often out on the road and don't have time to come into the studio to record a complete album. So it's not always their fault. They will be able to jump in and lay down a vocal track or perhaps add the lead guitars in between shows. But to spend countless hours recording everything? That just doesn't make sense financially to a band that is making hundreds of thousands of dollars playing before tens of thousands of excited fans night after night! Again, they can get an album done and out in the stores much more quickly this way. That is the recording industry's only interest. A record company doesn't make a dime from a band's live performances. They focus on sales. So they are always eager and anxious for more products to market from their best talents. I will never name names… I know in books like this you expect us to name names. I have named my share. I named my father and mother and will name my wives and other friends and comrades. What more could you want? I don't want to be accused of not giving you what you expect! I have always been one who put the fans first! But never will I say or write anything remotely disparaging about any of my peers when it comes to their private and personal choices.

Well, getting back to the story, though I'm not sure we ever left. I think if I were to actually tell you some of those who at one time or another used a surrogate in the studio you might be quite surprised. Perhaps you would discover that some of the "classic" albums you have come to know and label with that lofty nomenclature have actually been recorded or augmented by outside studio musicians. Never any Scorpion album, of course.

So basically from 1971 to 1976 I was a stand-in for many artists recording in the UK. It was quite often "work for hire", so I didn't always receive album credits, even though I know I was there. And the important thing was I think I did a pretty good job of playing, and built up a solid reputation. Studio work is great for polishing a player's talent. You can play and play and play with a band but never learn as much, at least as a drummer, as you can in the studio where precision is paramount! Having to play along with a "click track" or metronome to make sure the meter is consistent for the song, forces you to play with control. You can't just wildly bang away as is the normal approach many use on stage. Add to this that one day you might be playing for Gerry and the Pacemakers and the next for, say, Deep Purple... Keep in mind, I'm not naming names here! I never worked for either, so I do not know if they used session guys at any time. Don't start making enemies for me. I'm probably doing a good enough job of that on my own right now! Anyway, the point is, you work for a vast array of artists playing a myriad of styles. You have no choice but to learn.

I'll tell you something that always amazed me. As I mentioned before, I was enamored with Keith Moon of the Who early on in my playing career. His power and energy and then the destructive closing he and guitarist Pete Townsend used as a part of their stage performance was very intriguing. But by the early 1970's the Who had made a bit of a transformation of their own. The release of what I consider one of the greatest pure rock albums of all time, *Who's Next*, signaled a new direction for the band. Gone were the rough edges that so defined the traditional "skiffle" sound that was so much a part of their early recordings. It was replaced with a synthesizer that blazed a hypnotic-like underscore for the songs "Baba O'Reilly" and "Won't Get Fooled Again". However, what often is forgotten or goes unnoticed is the replication of that incredible music in front of live audiences. I so vividly remember the pictures of Keith Moon wearing headphones on stage in order to hear the prerecorded synthesizer's drone, or perhaps he was following a click track while playing these songs live to insure he'd stay right in time with what was being produced from a canned source. Remember, that was long before there was wireless anything on stage. I'll tell you, it's one thing to play along with meter in the studio or even along with a record at home when you practice, but when your adrenal glands get pumped up in front of an audience, it's a completely different form of playing. So his ability to control his own energies in front of thousands of people, well, that impressed me more than I can tell you within the pages of this book. I know from personal experience, it would have been very difficult for me to do. Difficult… Not impossible. But at the time it did help me to understand the emphasis made by my teachers when I was young.

So there I was, a German in London trying to make a name for myself in music. I did play with some bands during that time as you might well imagine, but there was nothing that seemed all that promising. Either I didn't feel comfortable with what they were doing or they weren't comfortable with what I did. The only band I did play with for an extended period of time was called Vineyard. They played music along the lines of the sound that came to be associated with Supertramp.

I knew in my mind, however, what I wanted to play and the kind of band I wanted to be in. Simply playing other peoples' music the rest of my life wasn't an option. I wanted more than that. I wanted to be part of a big band as I said. No, not like Benny Goodman or Glenn Miller. I meant a big name rock and roll band. You know, given the amount of turnover in the industry, I suspect had I just waited around rather than joining the Scorpions as I did, I may well have played as part of some of the biggest names in the industry. Heck, Uriah Heep alone changed drummers five times from 1969-1972. Yet they never once approached me. I was probably sixth on their depth chart. I'm hardly complaining, mind you, but if you look at the role call for a lot of bands, it is curious to me, at least, how the same guys kept turning up as part of different bands. You see that a lot more in the States than in the UK probably because there are more bands based out of there these days. However, I think for the fans, it isn't always for the best.

I left the Scorpions in 1996 on good terms because I just wanted to try some other things. They needed to find a replacement and wanted to keep going, so they did just that with my blessing, as you will discover later. But in some instances, and this is what does annoy me, there are four or five versions of the same band making the rounds. In fact, there are even some bands that feature none of the original, founding members and yet still have the "gall" to use the original name. To me this is completely wrong. It's not only wrong for the industry, but also wrong for the fans who will surely believe a band is, at least in part, consisting of original members. In my opinion, such bands are nothing more than tribute bands. I mean can you call the Jimi Hendrix Experience a band with Mitch Mitchell? Or how about "Herman Rarebell's Scorepions"? It sounds ridiculous, I know. But that's what you find out there.

You know, I have to admit, the loss of John Bonham in 1980 not only hit me deeply as a musician who was a big fan but also as an artist. After his passing, the remainder of the group so respected and appreciated that which he brought to the table, they decided to disband rather than just add one more player to fill in. Most bands would not have done that. And so my respect grew even more for the group. To this day I do not believe the other three have ever gone on stage calling themselves "Led Zeppelin". Page and Plant, yes. But not Zeppelin.

5
WELCOME TO GERMANY, HERMAN ZE GERMAN!

I have to admit, the time spent in England was good time for me in many ways. I was able to do what I love best. I also got to play my drums and get paid. But the English lifestyle was one that was quite in line with my tastes, at least at that age. Since I now live there, I guess it was and is in line with my tastes in general – except for the weather. I will say, as would anyone wishing to be completely honest, it wasn't then and still isn't exactly the best on the planet. (We sure as hell could use some "global warming" there.) I'll give that award to Los Angeles. I really doubt I'm the only one who ever tendered either of those opinions.

At any rate, being on my own for the first time in my life gave me quite a sense of freedom and independence not so unlike any that most other people have. I didn't have to sneak around with a girl to find a place to… I don't think I have to explain the obvious. What guy wouldn't like to have privacy when he watched television with his girlfriend? Keep in mind, television was still relatively new, and the BBC was very different from what we had in West Germany. But I did have one serious relationship with a girl named Sonya Kittelsen. She was 10 years my senior, though no one who ever saw her would have even for one second believed that. She was beyond beautiful not only physically, but the maturation of her years gave her an internal beauty as well which, of course, is always the most important. For time will erode that which faces the world each day, while the beauty one finds within another grows more and more attractive with each passing day.

It is quite synonymous with an analogy one might consider while buying a home. He sees two that he really loves. One is perfect. It has everything he could ever want in a home. The second, however, is just as appealing, even though it doesn't have exactly what the buyer wants or needs in every respect. It is still a beautiful home and has one bonus that the first one doesn't – a view from atop a mountain looking down upon all that is below. The buyer falls in love with the view and, of course, buys the home. A few months later, the flaws in the home begin to show themselves. He begins to regret his decision. Oh, the view is still there. But in all honesty, he hardly even notices it because he's seen it everyday, and it now contributes little to the attraction of the home. Anyway, the point is, Sonya had both beauty inside and out, and that made her a very special person in my life. When the time came, she would eventually join me in Germany when I made my "triumphant" return.

Actually, getting back to the story, television was quite an important part of the music scene in London. (I know some of you probably thought I was only making mention of it for the sake of a joke.) The predominant show for rock music was called *The Old Grey Whistle Test*. It wasn't, however, by any means a glitz and glamour kind of show. It was actually shot in a very bare studio, which was truly meant to highlight the artists, not the special effects. It featured some of the greatest performers the rock world knew, and, in some cases, didn't know at that time. Artists as diverse as Meatloaf, Tom Petty and the Heartbreakers, AC/DC, Rory Gallagher and the Eagles, all made appearances on the concert series. Most young, aspiring musicians were either in the audience or at home watching, as it was an open doorway to free concert performances, which was about all most musicians could afford. After all, they weren't part of the Mastermen!

There were other series on television as well like *Top of the Pops* which was an interview and concert style show featuring the artists who were on the top of the UK charts – probably akin to the *Midnight Special* in America. It was a much different show than the *Whistle Test* as the artists were from all over the musical spectrum. The Beatles made several appearances on the show, for example, as did the Hollies and the Dave Clark Five. Even the likes of Perry Como, Frank Sinatra and, incredibly, Telly Savalas were on the show. I guess the BBC loved him, baby. Yes, there were hard rock acts as well when they were on the charts. Deep Purple, Alice Cooper, Thin Lizzy and many, many others were all invited on. Even punk rockers like the Sex Pistols and Television had a spot on the show.

Yes, I could go on listing shows as rock and roll seemed to be made for television, and that was a fact that the BBC didn't overlook unlike the American networks that seemed to never let it go beyond their variety shows like Ed Sullivan, Sonny and Cher and, of course, the enigmatic Tony Orlando and Dawn, all of which I remember seeing at one time or another. Keep in mind, there was no home video at that time. There was no MTV airing videos… Kind of like today, huh. I, personally, can't remember seeing music programming on MTV in America for perhaps more than the last 10 years. But the point was, if you were a serious artist, the opportunity to see the stars perform was limited to your bank account, and so free, over the air broadcasts were quite welcome by all of us.

However, when we weren't sitting at home, my girlfriend Sonya and I would… Well, we did that, too… But when we weren't at home watching television or doing you know what, we would venture out to an assortment of clubs that were frequented by seemingly all the rock and roll musicians like one called The Speakeasy on Margaret Street in London. It was the local hangout for musicians. Every city, big and small has one – a gathering place for those who had a job as well as those who didn't, not to mention those who maybe had a job but were looking for options. Of course, it's also where the "groupies" were, and so it was kind of like going to the grocery store and shopping for the evening's meal for some who were well-known and established stars wanting a little companionship.

On one "fateful" night, and in literature there always are fateful nights in every story (There will be a few in this book as you will see.), I bumped into a fellow German musician named Michael Schenker at a place called The Ship on Wardour Street near the Marquee Club, which, itself, was another very popular hangout. (Kind of makes me wonder why I rambled on about The Speakeasy. Regardless. What's done is done.) Everyone knew Michael at that time, well, actually, they probably do today as well. I don't think he's been forgotten just because he's a few years older. But at the time he was the guitarist for the extremely popular English band UFO. They were riding high in the rock world with such songs as "Doctor Doctor", "Too Hot To Handle", "Only You Can Rock Me" and, of course, the anthem "Rock Bottom" playing all over the radio as well as being covered by bands around the world in clubs not so different than The Speakeasy or the Marquee club I'm sure. (I hope you caught the link I so gracefully made to the Speakeasy… Not every writer would, you know? Only a writer with training from the Saarbrucken Music Academy could have done it!) In the opinion of many guitar aficionados, Michael was Eddie Van Halen before there was an Eddie Van Halen. He sort of bridged the gap between Jimmy Page, Jeff Beck and Eric Clapton to the Pasadena prodigy.

Given that we were in a bar, some of the events of the evening are not as clear as they might have been if we were, say, enduring the monotony of a Woody Allen movie. There were plenty of distractions including a lot of good rock and roll. The Ship was a club that had opened its stage to people like Jimi Hendrix, Yes, and Pink Floyd at one time or another, and was considered one of the best places to go for rock and roll in the city. To answer your question, actually, I don't know if it's your question, but I will answer it regardless, of course, we spoke German, Michael and I. I mean, honestly, why wouldn't we? I know in English language movies people meet and always speak English regardless of who they are and where they are from. But this was reality, not a movie. Anyway, the point is Michael and I hit it off because we were both from the same country, and so that gave us an immediate kinship of sorts.

It was a few months later during a conversation we actually had at The Speakeasy that he mentioned to me that the Scorpions were coming to England, which, in truth, sounded a lot like a title for an Ed Wood movie from the 1950's. As he went on to explain, his brother Rudolf had a band from Hang, I mean Hannover, named the Scorpions, and they were coming to London to play one show at the Marquee Club and another at the Sound Circus. He told me to go and check them out because they were looking for a new drummer and, of course, I, being a former member of the famous Mastermen and Fuggs Blues, would be the obvious choice. And after that, he told me the one about some blonde chick and three bears. In case you haven't already figured it out, he didn't actually say any of that except the part about his brother's band playing in England, and the fact that they did indeed need a drummer. The funny thing is, there are actually people in music who, if someone didn't say something like that to them, they'd make it a point to say it themselves. You know the type I'm sure.

So I went to the Marquee Club and saw the band. After the show we all went to the Speakeasy, and I started talking with Rudolf and Michael. The drinks must have been cheaper there, which is why we went there to talk and drink. Rudolf asked me about the band, and what I thought about them. I told him that I saw two possible directions. One was in the direction of Hendrix, which I later learned was inspired and encouraged by lead guitarist Uli Jon Roth, and the other sound was more melodic, like Uriah Heep. The latter seemed to be much more in line with the tastes of the rest of the group. I heard originality in what they were doing, but they had to focus in one direction and not allow themselves to be split in order to provide a distinctive sound for the audience.

I got a call to attend an audition for the Scorpions the following week, which I thought was nothing more than a formality. My immediate thinking was, "Okay, here's my chance to join a touring rock and roll band." That's how they described themselves. I was gullible and naïve. What did I know? Well, when I got to the audition, my bubble burst quickly. There were 50 or 60 other drummers waiting for their opportunity to join a touring rock and roll band no one had ever heard of. Some of the guys I knew. Others I didn't. I was dumbfounded to say the least, as I honestly believed it was going to be a solo audition. Had I known I would be nothing more than part of a cattle call, you know, I don't know if my young ego at the time would have accepted that. And so history might well have been altered.

At any rate, the 50 or 60 of us were all asked to play three songs with the band, though I can't remember any of them at this point. The band at the time featured Uli Jon Roth and Rudolf Schenker on guitars, Klaus Meine singing, of course, and Francis Buchholz on bass. Considering I really didn't know the songs, I thought I did pretty well. But at the end of the audition, as I packed up and got ready to leave, I got the old crisp handshake and danke schoen, kind of in a manner reminiscent of Wayne Newton, and a don't call us we'll call you brush off that left me with the impression that the last thing they wanted was a drummer from the Saarbrucken Music Academy. Maybe I shouldn't have told them about that. Perhaps it intimidated them.

And so I left the audition with a bit of a stale taste in my mouth. It was not so dissimilar to that which you would have after eating some bad sauerbraten. And yet as I thought about it I realized that my life wasn't going to change all that dramatically as a result of losing out on one or another position in a band. Heck, they weren't so special – a German band trying to make it in an English world. The thought was ludicrous. I reached a point where I was actually happy they didn't give me the job! I was too damned good to play with a bunch of drunken Germans! That's why I left Germany in the first place! I wanted to play with a bunch of drunken Brits! (After all these years, I finally got there as I'm now playing with Pete Way.)

So I returned home, after spending a couple hours in the company of some fine English ale and by the following morning had all but lost interest in the band. The Scorpions. What kind of name was that for a band? Boy, were they a bunch of egomaniacs thinking they'd ever be anything more than just an opening act for KISS or Sweet in Hamburg or Munich?

It's amazing how quickly an attitude can change within seconds of a telephone ringing. I answered the phone and was quickly advised that I was the "winner" of the sweepstakes, which, of course, sentenced me to a return trip to Germany. I was beginning to wonder about this. I mean, I had left Germany only to return to Germany. I seemed to be losing ground. But I was told that the band had big gigs and a lucrative contract for recording and all sorts of malarkey that would only impress a run of the mill idiot. Well, I like to believe I was not run of the mill. (I'm not sure I really care for the way I put that.) But that's beside the point. The point is, unlike the 49 others they probably called before me who read between the lines (I want to believe I was at least ahead of 10.), I bought into it, hook, line and sinker, and literally within minutes I was meeting with the group's so- called tour manager, had my drums pilfered by someone who said they'd take them to Germany for me, and I was given a very suspicious looking plane ticket to the fatherland that I was told I could use at anytime to fly there.

Well, as you might imagine, I was not so travel savvy at the time and probably less so regarding the music world. Had I known what I know today about the industry, I would have given this guy half of a "peace sign" and walked out. But I didn't. All I knew is my drums were gone, and I had some sort of voucher in my hand that I immediately took to the airport, after explaining it all to Sonya, of course. As difficult as it might be to believe, except for those who have ever lived there, she was not exactly enamored with the idea of moving to Germany. Though, as I think I said, she did eventually join me there, but she was never very excited about it.

Upon arriving at the ticketing counter at Heathrow Airport, I was informed that the alleged ticket (I never called it that.) was, of course, worthless, which meant that I now had no drums and not much else, to be honest, and I had to pay my own way to Hannover,

Germany, in the hopes that I hadn't been part of some big scam. And so, without many options at hand, I calmly proceeded to buy myself a ticket (If you can call yelling and screaming "calmly proceeding"...), though not to Hannover but to Bremen (There were no direct flights to be had.) where I then had to catch a train to get to Hannover. When I finally got there, I was met by the former drummer of the band, Rudy Lenners, who I guess had graduated from drummer to chauffeur in hopes of having a real job that would please his parents I'm sure. He took me to an archaic German bedsit which was on the top floor of a building that had to have been leftover from the days of Kaiser Wilhelm I. Though I had no way to know it at the time, I won't forget the summer of 1977, not because of all that happened with the band, but because it was perhaps the hottest in the history of Germany. (I arrived in Germany on May 18. I remember the exact date because it was the date of Klaus' wedding.) Being in the "penthouse" (That's the way I think they described it to me when I was in England, though with the abundance of alcohol in my system, I may have misunderstood.) under a roof that had no vents or insulation, I felt every degree of every day regardless of whether it was measured in Celsius or Fahrenheit!

All of that aside, my priorities at that point led me to wonder the fate of my still yet to be seen and quite beloved drum set, however, which was a point of concern and stress to say the least. To hell with the band and the wedding! I had my priorities!

At any rate, it was hardly an auspicious beginning. I was, in fact, questioning my decision, and yet things went from bad to worse, if you can believe that. I did eventually find that everything was exactly as they had described it. How can that be bad? Well everything, in that case, meant everything except, of course, the gigs, the recording contracts and the tour. There was in fact nothing and not much on the horizon. So began my illustrious life as a Scorpion.

6

PAYING MORE DUES THAN A UNION MEMBER

So now the conquering hero had returned to his homeland feeling not so much like Don Quixote but more like Sancho Panza, a blundering sidekick conceived in the womb of abject failure. I mean the revelation at the airport in London was only a prelude to the disappointments that awaited me upon my return to German soil. In the simplest of terms, they promised me the elevator, and were in the process of only giving me the shaft. In retrospect, I have to wonder even more if, in fact, I was the first pick after the auditions, or if I was merely the first one stupid enough to believe the smoke that was being blown up my posterior. Even though I had been around the music business for what at that time seemed like a long time, I was still quite naïve and trusting. As such, I, of course, knew my fellow countrymen would never do something to hurt me. Boy, was I a complete moron... No, actually, I would have had to have been a lot smarter to be classified as a moron. Let's face it: I was an idiot!

As I went to pick up my luggage which I had stored at the train station, I couldn't help but wonder about the fate of my drums. I checked every pawnshop window I could find en route just as a precaution. I every bit anticipated finding them on sale in some underground pawnshop. (Remember, there was no EBay then.) If it hadn't been for them, more than likely I would have turned around at the airport in London and waited to reap the benefits of the harvest from Vineyard. (Maybe that was the entire plan. Kidnap the drums and force me to play with them!) I had never before been forced to pay in order to play. But essentially, that was what was happening. I will admit I was quite diplomatic when I finally reached the rehearsal studio. Being much more of a lover than a fighter, I wasn't really one to ever cause problems, and as soon as I saw my kit safely there, I was much more at ease.

However, my respite was short-lived. As I began to inquire in earnest and much more specificity about the gigs and recording and all the other normal questions anyone with half a brain would ask, I began to discover I had less than half a brain. With each question came a very different answer from those I heard in England. There were no gigs or at least very few. The band was not so very far ahead of the band I had been with in England. Hardly being just off a beer wagon, my disenchantment grew with each passing minute. I continued to develop a very solemn picture in my head which was the revelation that I left a pretty good situation in London to go to Germany and join a rock band with only a few gigs and a somewhat dubious or, at best, precarious album contract with RCA. To be honest, however, I quickly realized my options were quite limited at that point. The plane ticket did cost a great deal of money, since I had to buy it at the airport. I couldn't really afford to haul my drums and myself back across the Channel. There wasn't much for me to do except play out the string and see where it would lead.

You know, now as I think back about all of this, I am kind of glad I was a little naïve and trusting. There are those in the world who will say, "If I knew then what I know now…" about various things, and honestly, I am one who does on occasion as well. But in that one instance, being a little less insightful was perhaps the greatest break of my life. Had I been much more learned and hardened in matters of life, music and the business, I most assuredly would have packed up and left immediately. To coin a phrase that would eventually make me a lot of money, I was basically "another piece of meat" in the eyes of the guys in the band at that point. (No, that's not what the song is about. I'll tell you that story later.) Okay, so maybe they didn't see it that way, but if you look at the big picture, it does seem a bit suspicious. If you consider the realities of that time, it only made sense for the band to choose me over the other possible candidates that were available at the audition. For one, I was willing while perhaps some of my more worldly colleagues were not. I also was German and, as I mentioned, that might have been the biggest reason of all. Remember, at that time there was no European Union. And honestly, the Scorpions hardly had any connections at that point. As such, had they selected someone from another country, there would most probably have been immigration papers to deal with as well as other headaches that I'm sure they didn't want and definitely didn't need. I will admit that immigrating country to country in Europe in those years wasn't so difficult so long as you were from the west. But still, there would have been further complications for a band that didn't really have much more than a couple of, I'll be generous here, mildly unsuccessful albums. I really have to keep myself from laughing as I write this. But the point is, I think in the big picture, I may not have been the best drummer at the audition, but ultimately, given the circumstances, I may well have been the best option for the band in their eyes.

After the heart-wrenching dose of reality, I didn't waste too much time getting myself settled into the flat they had promised me in Hannover. No, not because I was readying myself for a quick escape like Rudy Lenners. The truth was, like most everything else that was part of being a Scorpion, there just wasn't enough to the place to take long to get settled. Then you can add to that the fact that I was technically "single", and I didn't really need very much. That was fortunate, actually, since I didn't have a whole lot at that point. The bedsit they gave me made the first one I had in London look like Buckingham Palace. But again, when you're young, what do you need? A little food, a roof over your head (And it was directly over my head...), and, of course, female companionship pretty much would normally suffice. Well, having a girlfriend really cut into the last one, but I made do in the interim until she joined me. In other words, I honorably honored my commitment to my lady – at least a little, anyway.

I didn't have a lot of time to rest, which may seem odd, given that that there was nothing going on with the Scorpions. It was more a personal choice, because I really didn't want any. I had to listen to and familiarize myself with the band's music in order to begin my transition. If I was going to be the new drummer, I needed to know what the former drummers had done. In all humble honesty, and I'm not trying to be haughty or conceited here, but I wasn't all that impressed by anything I heard. No, the music was good. Don't take this out of proper context. I just thought that it could have been even better, and I suspect so did the other guys in the band.

I began to get a little more background on the group as it was at that point. As would be the case for anyone with an ounce of curiosity and perhaps even less brains (The latter of which it seems I've already admitted I had.), I inquired more deftly about the circumstances that surrounded the departure of my various predecessors. The only one that mattered seemed to be the one immediately before me, who was, as I have mentioned, my chauffeur from the train station, Rudy Lenners. His reason for leaving wasn't because he was Belgian and thought it was beneath him to spend so much time with a band of Germans. It was because of health reasons about which I won't go into detail here because that is not my place. I can tell you it wasn't because he was sick of the other guys in the band. And, no, it wasn't that he was threatened by the other members to leave or they'd kill him. There was a bit more to it. On top of his health, he did, indeed, desire steadier work, though not as a driver. He wanted to return to his work with children as a teacher. So please, don't start playing games with this story. In this day and age, with all the gossip websites and magazines out there starving for information, the truth often takes a back seat to creative writing.

On the musical side, the album that preceded my entrance was called *Virgin Killer*, which itself was preceded by *In Trance*. Each, honestly, was a very interesting collection of songs. But that is what they were in my opinion – collections of songs. As I had originally discerned, the band really had no definable identity, which made the albums seem disjointed. The individual songs didn't blend with the consistency and precision, the fluidity, if you will, that seems so very much alive in most successful albums. I learned a guy named Dieter Dierks from Cologne had produced them.

Dieter Dierks was well-known within the borders of Germany at that time. I would say, if I'm allowed, he would in due course become perhaps the most recognizable figure in the development of what the press eventually dubbed "Krautrock". Having played in and having worked with several top local bands, his studio in Cologne would one day be a place where people like Michael Jackson and Tina Turner would go to to record albums. Neither I, nor anyone in the band realized it, but Dierks would become just as important to the Scorpions as any of the more public members. A producer, a good one, is perhaps the most vital element in the development, production and sound of a group. Time and again you can see how changes in that one spot on an album's credit list can bring about a recognizable and definite change in the direction and overall sound of a group.

Most people don't really understand or acknowledge the important role of a producer. According to the artist, the label and the management, it can, at times, be a thankless job, to say the least. Often, he is asked and expected to wear many hats as varied as a surrogate father, a psychotherapist and a whipping boy all without batting an eye or returning a coarse word. It is business. It's not personal. That is difficult for some to accept. Musically, he provides a band with an objective and stable (for the most part) point of view. It's not the same as an engineer. A recording engineer is a guy who basically turns the knobs and moves the faders and knows the technology of recording inside out. The producer isn't always so well-versed on such things. He's like a director of a movie when in the studio. His role is always that of trying to put the pieces together and define the feel and sound of the band in a way that will make them current, classic and yet original all at the same time. He is the one who, when allowed to do so by a band, can give it not five different and hardly congruous styles but one distinguishable sound melded from the heart of each member. That is what ultimately leads to success. However, the band has to be cooperative, and at that point, we were willing to listen to anyone who could help us take the next step forward.

There are certain producers in music who leave a definite and indelible handprint on everything they record. One that comes to mind is Todd Rundgren. He is a legitimate genius, and can make any artist sound better than he actually may be. However, there are downsides to such things. For one, groups often fail to emulate what he produces in the studio when required to do so on stage before a live audience. This can lead to disenchantment with fans who will feel cheated or even completely lose interest when the actual group sounds less than up to the level of their recordings.

Dieter was the right man in the right spot for the Scorpions. As his influence grew within the group, so did our sales. But, as you will also find out, familiarity did, indeed, breed contempt, because as his influence grew, so did the resentment within the group. But at the outset, he successfully reeled in the various egos, and focused the band in a unilateral and definite direction. Even with my limited knowledge and understanding of the music world, I knew that that was needed when I first heard them, and, obviously, so did Dieter. But sometimes change takes time, especially when you are toying with the overpowering egos of artists. The same ego that is necessary for the production and creation of most stars is that which can often lead to their eventual demise. Not everyone can do this job. It requires the three "D's": diplomacy, decorum and, most importantly, (self-) discipline. It doesn't, however, allow for the artist to know he's being manipulated even when he is. As I have said time and again and probably will a few more times within this book, I think every successful group has that perfect blend of elements that leads to its success. Those who may not be so much in the public eye but do their work behind the scenes should never be marginalized, but more appropriately, they should be celebrated. In Germany, many still consider Dieter our biggest name in production as I have already alluded. But when push came to shove at that point in time, the mid-1970, we were his boys, and honestly it's difficult to say who did more for whom. And so rather than worry about such things, I will just say that together we created the music that is the reason you are reading this book.

7
TAKEN BY FORCE

If someone were to have asked my opinion, though at that point, it was about as welcome as a rabbi at Ku Klux Klan meeting, the first order of business upon my inauspicious arrival in Germany, which I think I've made quite clear, should have been that of trying to put together some sort of tour or, at the very least, a few select concert dates someplace, so we could make a couple of bucks. Obviously, as I said, since I was the newcomer, I had little to no input into the decision-making process, and so I suspect it was probably more of a priority to me than to the others. Remember, by the way they were talking in England, I already thought the concerts were in place. But as became expected after the debacle at the airport and the other assorted anomalies, disappointments and exaggerations I encountered along the way, there was little to nothing in the offing within the foreseeable future. As it was, I seriously began considering the feasibility of doing a reunion tour with the Mastermen. At least we each made the equivalent of 150 Euros a weekend. (Again, for you literalists out there who might be poised to jump at the opportunity to put down my work, I know there were no Euros back then. I'm just putting this in modern terms to allow for the proper perspective.) By that time I would bet we could have made maybe twice that much. Sure beat the hell out of what I made the first few weeks as a Scorpion. Though the band was paying me a little salary, about 50 Euros a week (I'm not sure, but public assistance may have been more…) and gave me that luxurious apartment to live in, I was hardly in the position I expected to be in. I had assumed a position, all right. However, from my vantage point I was fully anticipating the next part would include a thorough prostate exam zealously conducted by a physician nicknamed Dr. Hook. Indeed, it did seem that I wasn't exactly taking steps forward in my career.

But for the tenured members of the band, those who actually had some say, recording remained the most important matter, and so rather than put together an extensive tour beyond the borders of West Germany (I would have been happy with an extensive tour of Lichtenstein at that point.), we began to work on the songs that would eventually make up my first album with the group, *Taken By Force*. What you have to remember is that was my first time working on an album in a group environment in the studio, which might seem odd to some of you since I had been working as a session player doing studio work for all those years in London. But playing on a session is very different from being part of a group. When you work within a group, there is a group dynamic that can never be overlooked or taken for granted. As I attempted to clarify earlier, it, the synergy therein, is what defines the sound of a group and alters its work from what could be considered little more than a collection of songs to a classic album.

We did play one show, probably hastily thrown together with the thought of appeasing the graduate of the Saarbrucken Music Academy (I didn't bother to tell them I didn't actually graduate. Why upset the apple strudel cart with a minor technicality?) It was in a small town hall type setting with no more than a thousand people. In truth, it was a far cry from the kind of shows I was expecting. Heck, I think I played for more people in Fuggs Blues. The more I think about it the more I wonder if perhaps the Scorpions would have had to open for one of my prior groups if we were still working.

We began our rehearsals not only for the concert but also the new album in a small basement in Hannover, which was pretty much in line with what I used to rehearse in when I first started in music. Again, that was called progress. Once more, you have to remember, it wasn't like it was in other bands I played in where we were simply copying or covering music from records. From little more than a series of chord changes and some "interesting" lyrics (And, honestly, I'm being generous in reference to the lyrics.), we began to put the original pieces together utilizing the creativity and imagination in each of us to build the songs for the new album. The songs were, for the most part, compositions from Uli, Rudolf and Klaus, though I did contribute one song titled "He's a Woman – She's a Man". I will talk about that in a bit more detail in a moment.

The routine was essentially the same concerning the presentation of a new song to the group irrespective of who brought it in. Honestly, the procedure never strayed very much from the established pattern throughout my time in the band. Uli and Rudolf both brought their songs in on a tape. After listening to the tape and hearing the ideas of the composer, we would then work together and jointly contribute ideas concerning our various parts. Uli seemed to have more of a sense of what he wanted compared to Klaus and Rudolf. As such, he would give me more guidance in his personal thoughts regarding drums, for example. But even he didn't overstep to the point of strangling my creativity and input.

As for "He's a Woman...", the music was written by Rudolf and initially had no lyric. He hummed the melody to me, and it kept rolling around in my head for several weeks after that. (There wasn't much else in my head, so it did sort of have room to roll...) It was during a promotional trip to Paris that an idea came to me, literally. We all drove together in one car, and I will tell you quite honestly, it was hardly a luxury limousine unless you consider a Volkswagen excessively decadent. Anyway, continuing the story, upon our arrival in the "City of Lights", we decided we would do a little sightseeing, as would anyone I suspect. Don't get your hopes too high, as we were hardly interested in landmarks like the Louvre or the Eiffel Tower. Those things were for tourists. We were all quite curious to explore the more important aspects of the city like the infamous "red light district". Keep in mind, we were very youthful and inquisitive 20-somethings at that point, and so we were a bit obsessed. That fixation really didn't change very much through the years. But still at that point, everything was interesting and peaked our sense of exploration. At any rate, as we were driving along one of the streets in that part of town, we saw this beautiful woman walking by herself. Being normal, hormonal, testosterone filled males, we summoned her over to our car thinking maybe she'd be interested in having a good time with some real-life rock stars or perhaps settle for spending some time with us. We gestured to her through the window, and it seemed to have attracted her attention enough to get her to come over and talk to us. As she made her way over to our car, slinking with a sexuality that would have made Marilyn Monroe jealous, we opened the window on the passenger side of the car and said a polite "bonjour" to which she replied in a very deep and definitely masculine voice, "Hi fellas". Well, within minutes, after getting over the shock of it and taking a long second look in the hopes that maybe it was American pop-singer Bonnie Tyler, I came up with the idea for the lyric. And the rest is Scorpion history.

As a result of my first endeavor into lyric writing for the band, it really didn't take the others long to recognize the fact that my grasp of the English language was perhaps a little stronger than that of any of them. They seemed amazed that I actually knew adjectives, adverbs and the always-confusing prepositional phrases! It was only natural, since I had lived in England for close to six years, though, honestly, if you ask me even today I will tell you I am still quite a novice compared to those with whom I've become associated over the years. Remember, I thought I knew a lot of English when I got to England in 1971. So my opinion really meant very little. However, as a byproduct of this perceived mastery by the other members of the group, and perception is everything in this world, I was given the task of writing more and more of the lyrics as the future albums illustrate, and, I guess, in a way, document. Rock and roll was and still is English language music as I've said, and so we knew the future for us was in that language. The band recognized that long before I came on board as I have already mentioned, and they sincerely wanted to upgrade the quality of their lyrics. I mean, really, "Streamrock Fever"? What the hell does that mean?

I will tell you one thing I learned early on: in a group situation, a musician needs to be a wee bit selfish in order to insure he gets proper credit for all the input he has on the production of an album. Percentages and credits sometimes referred to as "points" translate into cash, and so even though you may want to be a "team player", it is often better to be a little egocentric when it comes to such matters. In truth, I suspect I was deserving of many more points than I actually was awarded over the years, but you know, I'm not the type to look at such things that closely or worry about them as much as those who possess a much grander ego. My preference is that of peaceful co-existence within a group, and money is the easiest way to destroy a solid foundation and friendship. If a group really wants to maintain itself intact for a long period of time, the safest way to do it is to simply give group credits on all songs and equally distribute the points. In other words, at the end of the day, regardless of the contribution, every member of the group gets an equal share of the pie. In the long term, it will serve to keep the relationships cordial and the bickering isolated to the dominion of the wives. (I'll bet won't make many friends with that comment.)(Actually, I may wind up sleeping on the couch tonight.)

I know there are those of you who are reading this thinking, "It all sounds good, but so did Marxist communism… And besides, my group doesn't fight over money. We don't worry about that." Well, that's great! Let me be the first to pat you on the back. No, I guess I wouldn't be the first because obviously, you are already patting yourself on the back. Anyway, not wanting to be a harbinger of too many negative waves, I can venture to guess that your group, at least at this point, probably doesn't fight over who's going to drive the Mercedes tonight or which house in Beverly Hills you should buy for an orgy. So let me tell you from experience, money always corrupts. When you don't have any, you have nothing to fight about. It's when you start making money, real money, not 150 Euros a week, that's when the real inside arguments start. And even if there aren't any at that point, trust me, if anyone in the group happens to have a wife or serious and significant other (Remember I wrote "He's a Woman…") they will surely begin chirping in the ear of their "mate" and, of course, this will start him/her thinking. (I think it's a guarantee I'm going to be sleeping on the couch tonight…) So take Herman's word for it, the safest approach and the best way to keep friendships and rock groups alive is to distribute everything equally.

Throughout the rehearsals (Yes, believe it or not, I'm still writing about *Taken By Force* and the rehearsals therein. I realize that may have been forgotten with all of the side notes. I apologize for that. They couldn't be helped.) for the new album, I have to admit I enjoyed all of the music immensely, which was no surprise after the discussions I had previously had with Rudolf in London. We both shared a love of Led Zeppelin and sincerely believed that it was the direction to go for the band, given the tools we had at our disposal. So I was very happy musically. However, the rub within the group came from Uli's creative clash with Rudolf and Klaus, because he was more in line with the Hendrix school of rock and wanted the band to go there as I think I have previously mentioned. Heck, some might have considered him obsessed with Hendrix since he even went so far as to date Jimi's last girlfriend. (More on that in a second.)

So ultimately, there were, as you might well imagine, constant spats over our sound and direction. We fought over which songs to include on the album and which to keep filed away. There were also some that were permanently given a place in the circular file, or at least I thought they deserved that fate. You know, those would probably be worth gold today, I suppose. I often laugh at some of the re-releases that come out today on CD featuring "bonus tracks". More times than not these so called "gems" are little more than trash that the group hated playing, but because of money, they are now placed on a CD in the hopes that some poor schmuck will buy another copy of the album just to have those "collectibles". I will admit that there are at times some wonderful bonus tracks. Sometimes groups record and forget about songs because they continue to write new material and feel the newer songs are just plain better than the old ones. I'm no different as a composer. I will write a lot of songs and keep an extensive file. But when I write something new I'm always very excited about it, and for a period of time, it overshadows all of my old stuff. Only after a few months of playing and working with the song do I start to think of it equally with my other material and then objectively give it an appropriate place.

Well, as you can surely understand, a group that is constantly on tour is constantly writing on the road. It's either write, have sex with a groupie or drink and do drugs... Okay so the middle one might be most interesting. But honestly, even indiscriminate sex has its shortcomings. (No pun intended... For the record, I meant limitations.) I'm not exactly sure what the shortcomings are. But there must be. I mean, I'm sure for most male gynecologists the first few days in practice are probably a lot of fun. Even at that young and tender age, I was able to multitask, and many such interludes led to new songs. You see, I can even find a way to justify philandering behavior. However, at that point I wasn't married – technically only involved. So no matter how lecherous and lascivious my behavior may have been, I wasn't actually cheating on anyone who could file legal papers against me and make my life miserable. In spite of this, though, age has taught me many lessons and as I think back today about my behavior, my attitude was hardly anything to be proud of regardless of the circumstances. I will go more into that later in the book. But just know that I am now more of a realist with regard to this sort of behavior, and I see how I hurt a lot of people along the way. I will joke about it and seem to take it lightly, but I can't change history, and so it is a part of my story. But sometimes a person can "glamorize" inappropriate behavior, and it will lead to giving others the completely wrong impression. I do consider myself a "role-model" and hope that regardless of what I may say within these pages about my escapades and adventures you understand the remorse I now have for that which I did. Sometimes the context can be distorted and so just know that the ignorance of youth is not to be an excuse for what is morally wrong and undeniably deplorable and reprehensible. Keep in mind at all times, this is a story not a guideline for life or an outline for happiness.

Anyway, that said, the point I was attempting to make is, you can only take drugs, drink booze and have sex so long before it gets old. And so on the road especially, most musicians spend a lot of the down time writing, or let's say for the sake of the artistry, composing. I know that term seems better suited for Bach, Beethoven and the Starland Vocal Band. But I thought I would try to be a little more cerebral here for those who wish to live within a fantasy world as it relates to rock and roll. Heck, anyone knows if you write a good rock and roll song it's hardly so much a composition as it is something you have created. Most songs are not written out in musical script. Most are simply played, and the only thing written down is the accompanying lyric on a sheet of binder paper. Rock music, perhaps more than any other, although jazz musicians would have a serious argument here, is comprised of various musical elements. It is a creation from the heart, soul and mind of the composer. You write not only from the technical notes, meter and theory standpoint but also with feeling and internal expression!

Anyway, getting back to the story, most musicians who are touring or spending a lot of time on the road for whatever the reason (Some perhaps can't find their way home after all the drugs and booze.) write so much new material that, at times, it does most surely seem better than what they have on file. More often than not, however, the subsequent albums fail miserably when compared to a successful predecessor that might have been recorded after months of writing and even more time in rehearsal for a variety of reasons. First, albums recorded on the run are often attempts at imitation rather than original creations. The album a band or artist is touring to support can be so popular that the label will want them to do another just like it. At the suggestion of the label suits (Though demand might be a better word… By the way, a "suit" is a term we use for an "executive".), or perhaps in an effort to appease the critics, groups often make the mistake of trying to copy or duplicate their work rather than create original art. Many times this leads to disastrous results. A band will stop being creative and become formulaic and predictable. Though there does need to be a similarity in sound and production, there are extremes that can make a group sound like nothing more than a one-trick pony trying to capitalize on a prior success. Fans will quickly attach a negative stigma to them, and become wise to and quickly bored with such transparent exploits. I'm sure just about everyone can name a group or artist that falls into such a category. They tried to be who the critics or the label told them they were rather than simply being themselves.

Another problem many groups encounter is the fact that they are trying to reproduce an album in a manner that is quite different than the one they used to produce the original. By going in and out of the studio, adding tracks as time permits, they will come up with something that is a blend of styles and sounds caused by the lack of continuity in the studio. The chance to sit together in a studio and throw ideas liberally back and forth to get the best out of each song is vital. We spent a lot of time doing just that, which is why our albums were spaced so far apart. (I originally wrote, "spaced out", but I didn't think that sounded appropriate. That would much better describe a Frank Zappa creation.) But perhaps you can now better understand why an album that's a bit of a "disappointment" often follows an extremely popular album. A lot of times it is a matter of time. Often a group or label's haste to capitalize on the success colludes with their intrinsic greed to lower the standard from one of incalculable greatness to that of wretched mediocrity.

What we did on the road with regard to our creating new music wasn't so much writing as it was collecting ideas for future songs. For example, I would write lyric ideas on the road on whatever was handy like napkins, envelopes or on the butt of a groupie who just happened to be available when an idea came to me, and then come home and refine them. I admit hauling a groupie home was a bit cumbersome and a bit difficult to explain to my significant others, so I usually just copied the idea from her butt onto a piece of paper. Musical ideas, melodies and chord changes, by contrast, had to be worked out by the band to get the right feel out of each. (I was officially a piano player after my time at the Music Academy, and since we didn't have keyboards in the group, I had to keep ideas stored away in my head until I could get home or at least to a keyboard and pound them out a bit more completely. I'll tell you honestly, I lost several wonderful ideas along the way, and it was the reason I didn't write the music for many of the songs we recorded.)

So what about albums and the financial side of the group? I touched upon it earlier, but now let me go into a little more detail as to how it really works. What the average person doesn't really realize (I often feel I'd have to improve a great deal to be considered average...) is a group doesn't really make much money off of album sales. When we started, I think a group got about 1 dollar per album. It's more now, of course, because albums are more expensive. But imagine an album that sells 1 million copies, a "platinum album", would only give the group 1 million dollars. Yes, that's a lot of money until you begin to split the pie. With us, for example, there were five of us in the group. Add to that the producer's take for his labors. And, of course, we can't ever forget management's percentage. (If we do, they will remind us in a manner that would be about as subtle as a stripper in the backroom of a political convention.) Then subtract from all of that the deductions taken by the assorted licensing agencies and publishers to pay what at times can seem like a cast of thousands, and when you finally get down to distribution to the artist, what remains may still be a substantial amount, and yet it really isn't all that much when you think of what a "rock star" should be making in the fantasy world of the fans. Oh, and, of course, figure in the taxes at the end of the year... Can't forget those. Ask Al Capone.

At any rate, the bottom line is that a group doesn't really make a lot of money from album sales. However, the album sales boost the group's profile, which ultimately adds to their marketability and the related appearance fees. If a group is making a thousand dollars a night on the road and suddenly has a popular album on the charts, that price will jump substantially, perhaps to 10 times that amount overnight! It's all a simple economic matter of supply and demand. The demand for the group becomes much higher, and people are willing to pay more to see them. You see I did learn something at the school of economics. My father would be proud!

So, all of that is a preface into my first months with the Scorpions. Had I had someone's book to read that told me all of this, it would surely have made things a lot easier for me. And yet, we were a bit out of the ordinary, not just because of the fact that we were Germans but also because one of our most popular albums was not our first together as a group but the follow-up. However, we'll get there in a few pages. For the time being, we're focused on the still relatively unknown Scorpions and *Taken By Force*.

My initial reaction to the group's music was understandable to say the least. I had the sense, as I already mentioned, that they were trying to be a combination of many different groups that were popular at the time, and it showed in the compositions. Each song had a very unique feel from the others, which wasn't bad, but I thought it could easily keep us from having a recognizable identity. I felt that with Klaus Meine's very distinctive voice (In my opinion, he is perhaps the most underrated talent in the history of the genre.), the focus should be more on the vocal aspects of the group. However, the other musicians, other than Herman Rarebell, were outstanding players as well. In my opinion, both Rudolf and Uli were the equal of most any rock guitarist there was at the time. To keep them both happy was, of course, a constant point of friction and concern. And then add to this the fact that there was a continual "can you top this..." songwriting competition within the group as well.

Actually, that may have been one of the more important aspects of the group that over the long term helped guide us to success. With so much talent in one place, the pool from which we could draw songs was quite deep. But it also led to the aforementioned identity problems initially and, of course, the related conflict. That was where Dieter Dierks played his most significant role within the group. To blend the songs in a manner that made them indistinguishable from each other (in style) is the most important contribution a producer can make. On *Taken…* he had quite a tall order in that respect. When you have various songwriters you get a mélange of styles and thoughts involved. Look, for example, at the Beatles. In the early years, their songs were all just about the same. It was impossible to tell if John or Paul had written a specific piece. But as time passed and their styles evolved, it was quite simple to figure out who wrote what. And then, when finally they went off on their solo careers, it became even easier for even the least trained musician or listener to distinguish Paul's songs from John's, even though they were all listed as joint compositions within the Beatles catalog. And yet, because of George Martin's work on production, the most ardent fans never thought about the songs individually but the catalog as a whole even with Ringo and George making contributions. Every song was a Beatles' song.

In the end, Uli contributed three songs to *Taken By Force* – "I've Got to be Free", "Your Light" and "Sails of Charon". I think the former, "I've Got to be Free", showed that Uli was already contemplating his next step in music, which would be outside of and, he surely thought, beyond the Scorpions. It's actually easy for me to recognize his songs on all the albums he played on because they are "riff" driven. In other words, they feature a lot of guitar runs that give them a distinct feel and sound. Listen to the early Scorpion albums, the ones with Uli, and I am sure you'll see what I mean.

By contrast, the songs Klaus and Rudolf contributed, the remaining 5 songs for the album, were along a very different sort of line of thought. They were more "pop" oriented or at least more focused on commercial rock. Again, to a newcomer like myself, it was clear that something had to give, and being that I was in the Jacuzzi with Rudolf in our mutual admiration of Zeppelin and that ilk, I have to admit I did have my preference to be sure.

There was one interesting collaboration for the album that perhaps verges on a piece of rock and roll trivia for many. At that time, Uli was dating a German woman who was living in England and was quite infamous within the annals of rock and roll. Monika Danneman was arguably the person responsible for the death of Jimi Hendrix for those who wish to believe such rubbish. But she was Jimi's girlfriend, the one who supposedly gave him the sleeping pills he "accidentally" overdosed on because she improperly explained the dosage to him. At least that is the story I have always heard. Anyway, be that as it may, in the mid-1970's she had hooked up with Uli Jon Roth, and if you look on the album credits, you will see her name attached to co-writing credits on the song "We'll Burn the Sky". However, what is interesting or might be to those of you who like a good scandal, she didn't co-write it with Uli but with Rudolf. I just wanted to give "a piece of meat" to the rumormongers among you who like a salacious piece of trivial nonsense. As far as I know, there was nothing more to it than an innocent songwriting collaboration.

As the date of release approached, we had to decide upon and select the song we felt had the best chance to be a hit single. In the 1970's, the single was still vital, and the airplay tracks were the ones that spelled success or failure for the group. We decided that our best song was "He's a Woman... She's a Man". I can't say that I disagreed given my obvious vested interest therein. But keep in mind, the ultimate decision was in the hands of the record label, RCA, who, by some miracle, actually agreed with our thoughts. That was truly a novelty since no label ever seems to agree with an artist. You could tell most record execs the sky is blue, and they'd ask for corroboration just for the sake of an argument.

The album opened with a song that I think hinted at the eventual direction the band would lean toward. "Steamrock Fever" with its grinding, vinyl scratch-like intro that surely had to make many record buyers think their copy had a major flaw in the pressing (It's supposed to be the sound of heavy machinery used for road construction.) builds quickly into a heavy guitar drone reminiscent of something

Motorhead might have created but then sidesteps to what I consider can best be described as an orgasmic chorus section rivaling the most infectious "hooks" and melodic cliché refrains on the American "pop" charts anytime in the past 50 years.

You know, there is something that I found rather curious regarding the song. The lyrics are about something or other supposedly in Los Angeles. For guys who had never been to California, they seemed to have captured the essence of the state with the song. No, I don't mean the state of confusion, which I am sure many who have driven on the L.A. freeways could relate to. I just mean the spirit and feel of the area. I never remember asking Klaus where the idea came from, or why he chose Southern California to be the center for his "fever". I may have to remember to ask him someday. It's not as if the song makes any sense in the first place. So I kind of doubt there will be a conclusive answer.

The previously mentioned Schenker/Danneman collaboration followed, and I think it really gave Klaus his best moments on the album. It also illustrated or perhaps prefaced the sound that would become the Scorpions most universally recognized trademark – a slow, balladic guitar underneath a soft and sensual vocal that draws you in as it cascades into a section that reminds beyond any doubt you are listening to a Scorpions song.

"I've Got To Be Free" came next. It is a song that is exactly what I'm sure most of those who initially bought the album expected. Honestly, the album is on the softer side from those that were to follow in some ways as there was still the tug of war to be won and the final direction sustained and developed. A lot of input from outside can, most assuredly, cause this. Sometimes the identity of a group is compromised in favor of trying to be current. Well, at the time I do understand that we weren't exactly lighting up the charts anywhere, so we were forced to try and find a niche that our fans, at least those we thought we had as well as those we hoped to attract, would accept. However, as most of you know, once we did find that place, our "sweet spot" if you will, we stayed quite true to ourselves and, more importantly, to you the fans – at least for a period of time.

On the positive side, *Taken By Force*, though not selling initially in big numbers worldwide, did have its share of successes away from the charts and sales numbers. For one thing, it opened the door to the Japanese market where it was quite popular. It also attracted the attention of one of the biggest management companies in the entire world, Leber/Krebs, as well as some of the vital members of the media. It was an important stepping-stone upon which we could build, and we had every intention of laying every brick in just the right place. (That wasn't all we had every intention of laying... But that's another story yet to be told.)

Interestingly, the thing that brought us the most publicity for this album initially was not the music but the controversial cover. The original cover featured children playing with guns in a cemetery. Tell me what could be more wholesome than that? But for some reason, there were many who found it offensive, and so ultimately the original cover art was scrapped and that which was released in most markets was a cover that was simply a black shroud with pictures of us good-looking guys perched atop it! Beneath the black was, of course, the cemetery, but we never told anyone.

8

KIMONO BABY LIGHT MY FIRE

Like any great musical group, of course, we considered ourselves just that. We believed the new album was the "Son of Sam" of albums as we sincerely thought it was a real "killer", and it was definitely going to be our ticket out of the bowels of anonymity. The previous album, *Virgin Killer*, which in my opinion sported an even more appalling album cover than the original *Taken By Force* sleeve, had garnered the band a little attention outside of Germany for the first time, especially in Japan where hard rock music was quite popular. The polka never really caught on there, though I'm sure during World War II there probably was an occasional group sent over in some sort of cultural exchange meant for purposes of diplomacy. So, more than likely, we were the first group from the former Axis ally to obtain a bit of a following in the Orient.

But as we listened to the playback of each track, we were certain that the new album was what all the previous albums were not as we made sure to lace it with songs that were not too hard to overwhelm the fringe demographics and not too soft to underwhelm the hardcore rockers. However, as it is whenever you try to appease everyone, I suspect what happened was that we tried to be too much of too many things and wound up being a lot of nothing. The critics were not even that kind to us. Even though the style would eventually evolve into what most consider being the classic Scorpions sound, it was still, understandably, a work in progress. Regardless, we were happy with the result despite what the critics said. Remember, we were still a novelty to many – a German band singing in "broken" English. Broken? Hell, a compound fracture is more like it. Again, what the hell does "Steamrock" mean? (If we're going to be picky, what the hell does "Lovedrive" mean?) I guess that illustrated the reason the others felt the great Herman Rarebell would be their grammarian and savior in the lyric writing department. But honestly, at that point, I don't think it really mattered. Even in my wildest imagination, I can't believe that there were a lot of fans sitting on the edge of their seats in Lincoln, Nebraska waiting to hear from us or any other German. Nena and her balloons was still a half a decade away, and what kind of numskull (ie, dum kopf) in his right mind would have thought some goofy song about "99 Luftballons" was going to be a hit in America? Besides, she sung in German. The English version sunk like the Edmund Fitzgerald. (The ship, not the Gordon Lightfoot song…)

We explained all of this to our record company RCA, well, except for the part about Nena, as we tried to convince them that we wanted to go to America. But they laughed and said, "Yeah sure… They're just waiting for you guys to come over…" We had a really supportive label as you can tell. Really inspired us. As a result, rather than storm the beaches of California, we opted for a tour of Japan. In truth, it probably was the best decision for us at the time, not to mention the only option actually given to us as the fans there were rabid to say the least. No, wild animals hadn't bitten them. Please don't anyone write me a letter claiming that I'm slandering the people of Japan. In this day and age, a day and age with too many attorneys who have absolutely nothing to do, it seems, especially in America, one has to watch everything he says. But honestly, it was as if they really had been clamoring for us to show our obviously handsome visages and play our equally seductive music. We didn't believe that until the record label changed the cover of our album. I mean they preferred to feature our pictures rather than the kid with a machine gun. Must've meant they thought we were damned good-looking! In fact, *Taken By Force* took Japan by force, even with our pictures gracing the cover. It attained the level of a gold record there, which, at that time, was the world's second largest music market. But as I think back, I think I already said England was the second a couple chapters ago. Maybe it was the third largest... Or maybe England was number 3... Then what about Russia? Well, actually, no one can accurately represent sales in Russia, since it has been notoriously the center of a lot of black-market reproductions over the years. I'm sure there is someone there with a "Sorpeans" album thinking it's the genuine article. Anyway, the point is, who the hell cares? Bottom line... We sold a hell of a lot of albums somewhere. Does it really matter where? In truth, or at least in my opinion which I like to believe is the truth, this is completely unimportant, and I'm wasting time that could be better spent plucking my eyebrows! Anyway, regardless of the debate on size, after all as women often lie to their boyfriends, size doesn't matter, we felt quite proud of being popular somewhere other than Germany where, in fact, we weren't even as well-known as we were in Japan. We believed, at least privately, the accomplishment and the tour showed us what being a rock star was like and unlike our label, gave us a little positive reinforcement for our work.

We warmed up for Japan with a few shows in Europe. In January, we played in Stuttgart and Mulheim in Germany, which come to think of it, were quite cold, as were Amsterdam and Utrecht in Holland in the spring. Then again, Holland is always cold and, for that matter, wet. It doesn't matter when you're there. It's bound to be miserable. It is, in many ways, quite a contrast to the women in Holland whom we enjoyed. They always seemed to be quite warm. But that's beside the point. From there, we went to an equally chilly London with equally warm women for a show there prior to embarking on the 12-hour flight to Japan. You know, the more I think about it now the more I realize we hardly warmed up. I mean baseball players seem to have the right idea in America. From what I understand, they prepare for their season in Florida and Arizona.

If we had really wanted to warm up, we should have gone to Monte Carlo! But in reality, the only thing people in Monaco knew about Scorpions at that time was that they were extremely pricey Italian sports cars produced by the Lancia Company.

As you probably already surmised, I had never been on an airplane for more than a couple hours. So that, in itself, was quite an interesting adventure. Flying over the polar ice caps was not so different from Holland. I know it's not that cold there. Come on, have a little sense of humor. It's a lot warmer over the polar ice caps. Anyway, during the flight, I did come to realize that such long flights allowed for a great deal of interaction with the cabin crew and, in truth, the stewardesses were surely enamored with all of us because we were the Scorpions. We forced them to pose for pictures with us, and we gave them our autographs and hotel name whether they wanted it or not. We had a reputation to build at that point, so we didn't want to waste time! However, seriously, such behavior actually did eventually become quite commonplace as our flights went from economy to first class with our rise in popularity. I'm not sure if we were more popular with the stewardesses, though. Free booze and peanuts can be a lethal combination.

Actually, on the first trip over to the Asian continent, we flew on a DC-10 and travelled, via an unscheduled landing, through New Delhi. So much for the credibility of my polar ice caps story, huh? On future trips, we did fly over the North Pole. I took a little license for the sake of a joke. Not the worst of all sins, is it? The point here is we had to land for our own good according to what we were told, as there was a problem with the airplane. When you're 35,000 feet in the air and the pilot says there's a problem, there aren't a whole lot of people who are going to argue with him. I mean her... Or should it be it. Pick whichever objective personal pronoun you want. This political correctness stuff is a pain when writing a book like this.

Anyway, though it may have been good for the many, landing in India wasn't the best thing for the soon to be dubbed "Herman Ze German". We were told by the airline that they would put us up in a hotel while the needed repairs were being made, which was where we stayed until they were ready for us to continue our journey. I have to tell you, for some reason, a reason I regret to this day, I was quite hungry while we waited. I searched all over town for a good beef hamburger or would have been satisfied if I could have found a pork sausage or two. But there was neither to be found! So I made the mistake of opting for some innocent looking ice cream, which I came to find out was anything but innocent. As best as I can figure, it was directly responsible for bringing about a horrible case of Montezuma's revenge. (Like there's a good case...) Or perhaps it was Mahatma Gandhi's revenge? Not that it really mattered at that point because whatever it was called, I was sick as hell throughout the entirety of the tour. So if any of the songs on the recordings made of those shows in Japan sound a little rushed, well, you probably can understand why. The drummer sort of had to finish the set in a bit of a hurry.

Upon our arrival in Japan, we were met with something that I suspect was akin to a "Beatles-like" greeting. It was similar to the way I expected to be greeted when I first went to England. There were actual fans at the airport waiting in droves, and the terminal as well, to meet our plane. I harkened back to the memories of my youth. I remembered seeing movies and pictures of celebrities who were greeted in such a manner when arriving in different places, but honestly, I never did and still don't think of myself as a celebrity. This was shocking for me because it was not so long before that I played in an empty military club for a bunch of very genial yet quite stoic tables and chairs. So to have all these people actually recognize us and courteously welcome us to their country was something that did take a little getting used to.

As for the people of Japan, they were genuinely warm and friendly throughout our stay. We played only four shows... I know I have called it a tour. Four shows hardly seem like a tour. We played two in Tokyo and one each in Nagoya and Osaka. But no matter how long we were there, I myself was so taken with the country, not to mention the quite beautiful and alluring geishas we encountered happily as often as possible during our free time exploring the traditions of the Orient, that I wanted to proudly boast to all who cared to notice how special it was. I was so impressed by the people and the country I bought myself a kimono to take back to Germany with me, and I wore it everywhere. I admit it was a bit out of place with the Hannoveranian landscape, but I really didn't care. It did become quite a conversation piece as people were asking me about it… This especially helped with the ladies.

As you probably figured, since I briefly mentioned it, the shows in Japan were recorded during the tour. Those recordings, or at least various parts of those recordings and the eventually released album that is now considered a bit of a Scorpions' collectible, is called *The Tokyo Tapes*. The recordings do give a taste of what an early Scorpions concert was like, for better or worse. It also marked the last recordings made by Uli Jon Roth with us as his days with the band as "lead" guitarist were drawing to a close.

Uli was, without a doubt, quite a temperamental sort as an artist in perhaps too many ways. He was most concerned about every aspect of his music and always focused on the aesthetics first and foremost. He refused to compromise on his "art", and at times, that did make things more difficult for all of us. But I can understand completely and respect his attitude. Money can never be a replacement for self-respect, and at the time of his departure, he really wasn't giving up much monetarily. As such, his integrity was much more valuable. I do wonder to this day how it may have changed the band's destiny or Uli's had he stayed on. Such thoughts are interesting fodder for speculative conversation.

Something that may give you a little indication of Uli's borderline compulsive nature when it came to his music was the solo he played for the song "He's a Woman…" when we recorded it in the studio. He was never happy with what he did there for whatever the reason. During the tour of Japan, we had the chance to do a TV show. They wanted us to play our single which was "He's a Woman…", but Uli, who again was unhappy with the solo, didn't want to play it. He felt it was beneath his talents and would be an insult to his fans if he had to play it. In fact, he felt that way not only about his solo but also about the entire song mainly because he didn't write it. At least that is my opinion.

Anyway, getting back to the live album, for the most part, it featured songs from all the previously released albums as well as some, of course, from *Taken By Force* like "Steamrock Fever", "We'll Burn The Sky", and "He's a Woman..." – the latter regardless of whether or not Uli liked playing it.

There were also a couple of intriguing parts of our sets in Japan that appear on the album. Not that all of it wasn't interesting. At that point, everything was interesting because it was my first chance to play in front of thousands of people! Anyway, during that tour, since we really didn't have a large catalog of hits to choose from, we performed, at least in my opinion, some darn fine covers of classic rock songs like Little Richard's "Long Tall Sally" and Elvis's "Hound Dog". I guess most rock bands have a stable of old rock tunes they once played when they were growing up. So I know it's not really a novelty. But for us, it was something that our fans, I'm sure, may appreciate even more today than they may have then.

Allow me to interject something for the musicians out there again. I mentioned early on in this book that when I was with the Mastermen and Fuggs Blues, we tried to sound like the records when we covered songs. We copied, note for note and beat for beat, everything the originators did. But I will tell you, now that I'm on the other side of the spectrum musically, the fastest way to guarantee your being labeled a cover band is to try and play covers exactly like a record. However, if you take a popular song and give it your own identity, which I honestly think was best done by Van Halen early on with their covers of songs like the Kinks' "You've Really Got Me" and Roy Orbison's "Pretty Woman", you will discover that they actually can help you develop your own individuality in the music industry. People like "cover" songs when they are done well. Originality is always the key that separates a good cover from one that is simply a second rate imitation. If people want to hear a bad imitation, they

80

can get drunk and go to a karaoke bar. Actually, I don't know that there is any other way anyone in his or her right mind could go to such a bar. So use classic songs, all those except, of course, Scorpion songs, which certainly should never be tampered with, and build on that foundation something that makes you unique, current and original. Sounds change, but classic melodies never do.

9
GOODBYE ULI – HELLO MATTHIAS

We had some suspicions as we completed our "vast" array of scheduled appearances in Japan but nothing definite. It wasn't until we returned to West Germany that we discovered Uli had made up his mind and decided to leave the band. To put it simply, it was not only a matter of a directional difference and a general difference in opinion about where the band should go, but also, as I mentioned before, it was a matter of integrity that led to his departure. Uli believed he owed it to himself and our fans, all three of them, to stay true to himself, and that the band should remain more steadfastly in line with its roots as he saw them. He didn't like the commercialism that had seemingly become a part of all conversations about the future, nor was he pleased with the song selection and overall production of *Taken By Force*. I'm not even sure he was happy with the death of vaudeville or in our preference of Bavarian beer, but he kept that information to himself. So I guess we'll never know. He felt musically, however, we were becoming "pussified"! In other words, we were tainting our sound in an effort to mollify women who notoriously didn't care for real heavy music but preferred things more toward the midlands of rock and roll. He wanted to keep us on the hard rock side, which for him meant combining elements of classical music with a mixture of Hendrix thrown in for good measure. He just couldn't palate the "pop" influences that in his opinion seemed to be steering our ship and dominating our thoughts. As I understand it, Eric Clapton had a similar experience nearing the end of his tenure with the Yardbirds. Once "For Your Love" became a hit, his interest in the band waned. He was a serious blues player, and he didn't like the pop sound that the band was starting to incorporate into their music. The way Uli was talking, it was as if overnight we had openly embraced disco and were planning to record the follow-up album for Saturday Night Fever! Anyway, to make a long story short, which probably I have already failed to do, he left the Scorpions in search of artistic fulfillment and formed his own group with the Hendrix-esque name "Electric Sun".

There are always reasons that necessitate personnel changes in groups. Sometimes it's for health reasons as was the reason given for my having been recruited. Other times it is artistic as it apparently was with Uli. And at other times, it's simply because the guy is an asshole. In such cases, he can be forcibly removed from the band. However, in this case, as I said, it was completely Uli's decision, and that left us with a void that needed to be filled before we began work on our next album.

Despite still having barely even scratched the surface of the American market, we were certain our next album would be the one to open that door. We really were being the epitome of optimists. I suspect if we had been on the ill-fated Titanic, chances are quite good we'd have been wandering about the decks saying, "Hey, great night for a swim, don't you think?" But we were young... Well, relatively young... And so with our inner beliefs setting the tone and controlling our mindset, our focus became one of trying to write more commercial friendly rock that would allow us to hopefully get much-needed airplay not only in the U.S. but also around the world. Of course, in an effort to follow that line of thought, I wrote "Another Piece of Meat..." Hardly a song that would gain kudos from the likes of Donny and Marie (As if that would have mattered...), but for me, it was commercial!

RCA, our record company at the time, did what they could for us, at least that was their story. They felt by putting "Steamrock Fever" on one of their "promotional" albums, an album that went "aluminum" I'm sure (heard by maybe 10 people), since next to no one listens to such albums because they are handed out at conventions like jelly beans or given as "Christmas bonuses" to gullible, kiss-up employees of the label. But to the hierarchy at RCA, if you had heard them talk about it, it was as if they had just given us personally hand-engraved keys to Fort Knox! However, even with that incredible push, our *Taken By Force* album still never seemed to get off the ground outside of Japan and, of course, parts of Europe – most notably the Erbel, Meine, Buchholz and Schenker homes.

Having had so much success in finding a drummer there, though I still wonder if they thought of it as success or simply my youthful willingness to accept the crap they were feeding me, we decided to go back to England in search of another victim and maybe find a new guitarist, too. It was at that same time Michael Schenker had a parting of the ways with UFO for an assortment of reasons, which I guess you would have to read his book to find out. However, for our timing, it sort of worked out, as he was able to fill in for a period on stage, and even take part in the recording of the first tracks that would eventually make up the *Lovedrive* album. He was on board, in fact, for "Another Piece of Meat" and "Coast to Coast" as well as the title track while we sought out a new, full time lead player. (For those familiar with Michael's work, it's not difficult to pick out the songs on which he played. He is truly an incredibly gifted guitarist with a unique style all his own.) Michael would have been the best choice, of course. We all were unwavering in our agreement on that. But he made it very clear from the outset he was temporary and had other ideas and commitments not to mention a few of his own personal demons that needed to be exorcised completely. Those, however, he had yet to come to grips with.

We auditioned something like 50 guitar players in London before finally finding the one we thought was the best fit for our group.

Again, the fact that he was German, as was suspiciously the case with me as well, and from Hannover no less, Matthias Jabs seemed to be the right man in the right spot. (He also wouldn't need the use of the lovely bedsit I was so generously given…) However, whenever changes happen, comparisons immediately are made. Some of our fans, perhaps one of the three, were quite disappointed with Uli's departure while others really didn't seem to notice or care. In fact, in a way, Matthias's addition seemed to fuel yet still another slight change and helped complete the establishment of the band's signature sound.

What I think was, in all humble sincerity, the most important change in the structure and formula of the band may have been the addition of a handful of Herman Rarebell collaborations on the new album. Okay, so that's a bit presumptuous, but I did have a much more active role in the songwriting starting with *Lovedrive*. Many, to this day, believe it to be the quintessential Scorpions album. I can't say that they are wrong because it did seem to kick off our career as worldwide artists not just local and Japanese heroes. Anyway, my contributions on this album are, of course, noted and not noted as it is with everyone in the band. For writing credits, I did write the lyrics and some of the music with Rudolf for "Another Piece of Meat" which is one of my personal favorites and co-wrote with Rudolf and Klaus "Is There Anybody There". And surely, not to be forgotten is the song that would become our first real success "Loving You Sunday Morning".

The song "Another Piece of Meat" is, believe it or not, actually a true story like most all of my lyrics. And again, no, it's not a personal story about my recruitment/kidnapping to join the band! It's about a girl in Japan I dated during the first visit. She was in essence a gap filler in between visits to the Geisha houses, playing concerts and the countless trips to the bathroom I was forced to make as a result of the dish of Krishna and Kumar's ice cream I had in India. And, of course, let's not forget the general overall debauchery we partook in that became a way of life for all of us. This young lady, darling as she was, for some unexplainable reason, had an affinity for not only the music of the Scorpions but also the sport of Kickboxing. Don't know if there was a correlation, but I hope it was only coincidental not indicting through guilt by association.

Okay, to clarify for those of you who are not familiar with the so-called sport of Kickboxing, as near as I can figure, it was essentially the forerunner to what is called "Ultimate Fighting" these days. Or is it "Mixed Martial Arts"? I don't really follow such drivel to be honest, so you'll have to forgive my ignorance. The one thing that was clear and easy to identify was the fact that Kickboxing is very brutal. Kind of like being forced to sit through three consecutive Michael Moorer movies. I mean, maybe I'm weird, well, actually, I admit I probably am, but tell me how it can be entertaining to watch two guys literally kick the "manure" out of each other for an hour?

Well, anyway, getting back to the story. My young lady companion that evening wanted to show me what a sensitive and innocent lass she was, and so she took me to a Kickboxing exhibition of some sort on an off night I had during the tour, and I will tell you the truth, I was aghast by the violence. It was almost as bad as Hockey Night on Canadian television! However, my date seemed to think it was rather tame by comparison to what she had been exposed to within her life. (I guess she had been to a Sex Pistols concert.) But to me, in the end, after having had to endure more bloodshed than at a Jimmy Carter cabinet meeting, (Remember, for better or worse he was the U.S. President then.) I just flat out told her, showing my own decorum, sensitivity and chivalrous diplomacy, "Let's get the hell out of here. I can't take this garbage anymore. You're just another piece of meat to me..." You have to admit, even at such a young and tender age, I was still a hopeless romantic. And, of course, after that, given that she probably didn't even understand completely what I was saying, we went back to my hotel and...

As I mentioned with regard to *Taken By Force*, we did seem to be feeling our oats in a manner of speaking during that album because we had yet to find our place in the sun. But with *Lovedrive*, we were no longer tugged in different creative directions from within. The writing was shared, as I said, by just three voices that all had a common vision for the group. We were never going to be the next Led Zeppelin. Nor did we want to try to be. There was already one of those. We had to be the first Scorpions, and so as you will notice as you listen to *Lovedrive* and compare it to *Taken By Force*, the centerpiece of the band was no longer the guitars but the unmistakable voice of Klaus Meine. Putting him up front for all to hear may have been the best of all the decisions we made as a band as he gave us the distinctive presence we so very much needed. Buried as he was on prior albums, the vocals were seemingly never audible to a point of helping the band. He was simply an instrument, not an integral part of the signature, and that was something we wanted to change. What was the point in doing songs in English if Klaus wasn't going to be heard or understood? So putting the emphasis on vocals and using the guitars as a supplement seemed to be the key ingredient to making the Scorpions a true player in the rock and roll game.

A lot of this was a result of the added influence Dieter was beginning to have. He had earned our respect through his work, and we were quite open to all of his suggestions. He was instrumental in developing Klaus as a vocalist and giving our sound the needed "tweak". The difference between five and six on a soundboard fader doesn't seem like much until you start to mix in the other supporting pieces accordingly. He spent hours, days even, on all the instrument sounds as well. He heard something in the new material that perhaps he hadn't heard previously. He would spend upwards of 16 hours a day working on getting just the right combinations to make the sound perfect. I worked with him at some points to the extent of even falling asleep behind my drums. I once got a call and in mid-sentence fell asleep while I was talking to whoever was on the other side of the line. The days were quite long for all of us. We all did that sort of thing to make sure we were producing not just an album but a masterpiece.

Another important directional change was that of entering us into the world of "power ballads". We didn't realize it at the time, but the addition of the female friendly ballads would be the ingredient that would separate us from so many other hard rock acts and give us the needed element to become a success. As I mentioned, the world had a Led Zeppelin. But at that point, in 1979, there was no such thing as a power ballad. Yes, some rock bands like UFO did do ballads. But they were, for the most part, considered album fillers that a lot of listeners probably resented. I think we sort of redefined the art form in some ways to make those songs enjoyable not only for the ladies but for their dates as well. Finding the right combination that will help make a woman cry and get a guy laid is the key to any successful venture within this world be it music or cheeseburgers. Those two things, no not music and cheeseburgers, I meant sensitivity and sex, are the things that both respond to best! So between "Always Somewhere" and "Holiday", we began to establish an important precedence. Both were overlooked initially but did set the stage for things to come.

In the mean time, while we were still in he midst of recording the new album, hot off our "successes" in Japan, for some strange reason we began to truly get noticed by the press and media. The media of the day was quite different than today. Today we would have been ignored like Armenia's contingent at the Summer Olympic Games. But in 1978, we truly were considered to be a hidden treasure in the eyes of many who wrote for the various trade publications, and we began getting a lot of attention from abroad. Actually, we were getting a lot of attention from a lot of broads. But that's beside the point. Okay, so that's a really bad joke. But heck, once you've stuck your neck out like I have time and again in this book, what's the difference how far? At any rate, our management in Germany was still far from convinced that we could make it in America. RCA, who at that time still had our recording rights, was still of that ilk as well. We felt we deserved a little more support and were unhappy with the consistently negative attitudes we were encountering from those who were supposedly on our side. As a result, Dieter and his lawyer Marvin Katz, arranged a soiree with a new label, a German label called Harvest, which was a subsidiary of EMI and had an American wing, Mercury Records. RCA was hardly losing sleep over our departure. Though no label ever likes losing an artist, they were sure we would never be much more than we already were. So to them, our leaving was hardly a blip on the radar. (I wonder if today they even realize we were once on their label?) Anyway, from *Lovedrive* forward, we were a part of the Mercury Records family.

It was at that same time, roughly (Remember, I'm getting up there in years so my memory isn't exact on dates 30 or 40 years ago.), Peter Mensch of Leber-Krebs Management contacted us. Mensch called me, personally, now living in a spacious and luxurious, one bedroom apartment, to talk about the band and himself. No agent can ever seemingly have a conversation without talking about him or herself though to be fair, he did it much less than some. At the time, keep in mind, they were the biggest management company in the world. With a roster of talent that included the likes of Ted Nugent, AC/DC and Aerosmith, we were most certainly flattered and excited to be considered in such aristocracy. He offered to manage us and wanted to bring us to the U.S.. None of us had ever been to America, and so we prepared to take the country by storm! (We had failed to take them by force so we did the next best thing.)

The first stop was Cleveland and a rock festival featuring, not surprisingly, Ted Nugent, AC/DC and Aerosmith along with Journey and Thin Lizzy. I will tell you at that point, it was very much a learning experience for us to see how these much more experienced and polished bands handled crowds of that size, as well as watching their overall performances. Yes, I know most of you are thinking, "Cleveland?" Well, honestly, I had never heard of the place myself, but we were assured that it was a great city for rock and roll. Remember, that was before there was a hall of fame there.

I will say here that I could go on and on, as could many in the industry I'm sure, about the dubious nature of the so-called "hall of fame". But the record speaks for itself. We sold close to one hundred million records, which I suspect is about 95 million, more than some of those who have been inducted. And then add to that the mysterious exclusion of American groups like KISS, Journey, Ted Nugent and Grand Funk Railroad (To name but a few...), each of whom was, for a period of time, the biggest rock and roll act in the world, as well as overlooking a European group like Deep Purple while inducting such fringe artists as Elvis Costello and The Pretenders (Keep in mind, I like both, but that's beside the point.), well, it can't possibly make sense to anyone who isn't suffering from the residual affect of over-indulgent drug use. Well, if anyone were to ask me, I would tell him bluntly, I think it's a bit of an embarrassment to the rock and roll community and far from a true representation of the legendary status that should be equated with such places of honor. I suspect, like all things, it's all a matter of politics not influence or talent, and it's a shame because the fans are the ones who are ultimately cheated. They are the ones who make the stars, and yet their voices are the last ones listened to by those within the industry. Honestly, I don't care if we ever get selected for entry because I play rock and roll for the fans not for the critics or voters, and I think the same holds true for the opinions of Rudolf, Klaus, Matthias and Francis. I just think it's a sad reality, and in some ways indicative of some of that which has forever been wrong within the music world.

Well, I'll get off my soapbox now and continue with my story. Where was I? Or better might be to ask was I anywhere? Oh, right, Cleveland. No jokes. It's not like I said we were in Fresno. I know, please, no one in Fresno be offended. (I spent a month there one night.) A little later in this book I'll tell you something more about Fresno, California that you may not believe. But for now, we're in Cleveland where I understand they once had a lake that caught on fire! Tell me if that doesn't show just how special that city must be? It's not every city that can ignite a body of water!

So as we arrived in Cleveland on July 27, 1979, we were, of course, surprised that our first gig in the States would be in front of 70,000 people. All right, so there were only about 30,000 there when we played our set. But still, it was more than we expected, and the response was incredible to say the least.

Actually, I should preface Cleveland with a few other cities because, honestly, we did, once again, warm up in cold weather

90

places doing an assortment of shows in Germany, France, Scotland, England and once again ran through Japan. We also spent a lot of time making personal appearances at radio stations to push the new album in between. So by the time we got to Cleveland, it was the end of July, which as I understood was about the best time of year to be there. Hot, humid, mosquito infested. What more could anyone want? From Cleveland we stayed with Nugent and AC/DC and did shows in Chicago, Indianapolis, Milwaukee and Fort Wayne, Indiana. Sort of sounds like a "which one doesn't fit into this group" multiple choice, doesn't it? For a couple of the shows we opened for Pat Travers and Sammy Hagar. Remember we were the new kids on the block... No, we weren't a bunch of pre-pubescent teenagers singing horrible music they wouldn't even play in an elevator. I meant we were new in America, so really we had to make a name for ourselves. You have to pay your dues no matter where you go in music, unless, of course, your uncle is a label suit.

Truly, this tour was not the most well-devised one since we played a handful of shows in one country and then jumped to another, in this case back to Europe, and then over to Japan again, and then back to the U.S.. It was all part of paying our dues, and it did seem to pay off for us as *Lovedrive* actually began moving on the American charts. It sustained us in the States and established us as a viable act to be reckoned with. I think it eventually reached the mid-50's on the U.S. Billboard chart, which we thought was quite an accomplishment for a bunch of Germans. We were quite proud of ourselves.

There is, of course, a side note to the album itself. Once again, as had previously been the case with our prior albums, the cover was controversial. The original cover, as well as that which now is on the CD, sported a picture of a man with a woman whose blouse is open revealing her breast. However, her nipple has a piece of chewing gum stuck to it which is also stuck to the hand of her male suitor. We thought it was funny, to be honest, but obviously the American critics (who never had a sense of humor) and the label (equally devoid of a funny bone) didn't agree. As such, in a move to appease we eventually bowed to the pressure, which is why the original release, at least in the U.S., was covered with red vinyl to conceal what was to be the "Cover of the Year" as voted by Playboy Magazine.

The story behind the cover is a simple one really. I know, often, there are hidden messages or big elaborate tales about the creation of an album cover. But in this case it's really not such a big deal. Before the music had been completed, I told the band that we should employ the same company that did Pink Floyd's cover for *Wish You Were Here* and Zeppelin's *Houses Of The Holy,* Hipgnosis. So Klaus and I met with a fellow named Storm Thorgeson, one of the main guys at Hipgnosis, and we told him we wanted a really good album cover. (As if we would meet with him and tell him we wanted a crappy cover...) So a few weeks later he flew from London to Cologne, where we were working in Dieters studio, to reveal the results of his labors. He showed us about 10 different ideas for the album. Immediately, we all went for the same one and that eventually became the cover for the album. What I really didn't understand was why there was so much commotion and negative hoopla over our covers? Why were they considered so controversial while other bands, especially Roxy Music, who had naked women on the front of their *Country Life* album, had seemingly no one even batting an eye? At least the woman had a piece of gum covering her nipple. Hardly politically correct I admit, yet we always had the impression that America was the land of freedom of speech. We learned a quick lesson in American freedom.

It is true that Europe has always been a bit more liberal than the United States when it comes to sex and drugs. Anyone who's wandered the streets of Amsterdam can attest to the latter. But I will tell you there are times when I do wonder if such things are as necessary as they seem to have become. I am not one who believes in censorship, but a look around the music industry does make you wonder if a little self-restraint would not be perhaps more appropriate at this point. Teenagers and even young children are influenced greatly by what they see and hear. We learned this first-hand through our journey in the music world. An artist can make a lasting impression, good and bad, on young people. There is a responsibility that needs to be taken. I admit our album covers did push the envelope, but, honestly, they were mild compared to much of what I see and hear today. I know, I'm an "old fuddy-duddy" and perhaps a hypocrite in the eyes of some of you who are reading this. But I don't think our covers promoted or encouraged any improprieties. Sure there are those who'll claim our original cover for *Taken By Force* could have influenced some of the kids to take guns to school and shoot up the place if it had been released. But even without it, they did anyway. So would it have changed anything? Such accusatory individuals and entities are always looking for scapegoats. They must be, of course, quite sick people, those making the accusations as well as the perpetrators, because you cannot promote something through a song or album cover. You need to accept responsibility for every action you take and each decision you make. Behavior, of children especially, starts in their home. So even though I do not think the music or entertainment industry can or should turn its back on its responsibility, I think there is equal responsibility in many varying directions to be taken and given. Our responsibility is not only that of not promoting and/or glorifying improper societal behavior blatantly like some of the rap artists seem to think is cool, but to try and entertain through our art and bring happiness to the world. Regardless of what some think, a "tongue-in-cheek" album cover can't influence anyone unless there is an open door left by those who are with a person on a regular basis. And, no, it was not demeaning toward women. It was actually just the contrary. Think about it.

10
ANIMALS AND THE ZOO

Well, we were off to the races whether or not we realized it. I suppose we were a bit intimidated by the path we had taken, given the suddenness of our success. Just hearing our songs on the radio made us "giddy" not so much earlier. Seeing an album ranked on charts around the world was almost as good as sex! Although we were still years away from attaining the status of "superstars", all the important elements were there and we were garnering a level of respect within the industry as well as developing the all-important fan base in various key markets like the U.S., Japan and the always-pivotal Marshall Islands.

As the *Lovedrive* tour came to a close, and we began to contemplate and consider our next controversial album cover as well as the songs to put on the record inside, we realized how important a follow-up would be to our career. Having made a somewhat dubious reputation for obnoxious and offensive album covers, we really didn't want to stray too far from the successful model. As they say, negative publicity is better than no publicity. I truly doubt anyone bought our albums strictly because of the sexual themes on the cover, and yet it does make you wonder. However, if that was what motivated them, then I suspect the music is what eventually kept them coming back. The idea with an album cover is to attract attention from those who don't know what they want to spend their money on. If the cover looks professional and attractive, it will be much more interesting to a curious buyer than one that's plain and boring – unless, of course, you're the Beatles. *The White Album* pretty much answered that question. It may well have been the reason for the less than stellar sales of the *Taken By Force* album in some ways. Have to blame someone. So as a result of our successful effort to attain notoriety for our album cover, we again employed Hipgnosis and Storm Thorgerson to create the cover for our next offering *Animal Magnetism*.

I know what some of you are saying or at least thinking. Well, I don't, actually, but for the sake of rhetoric here I'll believe that I do, so please humor me. You are thinking why would something like a tiny little cover that no one really pays much attention to attract attention? Well I'm glad you asked. Honestly, you would be right by the standards of today. Most music is bought online today and that which is sold in stores is often buried in a rack that doesn't really allow the buyer to see it unless he's willing to leaf through the rack. What you have to remember is that that is only today. 30 years ago, as I am sure many of you recall, all music was bought in stores, and those stores had walls with posters and album covers plastered all over them! The albums themselves were not just fifteen centimeters square. They were about 50 centimeters square and attracted a lot of attention just by their size! Why do you think a billboard on the Sunset Strip in L.A. is worth so much to a label that they are willing to pay hundreds of thousands of dollars plastering the pictures of their latest and greatest group up on one for all to see? Records, LP's, allowed for the covers to become a much more visible part of the presentation. The music is what interested most buyers, but the covers would catch those who were not sure what they wanted. A lot of planning always goes into a cover, and so it was with ours.

But beyond that, we had to make some music. Releasing just a cover might have its appeal, but I don't think anyone would have paid us for that. So we had to create our follow-up in the studio. Having success is nice, much better than the other option, but it does put pressure on you to continually up the ante, and create something that is in keeping with what your newly acquired fans anticipate as well as bridging the gap to those who are not yet convinced that you are a great band! It's one thing to open the door. It's quite another to walk through it. To rest on our laurels would have been foolhardy and was never even slightly considered. As a result, *Animal Magnetism* rolled onto vinyl and finally established us throughout the world as one of the most important rock acts of the new decade. What time has a way of eroding is the exact moment that we began our ascent.

The first half of the 1980's was an interesting, and yet, to be completely honest, in a lot of ways, a horrible period in the world. No, not because of the economic woes and inflation and 20% interest rates or even the horrid fashions that now seem to be extremely laughable. But in music, it was a period of transition, and the transition seemed to leave hard rock on life supports. Perhaps at no time in the history of music were there more "one-hit wonders" than in the early 1980's. With the sudden demise of disco's popularity rose the "new wave" of rock and roll, which was little more than a melding of disco and punk or actually, more appropriately, a haven for everything that made little or no sense to anyone. Some of the rockers liked the new sounds. I personally loved Blondie, for example... Of course, I always fantasized about loving Blondie... If you're there Debbie, please give me a call. Another band I liked was the Talking Heads. I don't know how many would admit it publicly, but there were actually some very good acts that came out during that time. Yet as quickly as many arrived they disappeared because of their reliance on technology and the developing digital era. You can only attract attention as a novelty one time. After that you have to have something more than just synthesizers and drum machines. Artists like Thomas Dolby, Eddy Grant, M, the previously mentioned Nena and her balloons, The Buggles, The Flock of Seagulls, Modern English, Bow Wow Wow, Gary Numan, Dexy and his Runners, Men With No Hats... I could go on for pages, but I think you get the point. (If I left out one of your favorites, please let me know and I'll make sure to mention them in an offensive manner in my next book.) I guess the point of this is simply to say that we, the Scorpions from Hannover, West Germany, were an aberration in an industry that normally doesn't have an interest in such specters. We were ghosts from another era – a 1970's hard rock act taking wings and flight in the 1980's. I think even the most ardent fan would be hard pressed to think of another rock act that rose from the ashes and carnage of what was left of the 1970's rock scene when disco was ushered in and force-fed to the masses and then new wave took center stage for its 15 minutes of fame. Yes, there were the "glam rockers", but they didn't really attract a lot of attention outside of their niche. And there were the punk rockers and the new wave rockers. But they tilted in those directions which gave them an audience. It was a small number of "warhorses", holdovers from the 1970's who had already built a solid fan base, who created most of the music in the genre of hard rock where we were as the new decade began. Groups like Aerosmith, RUSH, Journey and AC/DC were at the top of the list. Ted Nugent was beginning to lose a little of his luster, in my opinion, the minute he lost his producer and my friend, Cliff Davies. You don't spend a lot of time on the road with a band without getting close to those who are in it. Being a drummer from England, Cliff and I had a lot in common and also had many mutual acquaintances. His impact on Ted Nugent's career cannot be overlooked, nor should it be. It would be like overlooking Dieter Dierks and his work with us. This is entirely my opinion, but I believe it is supported by what I've written previously about not only the Nugent band, but also about the importance of a producer. Many others in the industry share the same point of view. Anyway, the point here is that it would be another five years before hard rock really began its resurgence and yet, we were climbing the hill amid the sort of negative climate that existed for our type of music. When hard rock finally resurfaced as a viable commodity, much of the credit was due in great part to MTV.

MTV was actually responsible for the one-hit wonders of the 1980's if you wish to point fingers. Many groups were so fixated on technology they were able to produce great videos that were actually much better than their music. MTV needed product to air to fill up the airwaves 24 hours a day, and there was very little except an assortment of esoteric footage that might have been floating around from bands from past eras. So a lot of the bands that weren't actually bands but simply guys who perhaps had taken a few film classes at a university and knew how to shoot a video made a name for themselves as "rock stars" because they were able to get their videos featured twenty times a day on MTV, which at that time, was starving for something. Many became household names as a result of a war of attrition. If you force people to listen to you several times a day as they wait for a Rolling Stones video or something they actually like, just like bands that had songs in the top 40, people will start to at least not hate the songs and many will eventually embrace them. I know for me, I'll admit, there are many songs I hated when I first heard them. But now, as I look back, they are nostalgic remembrances of a bygone era in my life. I can remember the girl I dated when I heard the song or some other special event. Most of the girls I dated didn't care for my style of music just as I didn't much care for their likes either in many cases. But now, looking back, I can fondly remember where I was or who I was with as a result of a song that again, perhaps I loathed at the time.

Anyway, as time passed, MTV actually opened the door for hard rock's return to the spotlight. Bands adapted quickly to the new darling of the burgeoning satellite communications medium. Seeing the success of some so-called groups that frankly sucked, (Perhaps even in the eyes of their own label...), labels began putting a priority on video production. No longer was touring so perfunctory for a band – well, aside from the fact that it was still important for those of us who were interested in having a bevy of ever-rotating beauties to spend the night with in order to boost our much needed egos. (Many "big stars" in that era couldn't tour because their music wasn't really created by musicians. It was produced by electronics as was their tenuous vocals.) It's not so easy to get laid over the airwaves. Remember, in those days, there was no interactive television or Internet. Anyway, be that as it may, the point here is that a great video to accompany a great song or album was, of course, the pinnacle that could not only boost the visibility of an act, but also lend itself to immediate monetary returns via sales in the stores.

Our first video, since we are on the subject, was for the song "No One Like You" which, as most of you know, was on *Blackout*. I know I'm jumping ahead a bit, since we haven't even gotten through *Animal Magnetism* yet. Just allow me to stray for a moment, s'il vous plait. Anyway, we shot the video on Alcatraz, which I'm sure you know is in the most beautiful bay in the entire world that borders one of the world's most incredible cities, Oakland. And San Francisco is on the other side. The story was about a guy in prison visited by his girlfriend. As for production, well, I'm sure you all have heard the joke, "The coldest winter I ever felt was the summer I spent in San Francisco...", so you can imagine how we felt sitting out there on that little island as we were, exposed to all the wonderful elements that make San Francisco so attractive to those who are only there for a short period of time (Undoubtedly, passing through on the way to Oakland.). Having seen all of the great cities of the world at one time or another, I can say in all sincerity, the gray, misty fog rolling in through the Golden Gate Bridge in the late afternoon as the sun is slowly setting at the horizon, is a sight that is unmatched in majesty and beauty. Though it is cold, damp and quite windy, something I think made that prison the perfect prison, since inmates had to have felt the bitter sting of the icy breezes that seem forever invasive on that rock, we still felt it was an honor to be able to shoot our video in such a historic and awe-inspiring locale. However, that aside, we had to work late into the night and through to the next morning because Klaus had to shoot segments overnight with the female actress to obtain the affect we were looking for. As a result, we had to sleep in the cells, and I will tell you, it was cold, perhaps even colder in those cells than outside in the yard!

After the shoot was done, it was time to leave, of course, so we started off toward San Francisco on the boat we had hired. Keep in mind, we really were working on little sleep, a lot of coffee and other assorted stimulants, and so our focus wasn't all that acute. Within a few minutes of our departure from the dock on the island, we started asking each other where's Francis? We then realized that we had left him behind. Perhaps he took it as some sort of omen that he wasn't wanted or that he wasn't an integral part of the band. (In certain instances, subtler hints have been given to those who had overstayed their welcome.) In truth, given the events that later transpired, perhaps Alcatraz was... Well, I prefer not to get into that. I won't sully myself or this book with such matters. However, as he groused and bitched, we did do our best to explain to him that it was his own damn fault! He wasn't where he needed to be! Well, actually, as I inferred, maybe he was... Oh, well... Funny how sometimes things can actually work, huh?

Anyway, getting back to the story, we began working on *Animal Magnetism*. The title of the album came from my own personal philosophy of life because I sincerely believe in the concept of animal magnetism. My input on the album itself grew greatly beyond just creation of the title, however, as the other guys began to realize that I might actually know something. You know, it isn't always easy to convince your band-mates that you are not just the guy they added because the guy before you left. And so for me, the *Animal Magnetism* album seemed to give me a sense of acceptance. It's amazing, really, when you think about it. We had spent more than four years together, travelled the world, and even went to Cleveland. We had shared wine, women and songs (The middle one would make a book in itself.), and yet, in the eyes of the other guys I was still the guy they added. This wasn't their intent. But again, when you are new to something, you will always be thought of in that way. Think about how your in-laws feel about you. Do you ever really feel like you can just walk into their house and make yourself at home, or do you feel like you're always in the house of your spouse's family?

Anyway, the result of their confidence was a major contribution to the legacy we created together. The first single, "Make It Real", I co-wrote with Rudolf, and it was given the prestigious placement as the first song on the album. The first track on an album, at least in those days, was the most important, so to have one of my songs given that honor was quite an honor in itself. I also received co-writing credits for the title song as well as "Don't Make No Promises", "Hold Me Tight" and "Only a Man". And at long last, one of my own, personal compositions appeared on an album in the form of "Falling in Love" for which I not only wrote the words but also the music. In other words, I was now more than just the drummer in the Scorpions. I was a major contributor to the music.

We continued to develop our sound and style, and the commercialism that drove Uli out of the band was now firmly entrenched as the centerpiece of our success. As for Uli, he never once regretted his choice. He considered himself an artist, as I've said, and his integrity meant more than money and still does to this day. So in his eyes, he did what he felt was the right thing for him.

We wrote and recorded a great many radio friendly songs for this album like "Make It Real" which was under four minutes as well as several others in and around the three minute mark to hopefully garner more airplay at commercial stations that still favored the three minute standard for pop music. However, in America at least, the song that seemed to catch on the fastest was a five minute and twenty-eight second grinder by Klaus and Rudolf called "The Zoo" which, as most know, was simply our impression of New York City during our first visit there. Those of you who have visited the "Big Apple", as Americans call it for reasons I am not sure of, can perhaps relate to the analogous reference in our calling it a zoo. With a powerful opening riff that truly established the feel for the relatively "dark" lyrics and a voice box/wah wah peddle lead guitar sound created by Matthias to supplement the feel of the melody, it was truly a step in a different direction for us, and yet it was right in line with what our fans seemed to want, and it caught on across the pond. The album as a whole became so popular in the States that as we packed to begin our 1980 tour of the world, we knew we'd be going to America with much more confidence and ready to headline our own shows.

And then there was the previously mentioned, eagerly anticipated, controversial album cover. Everyone was fully clothed and unarmed this time, which we felt was definitely an appeasing step in the right direction. I will admit that I was partly responsible here as well. No, not for the fact that we were fully clothed and unarmed. That was more the idea of Thorgerson. Using my title as his lead, as I said before, he came up with one more design that would, of course, draw as much attention to the cover as perhaps the songs. To this day I don't know what was so offensive in the cover. I mean, a short woman standing in front of a tall man who is on a mound of dirt. Of course that wasn't how the press interpreted it. And tell me, what can be more wholesome than sharing the whole thing with your trusty canine? Believe it or not, we were accused of promoting not only demeaning and belittling behavior toward women but bestiality. How absurd! We had nothing of the kind in mind... At least I'll never admit it. I guess we just had a reputation, and people inferred the worst. But this time we weren't forced to come up with an alternate design, and so there is only one jacket for not only the record album but for the CD as well. This was true progress!!!

Atop the Mount Olympus of Rock

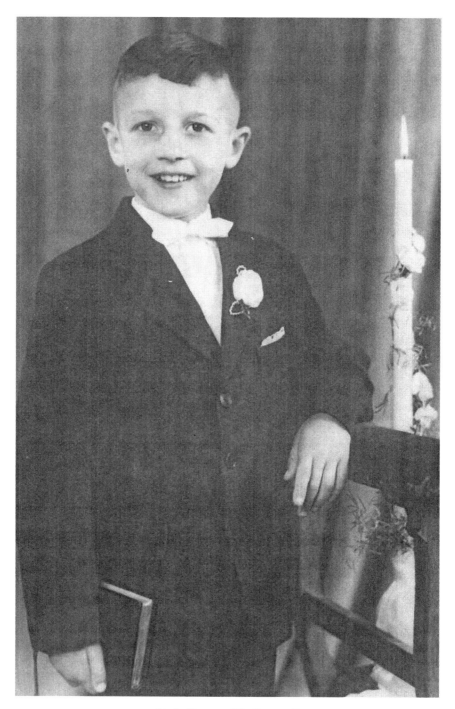

Little Herman "Ze German"

Mom and Dad

The Mastermen

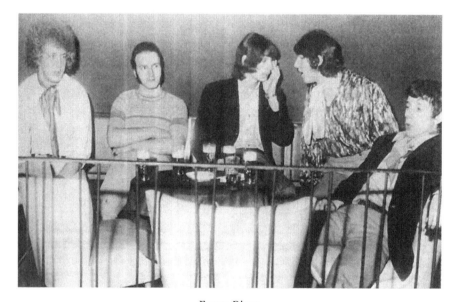

Fuggs Blues

R.S. Rindfleisch

The Scorpions

Foto: Udo Weger 1983.

Herman Goes Solo

My Daughter Leah

Prince Albert of Monaco and Me

11
ROAD WORK AND PLAY

We started the tour for *Animal Magnetism* in a manner that began to seem a bit redundant in some respects, though, at least at that point, still quite exciting. We were now firmly established and entrenched as headliners throughout Japan and most of Europe where we were fairly well known and considered not just a rock act but a major attraction. However, once we crossed into U.S. air space, all bets were off, and the best we could do was secure middle billing between a then unknown band by the name of Def Lepperd and still top "gun", Ted Nugent.

In case you didn't realize it, headlining a tour is quite different from being a support act. First off, there are the travel arrangements and accommodations. When you're a "special guest", you're hardly treated in a special way unless, of course, special means you are still young enough to carry your own bags, so you get to. You can pretty well rest assured you won't see the "Top of the Mark" or the top of very much else unless it's from the outside of the building as you perhaps are given the opportunity to clean the windows to supplement your meager income.

But let's not focus on the negatives. I prefer to be a much more positive sort of person. Let's look at what you do get! You get to see a lot of musty old motels with unexplained stains, spills and scents from unidentified sources emanating from the pillowcases, carpets and bathroom linen of your "luxury suite". Though they may provide entertainment by giving you the chance to play guessing games like "Name That Fungus", they do leave you wondering if it was such a good idea not to bring along an assortment of bug bombs, disinfectants, deodorizers and acifidity bags not to mention your mother for overall hygienic protection. Such places are, as you might well imagine, run by Norman Bates look-a-likes and are seemingly an ubiquitous fixture on every highway, freeway, turnpike and thruway in the United States. Whether it's got a six, quality, days or western on the sign, you know you've still got some work to do and some hills to climb in the rock and roll world. At that point, we could only dream of staying in places like the Howard Johnson's in Newark, New Jersey. From what I understand, professional wrestlers get to stay there, which probably says a lot about what it's like at the bottom of the music industry compared to being a part of the "real" entertainment world. Like my now late brother in arms Bon Scott sang in the AC/DC classic of the same title, "It's a long way to the top if you want to rock and roll."

Of course, there is much more than just the "incredible" accommodations package, which, if you're interested, is provided normally at the recommendation of the management but at the expense of the artist (Nothing ever comes out of their percentage…). Though I have no proof beyond speculation, in my opinion there is ample suspicion to cast the appropriate aspersions, as I suspect, in many cases, there are some "unscrupulous" management companies that probably get kickbacks from the motels. I know this sounds cynical, and yet it would explain why they endorse such dens of iniquity. I would hate to think they actually stayed in some of the places and liked them. (In our case, I think it was more of an economic consideration in the eyes of our managers. But again, they may have been the exception.) Keep in mind, it is interesting that when taking time out of their "busy" schedule to accompany their artists on the road (Normally when the managers are on the road, the band is playing in exotic or exciting locales around the world. Hardly ever see management in Bismarck, North Dakota.), the members of the management "team" will stay, not with the undercard but with the headliner at the local Hilton, Radisson, Novotel or Marriott (Again, quite often at the expense of the artist who may or may not even want them there or know that they are footing the bill. Honestly, management can, at times, appear to reproduce like rabbits once you are successful. There seem to be more and more of them materializing out of thin air everyday as your popularity grows. Many of the individuals suspiciously sport questionable titles and similar last names. By the way, this is an advantage to being a support act rather than a headliner.)

But as if that isn't enough (And if you hear the management normally talk about it, you'll believe that they really are doing you a favor!), while in the subservient role of support you can also add the extremely health conscious, gourmet meals you get to savor on a nightly basis to the extraordinary accommodations. I will tell you the truth, if I never see another hamburger or frankfurter, I won't be too disappointed. Yes, technically both are German creations. The names are pretty much a giveaway of the origins. But today most Germans don't recognize such foods as part of our culture or at least refuse to take responsibility for their creations after what the "Yanks" did to both. I doubt the Burger of Hamburg or Maximilian II would be too pleased with the current state of the "art".

Another part of being an opening act that is probably a bit unknown to most (Even those who may be the most fervent fans...) is the amount of space you are allowed on the mixing board or console at the shows themselves. As a general rule today, there are normally around 48 channels or inputs that can be utilized by the bands to mix their sound through the PA system. Of the 48, depending upon the act, of course, a headliner will use between 30 and 40 of those channels to get their sound exactly as they want it. Remember, they are the ones in charge. It is essentially their show, and you are just along for the ride. As such, opening acts are left with very little to work with. Often, if there is more than one opening act, they will have to "share" the remaining 8 channels. (Sharing is hardly the appropriate term. Trust me, the "negotiations" can often be much more merciless than even a week on Devil's Island. The ensuing and incurring fights sometimes are such that the butchery left in their wake would make kickboxing seem docile.) This, of course, means making some "tough decisions" on how to spread those channels around, which is never easy. During sound check, drummers, especially, nervously wait like virgins at a volcano eruption to see what sacrifices have to be made, because more often than not, it is at our expense. But ultimately, if it's done correctly and by a great soundman, the audience won't hear a discernable difference in the sound between the acts, and that is really what matters. I can tell you, for all that is his selfish reputation, Ted Nugent was actually pleasingly "notorious" for being one of the most generous when it came to leaving space on the board for his supporting acts. Perhaps it was simply because his band was a very basic four piece with limited vocal needs. Or maybe it was a conscious effort on his part to make the show the best it could be for the fans. I don't know. I just know that we had good experiences with him and from what I understand other bands had the same impression.

However, all of those wonderful things, the motels and meals, the space on the mixing board, etcetera, change once you achieve headline status to say the least. The motels turn to hotels. The hamburgers turn to steaks. And the conveniences in general all become much greater. After all, you're the star!

Also, as a headliner, there are countless intangibles. (Like getting to house the management and various members of their families at "Five Star" hotels in Rio de Janeiro. I never knew anyone could have six mothers-in law... Well, aside from Mickey Rooney.) This is something that cannot and should not be overlooked. One such intangible is the audience. Playing as an opening act, there was arguably an occasional night when there would be a smattering of people in the building specifically to see us, and other nights when perhaps there would be a handful of those who may actually have known who we were. But those occasions were the exception, not the norm. I doubt they ever outnumbered those who were at the shows exclusively to partake of the bountiful supply of available drugs. As you might imagine, our concerts typically tended to be played with the scent of marijuana filling the arena like incense at a sitar concert. As such, I am sure many in the audience were less than fully conscious, aware or even caring who was on stage so long as it was loud. Let's face it, unless you were at a New Christy Minstrels show, which is hard to imagine anyone would be, such things as drugs and rock and roll shows were pretty much synonymous. (Then again, I can't imagine sitting through a New Christy Minstrels concert without some sort of recreational supplement or stimulant to augment and enhance the performance or just keep me awake.) Honestly, we really didn't think much about who was in the audience, nor did it really matter. We played our best no matter what the situation was.

A lot of the time when you are on the road opening for a big name, it's in an effort to get exposure to a greater number of people than you could draw on your own as perhaps I've already made clear. Yes, there are instances when you are billed in support of another act and actually are more popular and well received than they are. (Remember the debacle in Moscow when Bon Jovi demanded to remain as the closing act on the bill?) At such times, the booker or management, whoever was in charge of the errant booking, will find his job about as secure as being the captain of the Exxon Valdez. He will be diplomatically "asked" by the headliner to remove you from the remainder of the tour. Their idea of diplomacy normally amounts to nominal threats of violence which include various suggestions to those in charge that they do to themselves things that I believe may very well be anatomically impossible.

On the positive side, a good opening act, and I believe we were, knows their place. Music is quite political, and you earn and garner respect from others in the industry by paying homage to the pecking order at all times. We knew when we "middled", for example, on a three act show our job was to give a tight 30-40 minute set that would get the audience warmed up for the "king of beasts" and feature none of the pyrotechnics, gimmicks, gadgets and/or gizmos reserved for the headliner should he choose to use them. It was always his, her or their choice, not our option. Some bands don't understand that and will do everything they can in a conscious effort to "blow off the stage" the others on the bill. This leads to dissension, as you might imagine, and can often harm a young band's reputation, and quite often, their career. Who wants to work with a group that is going to try to upstage them? Remember, entertainment is 100% about competition. As both Ted Nugent and AC/DC so aptly implied, it is a "dog-eat-dog" industry. The canine with the center seat at the food bowl is always under attack. Those at the bottom dream of being in his place and many have none of the scruples necessary to understand the concept of gratitude. The headline act doesn't really need an opening act to draw customers to a show. It is simply a courtesy, an opportunity, if you will, that is willingly extended to others. Every artist was at one time at the bottom and had to pay their dues – unless, of course, their uncle was a big shot in the industry. Such connections do have their advantages and tend to overcome lacks in talent when it comes to stardom. But for the rest of us who weren't blessed with the proper lineage, it is kind of a tradition that may date back to caveman. I mean I'm sure they had their form of entertainment then, too. As such, there must have been some sort of hierarchy to be had if you had any aspiration of ascending to the level of lead rock thrower or head fire maker. Anyway, the tradition is meant as a way of giving back by those on top to those who are just starting out. It's all a part of the fraternity called rock and roll.

Beyond that, though, as it pertains to a show, there is an audience psychology, an understanding of which makes for a good show. A good show, for example, is never selfish. The performers know they are there for the audience and understand the importance of building to a climactic crescendo. If you put the entire spectacle of special effects, etcetera, into the first act, what is left for the remaining acts? There is a subliminal seduction of the audience to be had. It needs to be caressed and massaged to allow for the passion to build up and lead to the ultimate and appropriate climax.

A fitting analogy might be a comparison to a narcissistic man who, while having sex with his wife, screams his own name and reaches his orgasm within seconds of beginning the romp. He is, most certainly, quite enamored with himself and his performance and is completely indifferent to the needs of his mate not to mention being obviously quite selfish. Eight seconds might be a good ride in a rodeo but for most any woman other than a prostitute, it's hardly enough. However, not to be overtly negative in my arbitrary condemnation, on the positive side, a "lady of the evening" will most certainly love him. So long as he's a cash customer, she won't care whose name he screams during the eight seconds so long as it's not "Vice"!

A good example of this, concert performances, not sex with prostitutes, I believe happened in Monterey, California, at the now famous 1967 Pop Festival that is so much a part of music lore. Actually, there probably were some very good examples of sex with prostitutes there as well, even though, as I think back, it was the summer of love, and so free sex must have been extensive. In such instances, no one could ever complain that he or she didn't get their money's worth. Then again, knowing the finicky nature of many in this world, there were probably those who complained about the quality therein even at that bargain basement rate. As for the concert, however, making an effort to get back to my original thought, although, in truth, it probably didn't originate with me as there were countless others who shared the same thought. You see, Jimi Hendrix was still an unknown entity in the world of rock music while the Who, another act on the bill, was pretty much at the top of the British Invasion roster. Well, Hendrix, being young and naïve, or perhaps not really giving a damn about protocol, did his normal act, which, of course, featured the destruction of his guitar at the very end. Well, who in their right mind wanted to follow that? But you see, no one really knew what Hendrix did in his act because it was essentially his first public appearance with his "Experience". And so, there waited the

Who offstage watching him simulate intercourse with his amplifier, bash his Fender Stratocaster into submission, and then systematically cremate it, thinking, "What the hell are we supposed to do after that?" And so when they took the stage and went through their act, which featured, of course, the destruction of guitars and drums by Pete Townsend and Keith Moon respectively, the audience sort of yawned because they had already seen that and wanted something new. By the time Woodstock rolled around a couple years later, well, other acts had wised up, and, as such, Hendrix wound up basically being the closing act of the entire show on the final afternoon.

A lot of very good bands fail miserably trying to be too big too soon as I have mentioned already. They really believe that a single hit record means they are worthy of top billing everywhere they go. As such, they will often go out on tour with their egos packing their bags rather than their common sense if they, in fact, have any. We had a lot of acts headlining over us while we actually had a record higher on the charts than they did. But what can never be replaced are the ingredients of experience, appreciation and patience. Our time would come. We needed to establish ourselves as headliners by proving our worth over an extended period of time. We needed to prove we could, in fact, draw money for the promoters. Fortunately, despite all the innuendo I've put here with regard to such entities, we had an outstanding management company. They didn't need another headlining act right away, since they already had several. This allowed us to have and maintain the proper perspective whether we wanted to or not. Many other so-called managers only see dollar signs and by any standard accounting method 15% of a headline act's fee is much greater than 15% of an opening act's take.

Being aligned with a great management company that had a stable of studs capable of carrying the load and putting "butts in the bleachers" on a nightly basis all over the world, truly did give us a tremendous advantage. Initially, I'm sure some of the negotiations they had with promoters included, "If you want Nugent or AC/DC, you're going to have to take the Germans as well."

Playing in front of 50,000 in a stadium is obviously better than playing in front of 500 at a small club or theater. We were not stupid enough to stomp around David Krebs' office screaming, "We have the #55 album in America! We should be headlining!" Actually, we probably were. But thankfully we didn't. Honestly, though, that's what a lot of bands will do and quite often it leads to catastrophic results. A lot of very talented bands fall prey to believing their own publicity rather than following the advice of their management. I will tell you again, however, there are a lot of cretins who claim to be managers out there. The stories are endless about artist abuse and the like, and I could personally name names here. By the same token, on the other hand, there are just as many stories, if not more, about artists who do abuse themselves and not with drugs and alcohol but with ego and stupidity.

As many who know me can attest, I admit I'm hardly the smartest dress hanging in the closet or even the sharpest knife in the drawer, but I do believe I have always found subjugation of my ego easy. That was the key, in my estimation. Perhaps it is the reason I have always been able to work with people throughout my career. Trust me, the music industry is filled with ego, selfishness and greed not to mention very demanding and temperamental artists. (Actually, the same could be said for life in general at least regarding the selfishness and greed.) Thankfully, I don't believe I am in either category, which I think has been the key to my personal longevity in the industry. I have been able to work with those in every categorization.

Anyway, whether or not I'm difficult to work with is subject to opinion, of course. Maybe it's just been that no one wants to tell me that I am a pain in the ass. Who am I to say? But I don't believe I'm bigger than the art or more important than the next musician. I have always known my place and been able to fit into a group environment. When in the role of a leader, I believe I have been quite capable of exercising degrees of restraint and understanding. Sure, I could have bossed everyone around and bullied him or her into following my line of thought. But such attitudes in all walks of life tend to be counterproductive. If you are part of a group, the group has to be bigger than the self. That goes for everyone in that group or body whether it's a rock and roll band or just a small business in Munich.

I think my latest album titled *Take It As It Comes* might best illustrate my attitude and approach. The album is listed as "my" album, but it is as much a group creation as any album I recorded with the Scorpions. Yes, there are some of my compositions on the album but also some by the other members of the band. We all put in our songs when we began rehearsing for the recording and then chose what we felt were the best ones to put on the CD. Yes, I have plenty of material written by myself that could fill several albums. But that wasn't the goal. The goal was to put out the best album we could for the fans, and since my name is on it, I want it to represent what I am about. I hope those of you who are reading this will take time to pick up a copy. It was for you that it was made.

Getting back to the Scorpions… It does seem as if I've strayed a bit, huh? I know, so what else is new? This whole book seems like an assortment of stray tangents occasionally redirected to a story about my life. But what you have to understand is life isn't just about playing in a band, but about an assortment of attitudes, beliefs and opinions that make a person who he is today. I have a public life in the music world as well as a private one outside of music. I would like to believe that you are interested in me as a person just as much as me as a musician.

At any rate, we, the Scorpions, were fortunate in our career to have the opportunity to work with some good people. Boy, I sound like a stereotypical, disingenuous "brown-noser", don't I? Kind of like I'm giving the sort of trite, insincere acceptance speeches that accompany induction into the Rock and Roll Hall of Shame, I mean, Fame. I know our getting inducted anytime soon has about as much chance of happening as I do of becoming King of England. King of Monaco, maybe. I think I was perhaps at one time in the mix there. Okay, so I wasn't. Humor me, okay. So anyway, to get to the point that I think I was trying to make a couple pages ago when we were talking about headlining over simply playing in support, when you headline, you are playing before people who are actually there to see you. I can tell you, it's very exciting to look out at an audience who not only knows who you are but knows the words of the songs you are playing. When you see their mouths lip-synch the lyrics you wrote, well, it's a "high" far above any that can be achieved artificially within this world.

Oh, I forgot, there is another thing about headlining compared to being in a position of support that might well be labeled as most important for many who get into music, and that is the women. I know there are those of you out there with saliva dripping down your lips saying, "Yeah, yeah... Tell us about the women..." Well, the main difference between opening and closing a show is the amount of alcohol you need to consume prior to leaving the bar. It's amazing how a half a dozen shots of *Wild Turkey* can take any woman from appalling to appealing! It's what some call the "Motel Face". "Tomorrow you'll look like hell... But tonight, you look swell!" Yes, I know, this is a horrible way to talk about this kind of thing. Keep in mind, most of the groupies drank right along with us, so perhaps they felt the same way about us. But as the song goes, in our honest opinion, the groupies that would allow us to defile their virtue, if, in fact, they had any, were and probably still are viewed by most in the music industry as little more than just "another piece of meat". I understand that some may view this as being awfully denigrating and demeaning to you ladies out there, but hey, we were the Scorpions and our album covers told the story! (By the way, I've never heard a man complain about that sort of attitude or labeling even though "ladies" on tour also take part in the same sort of late night athletics.) Honestly, we didn't feel that way. Our wives wouldn't permit it. But we had a reputation to uphold. Anyway, when you're an opener, you are forced to wait your turn while the groupies, justifiably, flock to the headliner first. They know he may not be the best-looking guy or even the best in bed. But he has all the perks... The luxury suite at the "Five Star" hotel... The round bed with mirrors on the ceiling...

Room service... What did we have to offer? A double-room at the Motel 6... A rust stained tub with a leaky faucet... Flea infested beds... A mirror in the bathroom... If they played their cards right, perhaps a Filet-O-Fish sandwich at McDonald's... However, since they all can't go to bed with the star, when they lose out with him, they come to us for consolation. It's a lot like the guy who strikes out with the girl of his dreams and winds up with her best friend – the cute, adorable sidekick.

Meanwhile, back at the story... Technically, we had headlined in Europe and Japan in previous years and even prior to travelling across the Atlantic to the U.S. in 1980 as I've already mentioned. Specifically, in March of that year, we opened the tour in Japan before returning to Europe to play dates in France, Germany, Belgium, England and Scotland. From there, our routing became a little more creative than perhaps we would have preferred. Ordinarily, European bands will fly to eastern cities of Canada or the United States to open a tour of North America for purposes of not only shortness of travel, which, of course, means lower costs for flights but also because of the time differences. Jet lag was always a problem. It really could cut into the time and energy we had after the shows for sex.

However, our management didn't care whether or not we had sex, after all, it was very difficult for them to get their "piece" of that action. (All puns are intended.) I mean, what were we going to do? Were we supposed to stop 85% of the way through and say to our comely evening's companion, "Well, that's all for me... Let me introduce you to my agent. He'll be finishing up..."? At any rate, our management, being fixated on our making money rather than concerning themselves with our sophomoric attempts to build what we felt would be the appropriate offstage repute, wanted to link us with one of their top guys as quickly as possible, as I mentioned earlier, so they sent us to California where Ted Nugent was in the middle of a tour, obviously in between hunting seasons, playing in San Francisco in an old relic of a building called the "Cow Palace".

Given Ted's propensity for killing livestock, I'm sure he had a twinkle in his eye when he first heard the name.

Along with Ted, we also played with what was then a very young band, Def Leppard, as I already said. (Weren't we all young once?) Though they were virtual unknowns in America at the time, we knew them from our time spent in England. They came as fans to one our shows in the United Kingdom, and we had met them all backstage. They must have had connections of some sort even at that point to be able to get backstage. It was great to see them again as they were and I suspect still are very nice chaps, and obviously, as history shows, they were on their way up. Granted we weren't exactly long in the tooth, but compared to us, they were children. For example, Cliff Davies, Ted's drummer, and I had to smuggle Rick Allen, the drummer from Leppard, into clubs because he was not only under 21 but jailbait as well as he was under 18 for Christ's sake! But even through thick and thin and under aged adolescence, we drummers, always stuck together. Sort of a fraternal bond there I suppose.

If you recall, our first tour of the U.S., such as it was with just a handful of cities involved, we really didn't venture beyond the Midwest, so we only got a small sampling of the States. This grand scale "tour de force" was really our first taste of the country as a whole, which honestly was much bigger than we expected. You discover that when you're on a tour bus for several months.

An interesting note, however, at least it is curiously interesting to me as I look down the docket of cities we visited and played concerts in, was the exclusion of several major markets during the tour. There was just not enough demand in the major markets for us at that point, I guess. We did have an offer to play at the Roxy Theater in Los Angeles, but the venue was so small we opted to stay with Nugent in a support role and play before much larger crowds. Most glaring, however, was the absence of stops not only in Los Angeles but in New York City as well. (Obviously, we latched on to Ted after he had hit those cities.) So the point here was that even though we had two successful albums, we were still yet to play in either of the two biggest music centers in the United States, and it did leave us wondering if we were ever going to be considered "big time" enough to play in Carnegie Hall.

Eventually, as you probably know, we gained a very large following in Southern California to the point where we would play back-to-back shows at the Los Angeles Forum. It was the same in New York where we sold out two nights at Madison Square Garden in the middle 80's when "Rock You Like a Hurricane" was on the charts. But I guess during that tour, we were still considered small fish in a very big pond and the pond, at the time, out west at least, was probably screaming out for more of the Knack.

One thing we did learn about the east and west coast was that New York was quite different from Los Angeles in musical mindset. Though both were and probably still are "cliquish" and quite supportive of the home teams, at that time Southern California seemed to be captivated by the new wave as was played by the aforementioned Knack and softer rock like that produced by the Eagles, Warren Zevon and Linda Ronstadt. Meanwhile, punk rock that was previously an underground rage, took center stage in the "Big Apple" during those early years of the 1980's with groups like Blondie and The Ramones who were very big there at the time. So even though our management was based in New York City, the closest we came to Manhattan was Buffalo.

However, even though things were going well for us, and we really had no complaints or worries, as it seems to be with all things in this life, when everything is going too well it's usually a sign of potential disaster. Of course, as still very young guys, we had a sense of invincibility that did not allow us to think in negative terms about our future. We only believed what our current publicity was telling us. The sky was the limit. However, in the sky above, there was a storm cloud brewing as we entered the final leg of our tour and started to plan our next album.

There is a little side story here, though, that should not be overlooked or forgotten. It was during the tour that the title song for the next album, *Blackout*, was, in fact, conceived. Actually, I don't know that that's the proper term, since it wasn't so much a conception as it was a simple reporting of the facts. And no, it had nothing to do with the storm cloud. Consider this analogous with the wispy cirrus clouds that often prelude the arrival of a storm moving in from the west. Anyway, it all began after a show we played with Judas Priest and Def Leppard in Dubuque, Iowa, of all places. I remember we all stayed in the same hotel, sort of like a Howard Johnson's, though I am not really sure after all the hotels what it was. I don't believe we had earned the right to stay at such an ostentatious establishment quite yet. (If you live in Dubuque, you probably know the hotel I'm talking about, since it's next to some shopping mall there. Let me know, so I can make the correction in my next book.) At any rate, as I looked out the window of my room, I saw the police arriving at the mall. No, not Sting, Stewart Copeland and Andy Summers... Nor do I mean rent-a-cops. We're talking authentic Dubuque gendarmes — cattle prods and all! Apparently, or perhaps more appropriately, allegedly, Rudolf was a bit over the top drunk and running around the parking lot in what probably could best be described as a stupor. If you knew Rudolf, you'd know this was nothing out of the ordinary. However, he was lost and trying very hard to find his way back to the hotel. I am sure the cops thought some long-haired subversive was perhaps trying to break into one of the stores that had long since closed up for the evening. Since he had no ID on him, and you have to understand in Iowa he did stand out a bit compared to the ordinary citizenry, they were about to arrest him.

Without enough time to make a quick trip to the local Winchell's to pick up a dozen donuts, I had no choice but to creatively think on the fly as I bolted out to the rescue. Upon arriving on the scene, however, the best I could come up with was an extremely feeble attempt to impress them with stories about my father and grandfather being such prominent members of the law enforcement establishment in our homeland, as well as explaining my respect for those who put their lives on the line in such dangerous places as Dubuque. I then proceeded to explain to them that Rudolf was with us (As if that was going to make them feel much more comfortable.), and that he had just gotten a little confused and lost trying to find his way back to the hotel, since English wasn't really his first language. The fact that there was a giant sign right in front of him saying the name of the hotel didn't help my case, of course. But I figured maybe they would just think he was a foreigner and unable to read English so well. Okay so it was a stretch. What else did I have? Ultimately, and in all honesty, amazingly, they believed me, and turned Rudolf over to me, and went on their way. Actually, I don't know if they believed me so much as they just didn't want to bother with the paperwork. It was much easier to simply reprimand him to my custody, since I did, I guess, seem cogent and sober, and leave it at that.

Happy ending, right? Wrong...

As if that wasn't enough of a scare, however, the story was not quite over. There was still a little more of a performance to be had. I went with Rudolf into the lobby where there was a place in the reception area that you could buy a beer at. I'm not sure, as I think back, if it was a bar, per say, but you could buy beer there. Well, as you can probably surmise, the last thing he needed at that point was another drink. But Rudolf was one who never saw a Budweiser he didn't like... Or for that matter, an Amstel, or a Lowenbrau, or a Duvel, or a Tuborg, or a Cerna Hora, or a Baltika, or even a Kilikia... He wasn't the most particular drinker. And so, probably by instinct, he made a beeline for one he noticed sitting harmlessly on a table next to a guy who was transfixed on a small television watching whatever mindless event was taking place thereon. (Let's see, there were tables you could sit at and you could buy a beer and there was a television there... Hell, that does sound a lot like a bar, huh?) Rudolf quickly procured the fairly full pint of brew as he stumbled through the sitting area, not to drink, as I suspected he would, mind you, but inexplicably to pour on the television. To this day, I'm not sure if it was his way of critiquing the crap that was on the tube, or if he simply thought it was the right thing to do for whatever the reason. You have to admit, it really isn't something you see everyday, at least in Iowa. There were two guys from both Def Leppard and Judas Priest sitting there flabbergasted. They just couldn't believe what they were seeing. Perhaps they wondered, since we were the only German rock band in existence, if it wasn't some sort of standard Bavarian custom. Somehow we were able to get Rudolf to his room where he passed out on his bed.

But, believe it or not, this was still not the end. There was a third act following intermission.

The next morning, having sobered up, Rudolf not me (For perhaps one rare occasion in my life, at least at that point, I hadn't drunk to excess the previous night, and was the most coherent individual in the general vicinity.), I told the story back to him about the previous night's chaos, curious to know what the hell had happened. However, as I told him, a look of disbelief filled his eyes. He was completely unwilling to believe me. It was clear to me that his loss of memory, temporary as it obviously was, must have been caused by some sort of alcohol-induced loss of consciousness, or more simply, a blackout. My story was confirmed later in the day by the guys from the other bands who were there watching the whole thing unfold. So, in a roundabout way, Rudolf, being less than in control of his faculties, actually contributed to a multi-platinum album by simply drinking himself silly! (I'm sure as he reads this, he's probably toasting the thought!) (If not, I'm sure Pete Way will for reasons only he would know.) I immediately made some notes to myself about the event, and the rest is Scorpions history. So no one should ever say that there are no positives in abusive drinking – at least abusive drinking in Dubuque, Iowa.

Oh, in case you are curious, it's not Rudolf on the album cover but the artist who created the cover, Gottfried Helnwein. It was a self-portrait, he claims, though I can't honestly say I know for sure he was ever subject to a blackout himself.

12
SORE THROATS AND BLACKOUTS

After leaving the states at the end of the summer, we really didn't tour continuously through the fall, even though we were playing steadily. There were various one-nighters in places like Sweden, France and England as well as concerts in those countries. There was also a return trip to Japan in early November. As I said, it may not have been technically a tour, but still it was grueling nonetheless, given that we had just come off a long road. (How much sex can one man take?)

However, as these dates drew to a close, perhaps as a result of the extensive number of engagements (We weren't sure at the time.), Klaus began to have some troubles with his throat. Contrary to what many may believe, a voice is a form of a musical instrument. The main difference is, however, when it wears out, you can't just put on a new set of strings and keep playing. Of course, initially, we thought it was nothing more than just a severe case of ordinary fatigue similar to what nightclub singers call "Vegas throat". Vegas throat is what happens to many who work the arid desert resort because the dry air of the climate can, at times, cause dryness in the throat. This often robs a vocalist of his range among other things. None of us had ever been on such a rigorous tour in our life, so we suspected the wear and tear, the daily grind, if you will, had been just a bit too much for him to take, and a few days off was all he really needed.

Figuring a little well-deserved rest was, as Nugent would surely have put it, "just what the doctor ordered", we began to work through the songs that would make up the most ambitious and well received album cover to date giving little further thought to Klaus's vocal qualms. Actually, quite surprisingly, we no longer felt we needed to have controversial album covers, so the *Blackout* album was more about the music than the cover, and that is the way it should have been from the start. Our music was indeed catching on. Both *Lovedrive* and *Animal Magnetism* were fast becoming as well-known for the music as they were for the controversial covers. Each had actually attained gold status and were headed toward platinum. And so the follow up for *Animal Magnetism* was going to truly make or break us. (Such insecurity is what keeps you on top. The minute you become complacent, you lose whatever "edge" you might otherwise have.) Some bands can produce one or maybe even two popular albums. Honestly, in our opinion, we had yet to produce the perfect Scorpions album, but we were getting closer with each offering. So *Blackout* was a major production in our all-out effort to keep the already established momentum going. Our hope was to prove to even the most cynical misanthropist (Which might be a lovingly generous term for most "critics".), and trust me, there were many, that we could sustain and were there for the long haul. We were always aware that lurking not too far in any non-positive direction was the omnipotent and capricious grim reaper of rock and roll who might want to hasten our departure from the spotlight even before it really began. I suspect no matter how big you may become, you always have that fear lingering in the back of your mind.

As had been the case with the prior albums, the songwriting was split between Klaus, Rudolf and myself. Some of the songs, as you may be able to tell if you know our lyrics, were written, at least in part, while we were on the road. However, some were nothing more than ideas that came to us during the tour that needed to be developed. For those of you who are reading this only to hear about the women, and honestly I would hope that's only a very small portion of you, well, the song "Arizona" I wrote with Rudolf, kind of tells a little tale that perhaps will satisfy and, at least temporarily, pacify your salacious curiosities. But I don't wish to shortchange the women from other places in the States. I personally can testify to having enjoyed all of you. So I'll get to the story of "Arizona" in a couple of paragraphs.

But first, let me talk about the overall writing itself. As I started to say, it was truly a group effort, at least between the three of us, though both Francis and Matthias did have their input as well once we began to rehearse the tunes. However, to be completely fair, I did write a couple of songs with Matthias over the years, "Don't Make No Promises (Your Body Can't Keep)" from *Animal Magnetism*, and "Money and Fame" and, of course, the hit song "Tease Me, Please Me" both from *Crazy World*. The songs, as a whole, show that element of consistency in their blend. As I have said, a lot of times when various people write songs, the feel of each song is quite different as it was when Uli was contributing his pieces from outside the Scorpion model. It is also the reason why a "one-hit wonder" becomes exactly that.

Most single hits by an artist are one of two things: either a contrast to the group's normal music or artist's normal style or a song covered by a group or artist written by someone else. The latter of these two reasons is the most obvious. If an outside, third party, writes a song, it often is just a fluke in the repertoire of a band. The remainder of their songs may be penned by other people or by the band members themselves and will be far different from the hit. The former reason, well, that's a little more difficult to explain except to say that an artist or band can often come up with one really good song, but to follow it up is not always so easy. Before you have a popular song or album, there is little to consider as you are still trying to find the right combination. But once you hit on something special, the fans, being fickle as they often are, expect every follow up to sound exactly the same. This, of course, is impossible since you can't cut and paste the melody and have a new song. Anything that doesn't sound like the hit, note for note, can often be uninteresting to those who listen to the top 40. That is the reason you find so many bands copying the sound of a popular song or group.

They are just trying to capitalize on that which is the current rage. Of course, quite often, by the time they finish writing and recording the song and get it released, the trends have changed and they discover they are way behind the curve. The originators themselves will often fall into the same trap recording song after song that is identical to what brought them success not realizing that some change is needed to give a little variety to their albums.

A good example of a formulaic album that never really sold like the hit single might be from the new wave group the Romantics. Their song, "What I Like About You" is to this day a staple of FM rock stations around the world and has been featured in countless films as well. However, the album from which it originally came is hardly one to brag about in terms of sales. Though it had an eventual "monster" hit (Originally the song was only able to crack the top 50 in most places.), the album sold poorly. If you listen to it in its entirety you may discover the reason why. The album is filled with songs that sound exactly like the hit. I am not kidding. Almost every song on the album has the same basic chord changes and beat. Even though it is enjoyable and melodic, it does become a bit monotonous after a while. That is probably why the song's popularity was mainly built through its appearance on countless compilation LP's and soundtrack albums.

Anyway, getting back to our story, as I mentioned earlier, though some of the songs were written while we were on the road, the majority were pieced together and completed after we finished our tour when we were back in Hannover. In the case of the song "Blackout", for example, even though I wrote it about that incident in Iowa, my then girlfriend, Sonya, had a little input into the lyric that made it tighter.

Of course, in our situation, having the consistency and stability in the production booth given to us by Dieter was also a major component in the true Scorpion sound coming to life and prospering in the land called harmony. Regardless of the writing, it still was the "magic dragon" breathing fire behind the mixing console that brought life to the songs. However, for the record, you will find my name attached to "You Give Me All I Need", "Now", "Dynamite", "Blackout" and

132

"Arizona", and I guess you could tell by the basic storyline in so many of our songs, we were all quite engrossed with and appreciative of the abundance of female attention we were receiving. Yes, I know, some of us were married at the time or were involved in long standing relationships. I won't pretend that we were doing the right thing or even try to defend it. But you again need to remember, there is that same fraternal sense of brotherhood on the road that I know wives and girlfriends don't appreciate. One of the "rules of the road" within our "secret society" was and still is basically that of turning a blind eye toward all that is or may have been taking place around us. I am not one who will tell stories outside of school, and so any such talk will only be about my own errors in judgment, though at the time, I hardly thought they were errors. I could always find ways to justify my own indiscretions. Kind of like the guy who says, "I didn't stab him 12 times. He just kept running into my knife with his gut!"

Okay, I mentioned earlier that I would tell you the back-story to the song "Arizona". Don't wish to forget, though, at my age, forgetfulness is something I am always leery of. It was actually another very true story. I know you always doubt the authenticity of a story told to you by a philandering rock and roll guy. How can you trust someone whose reputation is already built on lies and deception? But honestly, this one was true. I was "picked up" by a beautiful woman in a black limousine who took me out into the desert on a clear and starry night. For those of you who have been to Arizona, you know, the desert wasn't all that difficult to find. Anyway, as the song implies quite openly, we did a lot more than just read the sonnets of German poet Johann Wolfgang von Goethe to each other by the moonlight... As you can imagine, it was true love, whatever her name was, and Arizona will forever be one of my top 50 favorites of the United States. The story was a bit of a letdown, huh? Well, you asked for it. Honestly, the fantasy of what might have been is often more interesting than the reality.

Anyway, taking time to drift back to the story... As we were nearing the completion with regard to the writing for the album and getting close to the point when we were going to start recording, we knew we were on to something very special. We also knew Klaus was having more trouble than we originally suspected, even though he wasn't letting on. That was quite disquieting to our own peace of mind, as you can surely understand. Here we were sitting on this incredible body of music, and we weren't even sure if or when we would complete it!

When time came to actually start the recording of *Blackout*, Dieter rented a big villa in the south of France, Grasse, to be exact. It was an incredible house, to say the least, as it had seven or eight bedrooms which we, of course, took advantage of not only for sleeping but also for other more entertaining activities. (I never realized there were so many different ways to play Solitaire.) Maybe it wasn't a villa. It could have been a chateau. Villas are in Spain. Chateaus are in France. I know this probably doesn't interest you, but I just want to set the record straight in case one of the other Scorpions writes a book like this and calls it something different. Don't want you to accuse me of lying. (Actually, I doubt any of them would write a book like this. They take this all much more seriously than I do. I doubt there would be many laughs in their book. Then again, to some of you that might make theirs exactly like this book.) Anyway, the reason for choosing a big house (How's that for diplomacy?) for the recording was basically the acoustics of the large rooms. No matter how hard you might try, you can never replace or replicate the natural room sounds you can get within a "real" space. Even utilizing the most advanced digital technology available today in any studio, I believe you would still come up short. So remember, 30 or so years ago, we were dealing with Jurassic technology. Sounds could not be enhanced or produced as easily inside a studio, and so we had to "stoop" to working within an authentic space. Truthfully, there is nothing like a genuine marble floor or wood paneled wall with 20-30 foot high ceilings when it comes to creating a specific sound, if that is, in fact, what you are trying to capture. Canned reverb and other effects may be fine for those without any other option, but it's nothing like that which can be produced within the realm of the living. Obviously, perhaps the chateau was a bit of a giveaway, we were blessed with a substantially larger budget for recording as a result of the success of our prior albums. But we weren't about to spend every waking hour counting our money or resting on our past laurels and accolades. We wanted to "up the ante" and decided to spare no expense in production to insure that we would have every opportunity to produce a classic.

Upon completing our work in France as well as the rhythm tracks there, we went to Dieter's studios in Cologne to add the instrumental solos and vocals. However, Klaus continued to struggle vocally, so Dieter told us about a young singer named Don Dokken that he knew. He said he was more than capable of singing backgrounds and perhaps putting down a test track lead for us to follow so we could complete at least the instrumental portions of the album.

Meanwhile, after taking time to consult with several doctors, it was finally determined that Klaus was going to need surgery on his vocal folds to remove some polyps that had developed over the prior year. At least that's what I recall. The rigors and demands of touring were indeed the most likely culprit and had truly taken a toll on his voice. That part we were right about. I have to be honest, Klaus was a team player, and I suspect it was the sense of team that kept our group together for as long as we were. A lot of groups suffer from ego conflicts that internally destroy a group as I've said. That's the reason so few sustain with the basic core players for more than a couple years. (If you look at our longevity, the same basic six people (including Dieter) were together for more than a decade. What other group in the history of rock and roll can boast an endurance record like that?) But it wasn't that way with us. We were a tight unit, and there was friendship and camaraderie that was in some ways unique. We noticed that most clearly during our tours where we would see the divisiveness and backstabbing that was so much a part of other bands we would encounter. There would be many who were four or five totally different people with completely different agendas. They were only together because fate caught up with them as they were immersed in the general transience that is so much a part of music. Players will jump from band to band because they are looking for the best gig. They aren't really looking beyond the next casual or club date. They figure they'll only be with the group when time permits and will play with half a dozen bands at one time in an effort to pay their bills. Well, when circumstance steps in, and one of those bands actually gets a call from a label that liked their demo, the current line-up, whatever it may be, tends to be the one that signs on the bottom line. Many times, the group isn't really a group. It is just a handful of musicians who happen to be in the same place at the same time. They may not, in fact, even like each other. And so the longevity of their tenure as a group may be considered tenuous at best. Perhaps it is the reason so many groups in rock and roll come and go within hours of being discovered.

However, in our case, we were actually friends. Yes, I know, Matthias and I were, of course, "recent" additions in many ways, but the chemistry between all of us was more like brothers than it was just adding two complete strangers. Again, in part, this may have been the result of our all being of German ancestry. I don't know if this went into their thinking when they decided to add me to the band, nor do I recall if that thought came to mind while we were auditioning guitar players. But ultimately, the similarity of lifestyles and backgrounds proved to be quite important over the long term of our band. We understood where we all were and where we all had come from. No matter how insightful a person might be, he can't possibly see or know how it feels to be someone else, or what it's like to grow up in a country other than his own. The perspective afforded him by his own life will forever limit him.

We all knew and understood that Klaus needed surgery, as I said, and so we made it clear to him that regardless of his thoughts or even wishes, we would wait. The surgeon, an optimistic sort, said there was a chance he might never sing again, but at the very least, it would be several months, perhaps even a year, before he could sing anything at all. Klaus, in response, once again reiterated that we shouldn't wait for him. We should go ahead with a new singer. But we were a family, and families don't turn their backs on their blood. Besides, Klaus was a key ingredient in our sound and could never have been replaced without a noticeable difference to our fans that we were just starting to attract in large numbers. I think, to be completely honest, in some ways, he may very well have just been feeling very pessimistic pangs within his heart and maybe a little guilt. So perhaps he felt that we would be upset with him if he were never able to sing, and we had waited for him. I think most people feel that way when something happens to them. They reach a point of helplessness and suspect the "end", whatever that might entail, might be quite near. So Klaus was trying to be positive in public, but I suspect, in his heart, he thought his career as a singer might have been drawing to a close.

We were, most assuredly, worried and rightfully so, given that we had finally cracked through the worldwide market only to discover our fame may become as short-lived as the Soviet political career of General Secretary Yuri Andropov atop the Communist Party. It isn't easy to replace any member of a group as fans can become quite difficult to please; most certainly rumors would abound as to the reasons Klaus left the group. Such scandal could be devastating. A singer is irreplaceable. I know there aren't many who will admit that. But it's quite true for most bands. Yes, anyone can sing a song but to make it convincing and not sound like a poor man's karaoke, that's a different matter altogether. A band's sound is usually most recognizable to the general public by the lead singer's voice. The more unique or interesting, the more important he becomes. Truthfully, no one could replace Robert Plant in Led Zeppelin or Geddy Lee in RUSH. I doubt there are many who would argue with this assessment. And we felt the same about Klaus.

Please don't take this out of context. I am not saying that every group has floundered or folded after losing a vocalist; some have gone on to have arguably more success with a replacement. And yet, I think what has to be noted is the circumstance behind the change in personnel. The perception in the minds of the fans can be more important than the actual change. For example, Bon Scott died. That pretty much was about as definite as anything you can find within this life when it comes to the concept of termination. AC/DC really didn't have much say in that. And so when Brian Johnson came aboard, the fans chose to embrace the new sound the band created rather than criticize it.

And so we waited. As history shows, it was a wise decision. After recording the basic tracks with Don Dokken as a guide only, Klaus was able to make a full and complete recovery and once again give his very unique and distinctive vocal styling to the songs. Of course, the rest really is rock and roll history.

13
WELCOME TO MY WORLD

With his vocal problems resolved, at least that was what he told us, though in truth, we were still more than a little skeptical, we completed the recording of *Blackout* in early 1982. I won't go into too much detail about the recovery because, honestly, it isn't my story to tell, and I'd probably get it wrong. I know Dieter spent a lot of time working with him, and we also hired a vocal coach as well in an effort to help him learn techniques and tricks to preserve his voice while handling the arduous task of singing several nights in a row. All of that actually may have benefitted us because staying power is a part of our résumé. Had Klaus not had the troubles when he did, it is very possible he could have done even more, perhaps irreparable damage to his voice and ultimately been completely rendered useless at a very young age. Anyway, for my story, you know he recovered, and we continued, and so if you are curious, and Klaus ever decides to write a book, I'm sure he'll be able to explain it all to those of you who are sincerely interested in a good night's sleep!

Released on April 10, 1982 and gold (Certified sales in excess of 500,000 copies.) by June, *Blackout* pretty much secured the Scorpions a spot on the top of the worldwide stage. "No One Like You" eventually rose to the level of #1 on the Rock Singles chart, and we were off on another tour of the world, one that would run on for the better part of a year.

Beginning in March of 1982 and continuing to November and then resuming the following year with spot dates while we tried to produce our next album, we basically toured the hell out of the album. Our first stop was Paris in March... Springtime in Paris... Such a romantic thought. Though honestly, if you ask me, it did not seem so very different from summer or fall, in my opinion, and only slightly different than winter. Paris was followed by stops in Spain and Italy before we spent the month of April in the United Kingdom playing to sold-out houses throughout England. 16 stops in 25 days. Much like a liberal American politician, it was taxing. I'd be lying if I said we didn't have concerns about Klaus more than the overall schedule. The tour was much more stressful than that which we had done in 1980. So surely, thoughts of a recurrence or relapse of his troubles were always in the back of our minds.

After a few more stops in Europe, notably in Amsterdam, and then three more dates in our native Germany (with three different girls...), we were off to begin the summer tour of North America. This time, thankfully, we started on the east coast, which, as I've already said, is a much easier adjustment for the body to make time-wise than travelling across eight or nine time zones from Europe to California. From mid-June through mid-September we played 52 shows in what amounted to about 90 days, spanning the entire continent including many Canadian dates. We finally got to play the "big rooms" in New York and Los Angeles as well as headlining stadium concerts in a great many of the stops. In support for most of the tour was a non-descript band called Girlschool who pretty much vanished from the face of the earth soon after their part of our tour, at least to the best of my knowledge. I'm sure I'll get letters from their fans giving me the entire history of the group. But for me, they were just another band of girls – nothing out of the ordinary.

Anyway, they were replaced or followed (I don't really remember if they were canned for being horrible or simply done with our tour, so I don't want to speak out of "school'…) by a then unknown band that went by the name of Iron Maiden. Though I couldn't have cared less about Girlschool (Mentioning them in this book might be the most publicity they have ever received…), I did watch Iron Maiden a few times from offstage, and I was very impressed. Though the music was much harder and different from what we did, they still were a hard rocking band with a lot of good energy that I knew would be going places.

Finishing off North America in September, we then went across the Pacific to Japan stopping briefly to play a show in Hawaii along the way and to take a well-deserved breather. I loved Hawaii. Who doesn't? Having never been there before, I was given the opportunity to not only scuba dive for the first time but do another form of diving as well. I didn't miss any chance presented to me to dance a private hula with many of the local wahinis.

From the Orient, we were then back to North America and a couple more shows in Canada, before heading home. We were justifiably tired, and yet we were ready to do it all over again. It's amazing how a couple of days of rest can help you to forget any negatives. Yes, there are always negatives while on tour outside of just having to live out of a suitcase. However, at that point, there weren't all that many. For the most part, everything was quite positive and exciting! We were the main attraction. We got steak rather than hamburger. We got the good-looking women. And we even got to stay at a Howard Johnson's!

Back home, there was, of course, business to attend to like writing and recording a new album. That, actually, seemed like much harder work, and it was exactly that – work! Though writing isn't like digging a ditch, it can be stressful in its own way. There is only one person whom I've ever known to never suffer from "writer's block", or at least he has told me that he has never had any such difficulty, and that is the guy I worked with on this book. I have seen Michael sit down at a computer and start writing without any idea as to where he's going or what he's going to write and turn out 20-30 pages inside of a couple hours that will all be poignant, focused, concise and, most importantly, very entertaining! But such people are anomalies. I guess, in his own way, he could be classified as a genius though he'd never be one to think that way. He is one of the most sincerely humble people I've ever known. I will say, though, right here on the record, I am more than a little bit envious of his talents, and honestly I'll tell you, he, personally, is not all the comfortable with my saying this about him. But to hell with humility! He deserves to be given appropriate recognition as the genius he is. So there! (By the way, his new novel titled "Tomorrow Will Be Yesterday-The Story of BASH is wonderful romantic comedy about a "fictional" rock and roll band from the 1970's. I recommend it to everyone.)

However, returning to the date we brought to this dance, technically, the *Blackout* tour was not yet over. As I said, we toured the hell out of the album. For the next year we would venture out to various locales playing shows not so much on a tour but simply to keep our name out in the market place while we recorded our follow up. We believed we would have all the new material written and the album recorded and released by the following summer. But sometimes the best plans don't always come to pass.

One quite historic stop during that time was in the middle of nowhere. No our tour bus didn't break down on a dark desert highway where there was cool wind in our hair… Wait a second. I know those words. Sweet smell of colitas… Rising up in the air… Oh hell, that's "Hotel California". I'm sorry. Sometimes my mind drifts. Give me a second to remember where the heck we are. Oh, right… We played the middle of nowhere, California, though in musical terms, as I have come to learn in recent months it was near "Route 66", and perhaps that is where the "Hotel California" supposedly was. Who is to say except Don Henley and Glen Frey? Anyway, the point is, we played someplace in California's Mojave Desert, they told us. The concert itself was something called the "US Festival" in the spring of 1983, the 29th of May to be precise. I cannot tell you for sure if "US" meant U.S. like "United States", or if it meant "US" like the mantra of the "Me Generation" that was just beginning to come into vogue.

Anyway, the US Festival, regardless of all the rest of the crap I wrote, was one damn big show. That's what mattered. Truthfully, it was the most amazing event I've ever seen and definitely the biggest I've ever been a part of. People as far as the eye could see. I'm sure there are six million people today who claim to have been part of the reported 500,000.

I remember getting to the concert was a bit complicated. On the morning of our performance – keep in mind, we weren't scheduled to play until late afternoon/early evening – someone had the nerve to call us at our hotel, which made sense since that was where we were staying. I know, given what I've said about our promiscuous nature and philandering behavior, there's no telling where some of us may have actually spent the night. But for the official record, we were staying at our hotel in California, and, yes, there was the sweet smell of colitas, rising up in the air. (Glen, Don, are you listening? It's not plagiarism if it actually happened.) Anyway, we were told that morning that we were going to have to be brought in by helicopter because all of the roads were jammed, much like it was at Woodstock in 1969 I suspect. It actually turned out to be a gift from the heavens, even though initially I had some trepidation about it. But the short journey by whirlybird allowed us to get a bird's-eye view of the mass of humanity below as we circled high above the crowd prior to coming in for a soft landing. I had never flown in such a craft before, which led to my initial concerns. It can be a bit scary to look out a window and not see any wings. But I survived.

Upon arriving, which meant landing in a dirt field behind the stage, we were picked up by a limo. No, it wasn't the same one that picked me up in Arizona… We weren't that fortunate. This one merely picked us up and took us to the stage area. Van Halen was the headliner the day we played, which was the second day of the three-day event. The first day, I think, was for new wave and punk with bands like Oingo Boingo, INXS, Flock of Seagulls and The Clash. The third day was for more pop-oriented rock like David Bowie, Stevie Nicks, Joe Walsh and Quaterflash. With us on our day were the usual cast of characters who were still alive and well plucked from the ever-dwindling talent pool of survivors playing in the genre of hard rock. The number of those that were still hanging on was quite small at that point, which is why you keep seeing the same names time and again throughout this book. Judas Priest, Triumph, Quiet Riot, Motley Crue and Ozzy Osbourne along with, as I said, headliner Van Halen, pretty much ran the gambit of viable rock acts available within the "class" of 1983. However, if the truth were to be told, in all humility, I think we received a much better response than Eddie and his guys. I attribute that to a lack of self-discipline when it came to drugs and alcohol on the part of VH front man David Lee Roth. As I recall, he unwisely took a bottle of Jack Daniels on stage with him. As you might imagine, that did very little to enhance their performance that evening.

However, as incredible as the music may have been, as was normally the case at most of our shows to be sure, there were some backstage "shenanigans" that still provided the most interesting story. After we finished our set, I found what I thought was a pretty normal post-concert grope taking place between one of my band-mates who shall remain nameless and one of the always-available groupies inside our dressing room trailer. That, of course, included some very deep and passionate kisses of the "French" variety among other things. Keep in mind, such things were so ordinary that really we hardly ever even took note, and, in truth, I was a bit preoccupied myself, if you get my drift. But the fair maiden looked familiar, so I took a bit of a closer look. I was never one to gawk, mind you, but in that instance, I was curious. Upon further inspection, and I will try to be as delicate as possible with my description of it, I recognized her as the same young lady whom I had seen not more than a few minutes earlier "tickling her tonsils" with some of the male "members" of our road crew just behind the stage near some portable toilets.

Well, being the caring and fatherly type I always have been, I would not have been able to live with myself if I were to have ignored it altogether. And so after the nameless band-mate completed his work, I felt obligated to provide him with some inside information. The fact of the matter was, as I explained to him, his accompanist in his "tongue tango" was the very same young bird who had just had her lips precariously close to and at times making use of some of the available "tools" for purposes of pruning an assortment of protruding "limbs" and rigid "branches". Upon obtaining the knowledge that he had shared saliva and other now suspicious bodily fluids with the same girl whose mouth, throat and larynx had most likely frequented places he would never want his own to come close to, and that she had probably, at least by circumstance or happenstance, sampled some of the "forbidden nectar" from the "Peter Johnson" family "tree" as part of her sincere effort to earn an opportunity to rumba with one of the actual "members" of the band and perhaps play with his "instrument" (We didn't have an organ in the band...), he proceeded to unceremoniously "lose his lunch". (How was that for being politically correct?)

I know, even as sterile and clinical as I conscientiously tried to be in the last paragraph, there will be those who will read this book thinking it's the sequel to *Heidi* or maybe that it's a book about bugs and insects and as such will say, "That was unnecessary and uncalled for. It was indecent!" Well, I have to be honest with you, though I am quite sensitive to the feelings of others, we Scorpions did have one definition for the word indecent... "If it's in hard, in long and in deep... It's in decent!"

As for the onstage concert itself, playing with a veritable cavalcade of artists that perhaps could have been considered a "who's who" of rock music at the time as I've said, we were told there were more than half a million people looking on when we took the stage. It was a scene one can hardly ever forget. If you look on the inside foldout of our *World Wide Live* album (or just take a gander over my right shoulder on the cover of this book), you will see a panoramic picture from behind my drums surveying the mass of humanity that stood before us. With the sun setting at the horizon to the west and a slight haze hovering above (More than likely produced by marijuana, though in Southern California one never knows for sure.), the scene was as impressive as it was inspiring. For me, it will remain one of the greatest memories I'll ever have on stage. Notice I said on stage.

14
SUN OVER BEACH

As much fun as we were having on the road, and trust me, we were having fun, it was time to solidify our place in rock music history. Okay, so at the time we didn't think in terms of our legacy or contributions to the genre. Our only desire was that of producing the best damned music on the planet!

At any rate, in late 1983, we began to show our true colors as we commenced the writing of what would be our *Love At First Sting* album. For those of you who wish to label bands and musicians as little more than pleasure-seeking, sexual predators, I suppose this album and the lyrics contained therein would pretty much guarantee us a permanent residence in any sort of hall of honor therein there might be. Hey, if you can't be in the Rock and Roll Hall of Fame, the Hedonistic Lecher Hall might be a fairly good alternative. In case you are curious, the then wives of the group, believe it or not, didn't seem to care. At least they didn't do so publicly, though perhaps they kicked some ass behind closed doors. Then again, maybe the fact that they were, in some ways, living a wonderful fantasy life themselves, made it much easier to ignore our obvious and probably transparent indiscretions.

I recall hearing singer Tom Jones, when asked during an interview about how his wife handled the scuttlebutt regarding women on the road, saying she never asked and he didn't tell. In all honesty, that is pretty much the only way a man and woman can keep a marriage alive if one or the other is involved in the entertainment industry.

Oh, by the way, don't for one minute think that sex on the road is an exclusive right of passage for men only. Women in music or, for that matter, any other part of the entertainment industry, are just as sexually active as men. Yes, that's right. It is, however, a much better kept secret and much more private and definitely less reported because, I suspect, it's just not appropriate to kiss and tell with regard to a woman. I, too, will honor that tradition within these pages, so please don't ever bother to ask. I will say, however, ladies are much more discrete, since you won't see most in public at bars after hours picking up partners for their private rendezvous. Many utilize what they refer to as "personal" assistants whose only real job is that of securing male companions on the sly for their employer in order to keep it as secretive as possible.

Anyway, the point to all of this is, even though our music was laced with true stories of our life on the road, and despite the hours I may have taken meticulously crafting a lyric, a large number of rock enthusiasts never really learn the words to songs they like. The reason probably goes back to the origins of the genre. Rock music has always been and will always be more about melody and beat than it is lyrics. However, interestingly, at least to me, there are many who will not listen to instrumental rock because there is no vocal. It is the hook, or the chorus of a song, that is most memorable, and we were quite famous for some of rock and roll's best.

As for my life, I was in a period of transition as well. Having been bowled over to a point by the sudden success I was a part of, it wasn't so long before that I was living in that dreary hovel of sorts in Hannover, if you recall. And so the spoils of our newfound riches gave me an opportunity to reach out and grab some of what I considered to be the "good life". Prior to the beginning of production on the new album (It would have been difficult to begin production on an old album, don't you think? Funny how stupid certain expressions and phrases seem when you put them in a literal context...), as a result of our playing there and in the general vicinity on several occasions, I decided to move to Los Angeles. What was there not to love about Southern California? Okay, so there was the smog, the traffic, the gang wars, gunfights, murders, rapes and assorted other anomalies that may not be considered part of a quiet, ordinary life. So what? You could see most of that in Hannover, but you'd have to do so while freezing your ass off. And so, ultimately, I was seduced by what I perceived as the "magic" of "Lala land" and decided to take up residence in the legendary "City of Angels". It was, actually, a toss-up between Los Angeles and Fresno… All right so that's a bit of an exaggeration. Just wanted to see if you were paying attention.

Initially, when I got to L.A., I rented an apartment in Redondo Beach overlooking the ocean. Being a land lover up until that point, I loved having the sea at my doorstep. (It is the reason, along with the weather that I now spend most of my time in Brighton, England, across the street from the beach.) But no matter how nice living at the beach was, and trust me, it had its advantages like bikini clad women strolling up and down the sands as if they were part of a fashion show, not just attending a public beach, after a short period of adjustment in the apartment, I decided to rent a house in Cold Water Canyon in Beverly Hills. I still think, to this day, it is one of the most beautiful areas for anyone to live in. Hell, at that time, I was a rock star and wanted to be part of the "jet set".

Anyway, the importance of this story, at least one important element of this story, took place on Halloween night, 1983. I was sitting quietly in a small bar with a very good friend of mine, music producer Ric Browde, as well as a variety of other acquaintances, drinking liberally and most assuredly under the influence while generally minding my own business. As such, of course, my resistance, if I had any, was lowered to the point of extreme vulnerability. I guess we all have our moments of weakness, though in that case, I really don't think it was. On that "enchanted evening", across the crowded room, I spied the most beautiful woman in the entire world sitting with a couple of her gal-pals waiting for me to enter her life. Okay, so maybe

I'm exaggerating a bit. Maybe the night wasn't so enchanted. Who am I to say? But the woman in question was incredibly gorgeous, and that is what really matters. Anyway, from my standpoint, after the incident in Paris and being well aware of the reputation of the local California customs and lifestyle choices as well as the community and its environs, not to mention the fact that it was Halloween, I wanted to make sure I wasn't seeing things, and that she was, at least anatomically, a woman to avoid making a complete ass of myself. But honestly, I couldn't resist her lure, nor did I want to. So I said to myself, "To hell with it! If she's a man, I may switch hit..." No, I didn't really say that or even think it. To set the record straight, and I mean STRAIGHT, since there are those who will take this out of context, I, Herman "Ze German" Rarebell am today and always will be 100% male. I do not lean in any direction other than that, and so please don't bother trying to twist this joke into something it is not. It is a joke. Okay? Do you see the kind of stuff one has to deal with in this world? And of course now, there will be those who'll claim I'm homophobic because I'm trying to simply clarify something. It's hard to have fun these days, isn't it? The point to all of this is that I am just trying to make clear how beautiful she was! And so, casting suspicions and concerns to the wind, and hoping I wouldn't find a "surprise" beneath her skirt, with reckless abandon, I went over and invited Tamara Ventrella to sit with me. From that day forward, we started to see a lot of each other. I guess that's one way of putting it, since she moved in with me, and eventually, we had a romantic Las Vegas wedding in June of 1985.

Surely some of you who may not really give a damn about my love life may still be wondering how the distance separation of me in L.A. and the band in West Germany worked with regard to the rehearsing and recording of the album. There were and are a lot of erroneous rumors with regard to the *Love At First Sting* album that were, perhaps, fueled by the situation. But I'll address that in a few pages. However, I just want to acknowledge that I do know this "love" stuff is hardly of interest to those of you who want to read about rock and roll. But trust me, with Tamara, there was a hell of a lot of rock and roll if you follow my thinking. We both lived the rock and roll lifestyle, and, in fact, we were very much in love with one another. At least until we got married… We spent many a night partying together at a very popular nightspot in Los Angeles called the Rainbow Club. It was a hangout for seemingly everyone in show business. The biggest names in entertainment frequented the club. But we didn't stop when they pushed us out the front door after last call. We would always keep the party going after hours by taking several groupies or others to our house until dawn.

Anyway, since this is a story about my life in one of the world's greatest rock and roll bands, I was only actually in Los Angeles for about six months, which I guess shows how much can happen in what amounts to a very short period of time. Honestly, at that point, we, the band, had all decided to take a break and write and work on material for the new album. No, this isn't the reason that rumors abound about my playing on the new album or anything like that. We just decided as a group after the long tour we had taken, that we needed some time off. This is one reason why our plans began to go awry with regard to the time schedule we had originally put in place earlier. And so when it came time to start work in earnest, Tamara and I packed up our belongings and moved to West Germany. Talk about coming home with more "baggage" than you left with… (Please, don't write me letters. Look, if I were to compare Tamara to a handbag, she definitely would have been a Gucci. She was truly the top in her field!)

Tamara actually became a bit of a happy co-conspirator and all too willing contributor and accomplice in my wild and unrestrained lifestyle. Just as an alcoholic hardly needs to involve himself with the owner of a bar, Tamara was openly bisexual, and as a result of that combined with her incredible beauty, she had a rack, I mean knack for attracting the most attractive women. So, as you can probably imagine, we did have our share of interesting flings, however, I prefer to wait for another time for that discussion if, in fact, it actually needs to be discussed.

At any rate, it was also during that time, the time in Southern California, that I began thinking about and working on the completion of my first solo album. In Redondo Beach, near the apartment where I first lived, there is a studio called Total Access. At that time, Don Dokken was out there working. He told me about the place, and that a mutual friend of ours named Michael Wagener was there as well. Wagener was a friend of mine from Dieter's studio where he was a sound engineer but had moved to Southern California and become a producer. He eventually made quite a name for himself producing, for example, Great White, Poison and Metallica among other big name bands.

I decided to meet with Wagener and told him about my solo album aspirations. I related to him that back in Germany I had already recorded an assortment of basic guitar, bass and drum tracks with my friends Dave Cooper, a guitarist I knew from England, and Pedro Schemm, a singer and songwriter from my RS Rindfleisch days. All that was needed was to have some vocals added to some of the songs. He immediately suggested that I go forward with the album and employ an assortment of singers and other musicians to add their special qualities to the album. The end result was that which ultimately became, *Herman Ze German and Friends*. And what friends I had! Aside from the three songs I did with Don Dokken on vocals, I had Charlie Huhn from the Ted Nugent band provide the vocals for, "Do it". Jack Russell from Great White sang "Junk Funk". And we brought in Steve Marriott from, of course, Small Faces and Humble Pie fame to sing, "Having a Good Time." The only song we kept pretty much intact vocally, which was done by Pedro, was "Rock You All". Instrumentally, we chose to redo the bass tracks with Juan Croussier from the band Ratt while keeping the original guitar tracks Dave Cooper had recorded with me. To this day, I'm still working with Dave. He co-wrote, along with Pedro and myself, all of the songs on the album.

Of course, no solo album by any drummer can ever be considered complete without the expected cover of the Safari's "Wipeout". Mine was no different. It is the only song I recorded in total in California using all of my friends. You know, as I think back about this album now, I may actually have been a pioneer in this sort of production. As most of you probably know, many artists today record albums like that and many have had a lot of success. Immediately coming to mind is Carlos Santana, who recorded several albums using a cross-section of singers from within the rock and pop fields. So perhaps, in a small way, my *Herman Ze German* album was the forerunner to those who have since followed that same line of thought.

As a side note here to lend perspective, if you recall, the mid-eighties was the "heyday" of MTV. Nothing could be produced without an accompanying video. You remember the story about the Scorpion production on Alcatraz. So I, too, decided to produce a video to accompany the album and hopefully help sales. It was pretty much standard procedure to be sure. At the time there were few labels that would even touch a project without some sort of video. As a result, I produced what I consider to be a "fun" video for the song "Wipeout" that helped propel it to some minor chart success in several countries, most notably England, where it reached #17. The video is available for viewing on my website if you are interested. I assume if you are reading this book you probably have already seen it. But I'm always interested in making new friends and fans as well.

Anyway, even though we recorded and completed the album in 1984, it didn't reach the shelves of record stores on Capitol Records until late 1985 or early 1986 for reasons that I really don't remember so well. As you will discover in a few pages, a lot of my memories of that time were and are shrouded by a dark storm cloud that was hanging over my head. I suspect if I were to guess, it was probably just simply a matter of shopping the album around to get the best deal we could. In all modesty, sales were very good. Not at Scorpion levels, of course. Few albums in the world sold like those. But still, in my opinion, the sales were good, nonetheless.

Meanwhile back with the Scorpions, upon my return to Germany, we began rehearsing the songs for the *Love At First Sting* album in

February and March in Hannover. Eventually, we decided to go up to Sweden to the ABBA studios to record. I don't really recall why we decided to use their studio, but for me, I really wish we hadn't. While in Sweden, I developed "health problems" as a result of my own stupidity, which consisted of basically my abuse of alcohol and cocaine. Keep in mind, I wasn't the only one with that problem as I'm sure you know. The industry was and still is filled with such problems. But for me, it was my burden. My dark storm cloud, if you will. My personal demon. One day in the studio in Sweden, I flat out collapsed.

The group decided that I needed to get dried out and off the booze and drugs, and so I went with Tamara to Sicily for a well-deserved and needed holiday on the beautiful Mediterranean. To keep things moving forward with production during my absence, Dieter brought in, with my blessing, let me repeat, **WITH MY BLESSING**, Bobby Rondinelli of Rainbow to play the drums. Also at that time, even though he was not having problems with abuse as I was, we simply weren't very happy with the bass sound we were getting from Francis, so we decided to bring in former Rainbow and later Dio bass player, Jimmy Bain. I knew Jimmy from Los Angeles, and I thought he was a very good choice and an outstanding player.

And so Tamara and I went south and began sunning and resting along the Sicilian coastline – hardly what I, or anyone this side of Lindsey Lohan, would call hardcore rehab therapy. Hey, let's face it, anyone who has ever been hooked on such things as drugs and alcohol knows that there is enough denial to go around, and, truthfully, we all were dealing with the same problems. We just didn't accept it as a problem, nor does anyone else who suffers from the affliction today I suspect. Well, tough as it was, I suffered through the hiatus on the beach as best I could. However, it was short-lived, as after about two weeks I got a call from Dieter who told me he listened to everything that the replacements had done, and said it didn't sound like the Scorpions anymore. **He (Dieter) demanded I go into the studio and play the percussion tracks for the complete album.**

In other words, I rerecorded all of the drum tracks for *Love At First Sting* **at his studio in Cologne.** And so, all of you rumor mongering, mindless simpleton "hacks" out there, who, for whatever the reason, claim I wasn't the drummer on the album, well, as far as I'm concerned, you can pretty much... Well, actually I have too much class to say such things. I won't even give you the credibility by mentioning you specifically here.

Anyway, my return to Cologne to record allowed Tamara needed personal time to go back home to L.A. to spend time with her family. I was aware that she was lonely and missed California. Hell, I missed California. It had to be a shock I'm sure to go from sunshine and blue skies to cold, gray, dank and generally miserable Hannover, West Germany. So I understood completely.

I will admit that I was not so much a part of the writing on the album directly as I had been with the previous two; the credits, thereon, bear this out. But at that point such battles were non-existent. The songs that were produced are a testament to what a band can do when it sets aside its separate egos and focuses all its energies on creating the best music possible! I did contribute the lyrics to "Bad Boys Running Wild" and "Rock You Like a Hurricane" which, in truth, as previously mentioned, were little more than celebrations of, or more precisely, remembrances of my nights on the road. Oh, I guess we could say that our English was so limited that all we knew were the things we saw in American movies. But who the hell would we be kidding? Anyone who took time to read the lyrics knew exactly what we were talking about. And yet, our music by today's standards would be considered tame if not innocent fun. I mean a verse like, "It's early morning; the sun comes out. Last night was shaking and pretty loud. My cat is purring and scratches my skin. So what is wrong with another sin? The bitch is hungry; she needs to tell. So give her inches and feed her well. More days to come, new places to go, I've got to leave, it's time for a show..." leaves very little to the imagination. It's quite clear I wrote it about a normal morning in L.A. driving on the freeway. Seriously, we were not trying to be the "bad boys" of rock music, but with our album covers and risqué lyrics, we were getting there quickly, and we weren't about to change anytime soon.

As I look back upon that time now, I can say there probably was an outside reason I only contributed two songs to the album. Remember, that was the first album we produced after I had started living with Tamara. Regardless of what anyone thinks, relationships have both good and bad sides. Ask Tiger Woods. His marital problems took him from being a peerless golf hero to being a footnote saying, "What could have been..." Having a relationship of any kind takes time and commitment. You can't divide yourself mentally or physically in various directions and still be focused 100% on any one thing. Before I was involved with Tamara, I had relationships. But living with someone is very different, as all of you probably understand. You have to work at a relationship of that kind much more and that takes away from your ability to remove yourself from the stresses created therein of managing not only your career but also your home life. Just remembering to put the goddamned seat down in the bathroom kept me on edge! It was difficult to remove myself mentally as I needed to do in order to write music. Before that, I had nothing to consider other than my music and myself even though there were those like Sonya who stayed with me for periods of time. In general, "relationships" were shallow and plentiful. But even though I loved Tamara, my attention was now divided, and that caused a form of writer's block for me, the likes of which I had never known. I just had a lot more on my plate at that time, and it made escape much more difficult.

To be fair and hopefully not viewed as being sexist... I know, why start now? But I do see both sides of the story because I'm sure women see the negative impact of relationships on their lives as well. There is enough stress in life to go around and adequate blame for a bad relationship for everyone involved. I'll talk more about those things in the next chapter, but for now, I just want to say I am certain men have the same impact both good and bad on the careers of women in and outside of the industry. I am, as perhaps you can figure out, limited in perspective, so you'll have to forgive me if I'm wrong.

As most of you know, when the much anticipated "...*Sting*" was finally completed and released in 1984, I suspect as a result of our successful tour of the States and much of the world, it didn't take very long for it to reach the top of the charts around the globe. Of course, as much as our hardcore fans lauded "...Hurricane", "Still Loving You" was the song that reached out to the entire world and I think created a legacy that will forever endure.

The album rose quickly to #6 in America, which, at that time, was unheard of for any rock band in America. The American music scene was dominated by new wave and pop as I've already made clear. But somehow we managed to do it, and "...Hurricane" jumped to #25 on the Billboard Pop Chart and #5 on the Rock Chart. As far as I remember, the album itself shipped platinum; in other words, one million copies were "sold" on the release day.

Around the world, though, as I already mentioned, "Still Loving You" was the song that brought many to the band and the album. Eventually, reaching the level of triple platinum, three million albums sold in the initial offering; we made the decision that it was time to plan our conquest of the planet! (Keep in mind, these numbers were exclusive of sales on the black-market behind the "Iron Curtain". I'm not really sure what the current count is as the album still sells very well, though.) An 18-month worldwide tour to make sure everyone knew who we were was placed on the table before us. The quite humbling truth was that demand was so high for us we very well could have toured for 36 months. Unlike previous tours, we weren't really in a hurry to get back into the studio because we were recording our next album literally on the run. It was during that tour that we recorded the tracks that would become *World Wide Live*.

Just to give you a little idea, we got to the U.S. in mid-March of 1984 and played there in every city, big and small, from New York to San Francisco until September when we jumped on a plane back to Europe to play some more dates there, as we had done from January to March. We tossed into the mix some quick jaunts to our second home in many ways, Japan, as well as our first journey to South America playing in Rio de Janeiro for roughly half a million people!

During the two weeks we were in Rio between shows, we stayed at the Copacabana Beach Hotel, where as far as I remember, all the good looking girls must have gone in and out of my suite from the disco. Sorry Tamara. Actually, I think she would have been envious had she known. Most were her "type". However, the one thing that really sticks out in my mind about the concerts in Rio aside from the women, and that is the heat! The second show we did on January 19th stands out in particular because it was so hot, temperature as well as our performance, we were literally dripping wet after the first song! Remember, January is mid-summer south of the equator. So Rio was not only hot in the suite of Herman Rarebell but also on stage!

In case you are wondering, and because there are those who will try to put together a perfect timeline of events in the life of Herman Rarebell for reasons which I will never understand, it was prior to going to Rio that I took a couple weeks off to spend time alone with Tamara at our house in California. This is when I shot the "Wipeout" video on Malibu Beach. By the way, if you go to my website to see that video, also check out the drum solo from "Rockin' Rio" in January of 1985.

The tour itself was a tour for the young but even our relative youth wasn't helping as we began to feel our years, or for that matter, the years of the Rat Pack, by the time it all began to wind down. Though we played again on top of an assortment of unmemorable bands and artists like Jon Butcher, Fastway and Mama's Boys during the tour, our most consistent companion, at least throughout the U.S., was a little known New Jersey band with a cutesy singer who the girls seemed to be quite enamored with, named Bon Jovi.

The way it came to pass that Bon Jovi was with us was a result of our being contacted by their manager Doc McGhee. When I saw Jon the first time, I knew immediately he and his band were going to be big stars. The girls went wild. I told Rudolf, "This guy looks so good, his looks alone can pay the rent." I still maintain a cordial relationship with Jon and the guys despite the discussion we had a couple years later backstage in Moscow. That wasn't personal in the least. It was just business. Even today, whenever Bon Jovi is touring in Europe, I try to go to one of the shows and at least say hello.

Upon our return to Europe, Joan Jett and the Blackhearts joined us on tour. We were now the coattails that were being spread for the younger acts handled by Leber/Krebs, and it was our turn to give back. As for Joan Jett, I personally thought little of her talent and was hardly a fan of her music, but I will admit, I did like her song "I Love Rock and Roll".

Believe it or not, I can say that there can be too much of a good thing as we came to discover. 12 months on the road was way too much, to say the least, and yet we upped that by 50%. We did learn a lesson from it. Overindulgence in any form is not good. Yes, we had fans who wanted to see us. We understood that. We wanted to see them as well. It was all quite flattering. But flattery isn't always sincere, since it can take its toll on other parts of a person's life. I enjoyed playing music. But there are always extremes and playing for 18 straight months on the road with only minimal amounts of time at home can take its toll not only on your health but also on your life. Changing water and time zones every couple of days can bring about an assortment of physical and mental breakdowns. Perhaps you can better understand why so many musicians turn to drugs and alcohol as an escape from the monotony. With my need to steer clear of such things, I had little else aside from sex to fall back on and use as my crutch. And trust me, I did my share of falling.

15

SECTS AND DRAGS AND A ROCKY ROAD

It is said that a woman spends two years of her life in the bathroom... It is also said that a man spends three years of his life outside the bathroom door saying, "Can we go yet?" I thought at this time, rather than perhaps bogging down the entire book with talk of my personal life, I would dedicate a completely separate chapter to a discussion of my thoughts and views on marriage and love. Not that I'm some sort of Dr. Phil, or even Dr. Jeckyll for that matter, but still, there are some observations I have made about relationships as a result of having had many myself. Some of this I've already mentioned, so please forgive me if I repeat something from a previous chapter. I just want to cover everything here in one place to kind of give you an overview of that which I have encountered and hopefully learned from throughout my life. Then again, when it comes to the "fairer sex", well, there is nothing that is definitely cut and dried unless, of course, you're talking about the marijuana you may share.

This chapter, actually, should and could be titled, *Do As I Say Not As I Did* because honestly, even though most expect to read about the myriad of sexploitations we had on the road, for me it is nothing more than a perfunctory act within these pages meant <u>only</u> for entertainment purposes as are all the tales in previous chapters.

If I had my life to live again, this is one part I would surely seek to change. Some may take it upon themselves to call me a hypocrite as a result of the juxtaposed positions I have on these issues when comparing my values of today with my actions from yesterday. So be it. I am in no position to argue. But people can and do change. Ultimately the only thing I can say to anyone is think how your behavior today will look tomorrow. If it is not something about which you will be proud of then it is not something you need to do. And so as you read the following read it knowing I do not judge. I neither condone nor condemn. I am simply relating the truth and hope that it will make you smile, laugh and, most importantly, perhaps learn something from. You have your own choices to make, and so if my admitted errors in judgment help guide you to make better decisions, then that is what will matter. Though I shared my memories herein at times with salacious relish, they are now sources of anguish and sorrow from within. For those who I may have hurt selfishly along the way, I hope you will accept my apology.

As I look at the world today I find there is no longer just the "opposite sex" to be concerned with. There are now vast arrays of "alternative lifestyles" that can never be overlooked. That is the first problem. Having had enough trouble trying to understand women within my life, you can imagine how easily confused I am now with the countless options that are always in play and on the table. There are now seemingly a million variations on the original, basic theme. In a world where you are told not to label people, it seems the same individuals who give that advice are the first ones who appear to have labels for everyone. And so along with the now quite ho-hum heterosexuals who have clearly become mundane to the masses and as such have fallen out of favor within our societal demands for more creativity and imagination, you now have the much more "chic" gays, lesbians, transvestites, transsexuals, bisexuals, bi-curious, homosexuals, eunuchs and he/shes adding to the already muddied waters, which doesn't even begin to address all the deviations therein and in between. The list is seemingly endless. I kind of doubt in the Garden of Eden you had so many derivatives wandering amongst the trees and plants. Then again, what do I know? However, in my opinion, all of these options have not only led to the confusion of many a man and woman who may just want to have a relationship but also within the general populace that seems to be unable to simply mark male or female on an application with all honesty because they fear they'll be categorized as insensitive or intolerant by others who live in a less historically traditional way of life. And yet convention seems to be shifting as well, so even that may not be appropriate to say. To me, in all honesty, it really makes no difference what you choose to do within your life or how you choose to live. It is your life. What matters to me is what is inside your heart.

Obviously, rock and roll and the rock and roll lifestyle (Obviously one more "alternative"…) are not conducive to happy marriages unless happiness means being completely without any emotional tie to the one with whom you are supposed to have emotional ties. That is a sad reality that almost everyone in music has to face and deal with at one time or another. There is guilt by association. Even if you are the straightest arrow in the quiver, the most loyal dog in the kennel, you undoubtedly will be expected to endure endless speculation, suspicion, allegations and questioning at the hands of your mate. The temptations are much more attractive and alluring than any drug I've ever been exposed to. You might love your spouse, and yet, in reality, the love you have for your art, as well as the so-called love which is actually lust that you have for the perks that go with a life in the spotlight can often make you less than a perfect husband or for that matter wife.

I will be blunt here at the outset. I was, as I've already sort of mentioned, less than a saint myself throughout my years in music inside and outside of relationships. To hell with being less than a saint, I was probably less than a jackass if you want to get technical. Some may think I'm wrong or improper in mentioning this. Well, maybe I am, but I am not one who is proud of my behavior, nor do I excuse it in any way. And yet, how easy is it to say no to another piece of chocolate cake even after you've eaten your fill? I don't and won't try to pass the buck for anything I did while on the road. I accept full responsibility for my actions, which in most cases included things that were not within the realm of a proper relationship of any sort. I insinuated earlier that perhaps some wives of musicians love the good life their husbands can provide. Maybe that allows them to accept the excesses on their part. This is, of course, nothing even remotely resembling the truth, I suspect, as no one can be so calloused when it comes to the concept of love and marriage. I will say, though, I do not doubt that there are men and women today who are married in name only, and the only love they share is the love of money. I could name a couple of marriages like that, but that's not my place. However, I doubt any of them kid themselves into believing their mates are faithful. But then again, maybe they do. I do not know. I can only speak in terms of my own life. With the bountiful buffet of enticements available while on the road, you would have to be gelded or exposed to a steady diet of Roseanne Barr "comedy" to remain stoic and steadfast to your commitments.

I will begin back at school… Yes, even in the Mastermen, the girls were everywhere! We had the advantage of having money when no one else did as I said earlier. That, of course, meant we could take advantage of the lovely young ladies at our disposal. I got my first taste of the good life when I was 15. Again, personal decorum prevents me from going further here.

When I started RS Rindfleisch, we were playing all night, every night, in clubs like The Coliseum in Schweinfurt. The owner of the club housed all the musicians, waitresses and Go Go dancers in apartments above the club. Human nature, of course, took its course, and so orgies were pretty much the standard, after-hour's bill of fare for the band since there were far more of the ladies than there were guys in the band. You can rest assured we didn't complain about the numbers or how they broke down.

I remember one Christmas night, for example. We had what amounted to a Christmas orgy. In keeping with the German Advent season candlelighting tradition called "Advent I Advent Ein Kerzlein Brennt", one of the girls felt she could adapt it to her celebration with our bass player. (As I have said, there was always a way to justify our behavior.) I'll tell you the truth, I don't know how much alcohol he had consumed at that point or how much in love he might have been, but I sure as hell would never let any woman under any circumstances insert a match into the tip of my manhood and then light it even in my most inebriated state! Talk about your bargain basement priced vasectomy...

Needless to say, we were extremely active sexually. (No kidding.) Actually, that would be an understatement. (You see?) Simply put, we took advantage of every female we could! (It does kind of sound like we were agents, huh?) Our feeling was, if she had a pulse, and, trust me, that was important to most of us, she was in jeopardy! Keep in mind, that was long before AIDS or some of the other worries of the current age had entered into the discussion and become a deterrent to such promiscuity. In reality, though, it actually hasn't changed anything, amazingly. I guess it should be remembered, there are those who enjoy playing "Russian Roulette", too. But when I was starting out, it was the late 1960's, and the summer of love had just passed, and so we were just sharing our love! We were flower children and I, personally, didn't want to miss any of the blooms that were available to me. Yes, I was abominable to say the very least. However, everything we did was consensual, so please, don't get the idea we got women drunk and methodically defiled them. It was nothing like that at all. We didn't need to get them drunk. We simply paid for enough drinks to take care of it.

When I disbanded RS Rindfleisch and went to Saarbrucken Music Academy, which, in truth, really cut into my sex life, I got a dose of reality. Remember, musicians at a music school are hardly a novelty, and so the girls there were not all that taken by us simply because we could rock and roll. As such, I had to learn how to date, go to etiquette school if you will, and ultimately spend all sorts of money on a girl just to get a kiss on the cheek if I was lucky! It was a lesson

I would have preferred not to have had to learn, and yet, I did learn a bit about how to actually court a young lady. I learned not every woman was "another piece of meat".

I decided my sex life needed some help, so I left school, moved to England to resume playing music again rather than continuing to learn about it and began trolling the fertile British soil, "planting my seeds" in as many places as I could in the United Kingdom. I did my share of "gardening", though hardly as much as the infamous Dr. Cecil B. Jacobson (The doctor in the U.S. who substituted his own sperm for that of his clients/patients at his Virginia fertility clinic in the mid-1980's.), or even, it appears, Arnold Schwarzenegger.

You know, there is something I am curious about with regard to that latter situation out in California. It is all over the news as I write this, so I thought I would chime in. As far as I understand it, Arnold was married to American television commentator Maria Shriver until it was discovered he did a great deal of "farming" himself outside of the marriage, which, of course, led to their divorce. I agree his behavior was deplorable, and I can sight my own indiscretions as collateral examples that do give me a potent measure of ironic credibility on the subject. I am not going to attempt to justify the general behavior he demonstrated nor will I try to validate my own at any point in this book. However, here is what I find curiously interesting. I wonder what Maria's opinion is of her uncles – President John and Senators Bobby and Teddy Kennedy? Being an, ahem, journalist as she is, she must be well aware of their alleged and acknowledged exploits, and yet, I have not seen anything on the Internet or on television or in any other form of media that sights her outspoken outrage at their extra-curricular sexual dalliances. I think Arnold should simply claim that he was "carrying on" in the family tradition! Like I said, it's just something I have found interesting.

Anyway, upon my arrival in England, as I said, I dated a lot to say the least. Truthfully, it wasn't the same as the old playing days in Germany, though. The "system" was quite different, and I genuinely had to learn and adapt. The routine was to take lady to a pub for dinner, or perhaps several dinners, if I had any hope of even getting a kiss. (Please don't take this out of context. The dinners were on separate nights, not all in the same evening!) I also learned if there was tea to be had at end of the evening in her apartment, it pretty much meant I would need my toothbrush.

My first "steady" girlfriend was Sonya who I met through my friend Ray Galton. Ray was and still is a very good friend. Sonya was married to a steward with British Airways, and the separation caused by his work left her quite lonely. It was all a "gentleman" like myself could do to console her and help her through the lonely nights by enjoying the bounty that nature had bestowed upon her to share with a young, noble, "sword-bearing" knight in shining armor such as myself. (Though, in truth, I was doing all I could to tarnish my breastplate.) She was 10 years my senior but didn't look or act it. Most who knew her thought she truly was one of the most beautiful women in the entire United Kingdom. Initially, the relationship was all about sex. How could an extra-marital affair (Hers, not mine at that point...) have been about anything else? I was 24 and near my sexual peak as a male and, of course, everyone knows a woman's peak, sexually, is supposedly in her mid-30's... As such, we were a perfect "match", and I took advantage of every opportunity she gave me to "strike" that match and light her fire. (You know, maybe I was a psychic. It seems I was already preparing for my life as a Scorpion.)

Soon after meeting me, Sonya left her husband, and we eventually got an apartment in Surbiton, Surrey, on Lingfield Avenue, where we lived together from 1974 until the time I departed to go to Germany to join the Scorpions. You see, maybe I was a bit of a rogue in sleeping with another man's wife... Actually, there's no doubt that, I was. And yet, I wasn't a "love'em and leave'em" sort in the least! I honored the love I espoused to her on more than one occasion. It is said men give love to get sex, and women give sex to get love. Not sure who said it, but here it was completely wrong. Sonya taught me so much about life and love that, to this day, I still hold her in very high esteem. She was and will forever be a very special person I was blessed to have known. I will always love her dearly.

I remember the day when I came home after the audition for the Scorpions. Sonya told me she would come to West Germany if things worked out. However, quite often people say things they don't really mean figuring that they will come across as being supportive while never actually have to follow through with the offer. Given my negativity immediately following the audition, I'm sure she never expected I'd be asking her to come with me to Hannover and live in a toilet. As you may recall, I did get the job and all the included perks -like the glorious flat! (Truthfully, it probably would have had to have been much nicer to be considered a toilet!) So eventually when she joined me, and after we spent the summer sweating under the non-insulated roof, she wasn't all that anxious to find out what winter had in the offing. I sensed the relationship's days were numbered. (Not much ever got past me…)

During the first few months of production on *Taken By Force*, the flow of women began to slowly return to that which was more in line with my youthful preferences. We recorded in Cologne, and for some reason, after exerting 16 hours of energy in the studio playing drums, I still found the energy to go out to the discos and pick up a girl. Dieter had apartments for the musicians next to the studio to allow us a place to sleep. However, sleep was hardly the first order of business or what I used my bungalow for. Do you see why I developed a cocaine problem?

And then there was the first tour of Japan as already documented. The girls were following us around like we were really rock stars! They were very cordial and proper in public, and yet they were just the same as anyone when the lights were turned down. As you may recall, it was during that trip that I met the girl who was the inspiration for "Another Piece of Meat".

Of course, the best stories in Japan came as a result of our numerous visits to the various bathhouses. For anyone who has never been to one, the bath consists of not only a washing of the body in a big tub, but also a massage done by one or more Geishas, as well as other very pleasurable contacts. I went each night after our shows in Tokyo and wished I could take the houses with me on tour throughout the world thereafter. Every man should experience this once in his life. If he does, he'll understand the true pleasures of the Orient.

For those who will claim this is quite sexist, let me tell you the Japanese culture doesn't see it that way. Geishas see it as an honor and a form of art. They take pride in their work, and again, those who think negatively I'm sure have never been to such an establishment. I can tell you, if you were to ask any rock and roll star who has toured Japan, he would surely confirm that which I have written here as being 100% true. I am certain no rock star ever played Japan without having this experience as the promoter gave it to us as part of the local perks. I'm sure the offer stood for all groups and artists who passed through.

Upon the return to Germany, I had been so taken by the people and the customs, as I mentioned, I wore the kimono I had purchased in Tokyo everywhere I went, and actually, that helped me with many of the ladies in Hannover. They were all curious about the origins of the bathrobe, and why I was walking around in public with such a thing on. (They sure as hell weren't curious about my "luxury apartment".) Some thought I was a nut, while others were actually drawn to me sexually by it. It might be the same reason as to why women are attracted to gay men. However, I wasn't gay and took advantage of that very point.

Obviously, when we got the invitation to return to Japan during the *Lovedrive* tour, I didn't need to be pushed onto the airplane! I pretty much ran up the ramp and took my seat. If the pilot had asked, I would have lugged the damn plane out to the runway on my back! Upon my arrival, I made a beeline to a bathhouse. Having more time during that trip, mainly because I didn't eat any ice cream in India, I had an opportunity to explore more than just the Geishas and bathhouses. There was a great disco called "Biblos" that was the "in spot" where all the celebrities hung out. (Curiously absent from the clientele during my time there was perhaps Japan's biggest star, Godzilla! Guess he was busy destroying a city somewhere to the north.) It was a wonderful place to find beautiful women.

Having become the scourge of two continents, I was more than ready to see what American women were like, and I took little time to find out. Upon arriving in Cleveland, even prior to our first show, I broke the showbiz axiom, which is not to allow women to weaken us in the hours preceding a big event. And so in the lobby of the hotel as we were checking in, I met this beautiful redhead, who didn't leave my side or other parts of me until morning. I can and will say she showed me a few tricks I never knew before which included the most extensive oral "examination" I had ever had the pleasure to be "exposed" to. I certainly believed at that point that it would have been good enough to earn her a PhD in most academic institutions. However, as I travelled more within the country, I discovered she wasn't the only one who could "blow my mind" (Remember what they say about men and their ability to think…). As the tour progressed I quickly realized and was quite pleased to discover the tracheal aptitude throughout the United States was, at least in my opinion, without peer within the world. And so my initial impression of the U.S. was quite positive to say the least!

During the remainder of the tour on all continents, even when we were only the opening act, I still managed to have more than enough female companionship. I can truly say I did the *Lovedrive* tour, and I did more driving than I ever thought I could! If there wasn't a hotel room handy, the backseat of the tour bus sufficed.

The picture through the years never really changed no matter if I was married or single. Like I've said, I was more than a scoundrel, and in retrospect, it wasn't behavior to celebrate. Yet at the time, the guilt was not so omnipresent as it is today within my remembrances. The routine rarely had variation and the sex was not about love or commitment but mutual primal lust and carnal gratification with no strings attached! Primal lust and carnal gratification… That would have made a great title for a Scorpion album, don't you think?

Anyway, to be unbiased, as if a book like this can be, most of the women who make up what the world refers to as "groupies" are hardly virginal, and their desires are published clearly for all to read. Some, who obviously had nothing better to do, followed us from town to town during our tours. There was one in particular in the U.S., for example, I have since privately nicknamed "JFK" because it seemed everyone took a shot at her in the backseat. (Please don't start making faces. It's a funny line! You'll probably use it at the office tomorrow.) And truthfully, it is fitting. Though I can't say in all certitude, mind you, since no one really ever kept score, but if I were to venture a guess I would think it might be a safe bet to assume the Bismarck probably had fewer men go down on it.

In fairness, she wasn't really alone. No, I don't mean she brought along a friend. There were countless others in just about every country that pretty much fit the same mold. (Some who did bring along a friend...) And so, the bottom line is, at least in my estimation when it comes to groupies in general, and I am sure they haven't changed much through the years, you can think what you will about those of us who partook of such opportunities, but keep in mind, it was always a two-way street.

On the flip side, as I mentioned, I met Tamara in 1983, and we married in 1985. As you may recall, she was (And I suspect she still is...) bisexual, which meant we both appreciated women. So when I was on tour, I am quite confident I wasn't the only one enjoying female companionship. That marriage was not really about love, though. It was a traditional Las Vegas marriage as I mentioned a couple pages ago, if, in fact, any such marriage can be considered traditional. Having done cocaine all night long, we got up early in the morning and had the bright idea to get married. Love wasn't a question. We just simply got married for all the wrong reasons, though at that age, sex was about the only reason either of us needed. In the beginning we truly thought it was about love, but that changed over time to being much more sexual than loving, and we, at least, were able to recognize it. Ultimately and actually in short order, we got divorced through an annulment. She, too, realized the marriage was a fraud. To this day, because of the amicable nature of the divorce, Tamara and I are still friends. We make much better friends than we did husband and wife. I will offer to all of you who divorce to consider the concept of friendship first.

After the divorce, I moved back to West Germany full time. It was during that time that *World Wide Live* was released. However, my stay was short-lived as in September of 1985 I moved to Monte Carlo for tax reasons. It was there that I met Anne Marie, though at the time I didn't realize it, but she was going to be my second wife and the mother of my only child – our daughter Leah. We started dating early in 1986 after having met in the real estate office where she worked. She was the one who got me my first apartment in the city. Though we met almost immediately upon my arrival there, she had the good sense not to want to be associated with a perhaps less than scrupulous rock star. Her initial opinion of me was far from glorious. Can't say that I blamed her. Her main concern was whether I could pay the rather lofty rents in Monte Carlo. However, I eventually broke down her resistance, and she fell in love with my irresistible charms. (Those were her words not mine. I knew I was the same jackass I always had been.) At the end of the day, I found not only a place to live but also someone to share it with me.

In May of 1987, after a long courtship, we married in Edinburgh, Scotland because the paperwork in either West Germany or Monte Carlo would have taken forever to process. Those who have had to deal with bureaucratic formalities in one country can imagine how much fun it would have been to deal with the "make-work" documentation in two countries. (Paperwork seemingly designed specifically to make jobs for people…) We would have had to diplomatically tolerate and negotiate the red tape and questionable competence not once but twice! By marrying in a neutral locale, Scotland, we were able to take our vows sooner and avoid a lot of the crap.

However, sadly, (Idiotically…) I still continued my old ways while travelling on tour. I admit that I was not the most faithful husband on the planet. She deserved better but was patient and loving, and as I look back, I do appreciate her so much more today than I ever did at the time. She was, without a doubt, the best mother any child could ever have. (I was a "mother", too, but that, of course, was a little bit different.) Our daughter is proof of her maternal instincts and talents. Leah was raised with class and dignity while being taught etiquette and propriety all along the way. (Quite a contrast to her bohemian father during those years.) I hope Anne Marie will read this and understand that I have finally grown up and recognize now how much I missed by not being a better husband.

The reception we eventually had a few days after the wedding back in Monte Carlo was sort of a perk of being a rock star, since I could afford a lavish affair. As a result of my success with the Scorpions and the accompanying monetary prosperity, I was fortunate that I could afford to have the sort of dreamlike reception for our families and friends that ordinary laborers could only dream about. How many people could have Rudolf Schenker and Klaus Meine serenade them with "Still Loving You" as part of the reception? The party lasted three days with friends, relatives and celebrities from all over the world. For example, my friend, the late Robert Palmer, was there.

I met Robert at Dieter's studio during production of *Savage Amusement*. I know I haven't gotten there in my story about the band yet. But I will. Anyway, he was interested in seeing Dieter's place. We were recording the song "Rhythm of Love", and for some unexplainable reason we hit it off. I don't know if the Scorpions had an influence on him, but his first music video, the quite famous "Addicted to Love" video, does suspiciously reek of something we would have produced!

As I said, marriage didn't slow me down on the road. However, thanks to Anne Marie, the marriage did last many years, through 1998. She was somehow able to turn a blind eye to my many indiscretions, at least for a period of time, though she never should have had to. She will be sainted for this in the next life I am sure.

Paternally, I admit there is very little for me to talk about. I was "too busy" with being Herman Ze German to spend a lot of time at home. I love Leah and I will tell you she has grown up to be a wonderful young lady. I remorsefully regret not being home and sharing her life more. Not a day passes that I don't look back in anger at myself. I cannot change it and such memories now are only distant. I wish I could do it all again. I know I would make better choices though, in truth, given the demands of my occupation through many of those years, I don't know that I could have been home any more than I was.

The remainder of the tours and women pretty much followed the same systemic pattern. Most of the women you meet on the road don't care if a man is married or not. They just seem to want the ability to brag that they've slept with this or that rock star. (I sometimes felt like I was just another piece of meat to some of them.) I don't understand why that was important. But I wasn't going to argue with the concept regardless of what my conscience would have preferred. As I've said, sex is in its own way a quite alluring and addictive drug. This isn't an attempt to justify my behavior. It is simply an admission of guilt and understanding. I was never right. I only write about it here because it was a part of my life. It is offered only as an admission of guilt – an open admission of stupidity in the hopes of turning that page and never again looking back.

There is nothing specific to mention about most all of the liaisons, which is not meant to denigrate any of the beautiful ladies whose "I's" I dotted and "T's" I crossed. I loved you all, at least superficially. The mere fact that I don't go into detail here should be testimony to the remorse and regret I now have and the associated guilt therein. It should also be a bit of a testament as to just how formulaic and matter-of-factly my life and life on the road in general became. It just never occurred to me when I was married, for example, that I needed to make an adjustment to my line of thought. It was, to me, just part of the normal routine. I mean everyday on the road was pretty much the same. Everybody was doing it. I'd play a show. Get drunk after the show. Take a woman to my room and have sex. Get up the next morning, and do it all over again.

To put this into perspective, as I mentioned previously, females in the entertainment field have "personal assistants" to help them secure male companionship, and keep those rendezvous as discrete as possible. We, as well, though not as concerned with discretion, had an individual on tour with us who sort of served in the same basic capacity. Rob Steinberg was the man we had in charge of "talent procurement". At least that is the euphemistic way to label his job. (It was probably the way he described it to his family and friends.) His main responsibility was that of securing women to party with the band after the shows. Quite often, for example, the parties began as I came off stage and would shower with one or perhaps two beauties.

As a point of interest, I think I can honestly say here that I do have favorite memories and favorite venues and cities. I mentioned that my favorite city in the world is Los Angeles. The girls in L.A. at the time were not the plastic, artificially enhanced sorts that roam those streets today. They were a bit more natural then. A bit… Not completely. However, up the highway from Los Angeles I believe are the most beautiful women in the entire world. Please, don't laugh… For me, as far as I recall, the most beautiful women I ever met and/or saw while on tour were in the city of Fresno, California. I know I've made a lot of jokes about that city throughout this book, but those were simply jokes. I'm being completely honest here. The ladies there were so natural and so very innocent in their own way that I couldn't help but have that feeling. They were the epitome of the definition "farmer's daughters".

Anyway, as I mentioned, my marriage eventually and sadly, though quite rightly, ended with Anne Marie in 1998. However, I was not quite finished with marriage. After being single again for a period of time, I fell in love again.

I received an invitation in 2002 from my former business partner, Prince Albert of Monaco (I will talk more about that association later.), to play a charity show for the benefit of the Special Olympics in Monte Carlo. Invited to that show as well was a saxophone player from Munich, Germany (As you may recall, by then the "West" had been dropped.), named Claudia Raab. Together we played with an Austrian band consisting of handicapped musicians called "The No Problem Orchestra". Well, upon staring into her big, blue eyes, we were soon making much more music offstage than on. However, I had to jump through a few hoops just to interest her in a private concerto.

We started dating, though it was a long distance relationship, my being in Monte Carlo, and her being in Munich, and went back and forth for nearly a year until March of 2003 when I finally convinced her I was the man of her dreams. If you get a chance to visit my website, you will see her as the saxophone player in my music video "Take It As It Comes". You will surely realize her dream had to have been a nightmare to actually concede to marrying a man of questionable repute past and present as part of his résumé.

For the first time in my life, however, I met someone who could really understand me from all aspect of my life because we were both musicians. Having a similar interest of that nature, especially in a field like mine, is so incredibly helpful. There is more to being a professional musician than just playing music. There are the constant ebbs and flows within a career. There are the highs and the lows and a great many points in between. Things are not always smooth sailing, and so there is often a need for support and understanding that many people outside the industry can't understand. Money isn't the cause of anguish. In fact, if you want my opinion, it is just the opposite. The angst is a result of a life in the public eye and the continual scrutiny that you are confronted with. No, it would not help anyone to understand the philandering, nor would it ever be right to even ask that of another person. But, as it should be in most lives, you get a second chance, and, hopefully, you have learned and grown from your previous mistakes to make better decisions. It is almost a certainty that temptation will time and again rear its ugly head. However, now I realize the errors in my past ways and see the truth as I should have many years ago. And so to have someone in my life today who understands my industry is something I never had before. I just never realized how important it was until we met, and now Claudia and I are inseparable colleagues not only in love but also in life.

This chapter is sub-headed Sex, Drugs and Rock and Roll, or at least a reasonable facsimile thereof. So, now come the drugs. Yes, drugs are a realistic part of music; too much so in all honesty. The promises of those synthetic highs have been the downfall of far too many talents within our world. At this point, however, I do want to make clear that I am one who doesn't understand the world's hypocrisy as it applies to "drugs". I cannot understand, for example, why it is that someone can be allowed to drink alcohol but not be allowed to smoke pot. I'm not going to waste a lot of time going through the various reports that contrast and compare marijuana and alcohol because in all honesty I'm not sure of the reliability of such information. (I suspect most of those who make up the statistics are probably stoned.)

However, my feeling about other more potent drugs is quite resolute. Hard drugs like heroine, cocaine or other "recreational" narcotics dabbled in by too many today are quite dangerous. As I've already mentioned, I can speak from experience as it applies to cocaine. It is a stupid drug that only gets you high for about thirty seconds, and then you need more. That's the problem and the cause of addiction and death.

Be that as it may, my position on drugs is really unimportant. There will be those who will use such things, and those who will abuse them. As I have mentioned, I did more than my share of cocaine. I could not even begin to tell you why I did today, but I am thankful I survived. There are many who didn't as the record clearly shows. So for that I count my blessings. I am here to write this book while many others are not.

I do have one anecdote about drugs and rock and roll that you may find amusing. We were playing a concert in Kuala Lumpur, Malaysia. As most of you know, we were well-liked in Asia. The promoter for that particular show was so very appreciative that we would come there that he wanted to make sure he showed us a good time. It was clear he had read his share of rock and roll magazine articles, and believed everything he read. As such, he gave me a bag about the size of a pillowcase filled with marijuana. He must have thought every musician was Bob Marley. The sad part of this story is, at least in a manner of speaking, we had little choice but to try and finish as much of it as we could before getting on the plane because I couldn't risk taking such things through customs and didn't want to waste any of it. (I had already seen Midnight Express… Talk about being scared straight!) And so we, the road crew and I, were chain-smoking the stuff all the way up to the security checkpoint at the airport. There was so much smoke residue on the tour bus that Klaus, Francis and Matthias, who didn't partake, got high just by inhaling. Anyone would have just walking in the door. (Except maybe Bill Clinton since, as I understand it, he wouldn't have inhaled.) I'm amazed the driver could find the airport!

Anyway, drugs are a reality in music and entertainment. I am certain they were there 100 years ago, and I am sure will be there 100 years from now. The demands of the road and performing night after night not to mention the countless idle hours each artist has during the day leads to this sort of lifestyle for better or worse. I admit, I have met some musicians who were not interested in drugs, and yet they found their own personal solace inside a bottle of whiskey. Others found their release through sex. Some, like myself, combined all three. There are, however, traditions that are eternal even in literature. There are many people who buy a book like this explicitly to read chapters about this kind of thing. But for me, this chapter is a confession of stupidity in many ways. Promiscuity, drug and alcohol abuse… These aren't things that enhance a life, nor are they anything to be proud of. They are things that ruin lives. You have your next breath. That's the only "high" you need. But not everyone sees it that way. I know that I didn't at that time. There are times you drink more on any given night than is ever consumed in the entire State of

Utah in a month. No, that's a bad example, huh? How about in the entire state of Nevada? That's probably closer to reality. The question is why? The same holds true with regard to the use of drugs. You arbitrarily use them in an effort to attain a "high" not worth having, though you don't realize that at the time, never worrying, even for a second, that perhaps the next snort or injection might be your last. This is selfishness. This is true gluttony and greed.

And then there is the drug of sex...You have a loving spouse at home, and yet you feel the need to prove your manhood, or reinforce your femininity (If you're of the female persuasion or... No, I won't go there even for the sake of a great joke.). Why? I suspect a lot of the indiscriminate sex is related not only to addictive obsession but also to insecurity and vanity, though no one would ever dare say such a thing. I am not a psychologist, thank God, and only have personal experience to draw upon. So I can only tell you the conclusions I've been able to formulate based solely on my own life. Human nature, it seems, is to assess your place in life, and take advantage of that which is available to you regardless of what is right. As my friend Michael, my co-writer on this book, so often says, "There is that which is your right, and there is that which is right. Learning to see the difference is what leads to happiness." I think the profundity within his thought speaks volumes about his character. The point is, obviously, even though it may all be fun in the moment, it is not something you should or will be proud of in the future, as I have already mentioned. Happiness is not that which you do for yourself but ultimately what you do for others. Drugs are only for the self as is alcohol and philandering. None of it will last and yet it will forever remain. What damage you do to your body, your mind or your life in general can never be fully repaired. In the end, you have nothing and have given even less to others.

For me at least, when I learned about putting others before myself, that is what changed my entire life. Understanding that a look back from the future will guide you in the present can allow you the perspective you need to make the right choices If tomorrow you will say to yourself you didn't really need it, then you don't really need to do it. Perhaps if those who have gone on to the next life prematurely as a result of such abuses had thought it through, the choices they made along the way would have been different. I was quite close to joining that group, so I do know what I'm saying. I survived the ignorance of my own youth, and that isn't something everyone can say.

16
YOU PLAY 18 MONTHS AND WHAT'D'YA GET?

And now, back to our story...

As we returned from... Actually, I don't know if "returned" is the proper word since, much like the *Blackout* tour, we spent the last six months not really touring so much as parachuting in for our shows. But after roughly 18 months on the road, testing our fitness along the way, and, in some ways, feeling like we were giving Darwin's Theory a run for its money, we were finally "home". However, the prefacing retrospective commentary aside, it was far from a negative experience. How can it be bad to spend so much time in the companionship of some of your closest friends? No, I'm not talking about the others in the band or even the perpetually horny members of our road crew who seemed to walk around in a constant state of arousal...

Seriously, well at least sort of seriously, if I might digress a bit, road guys, at least those we found to work for us, tend to be some of the greatest conversationalists the world has ever known if you favor an unrelenting slew of "colorful" verbiage as part of your preferred discourse! Hard as it may be to imagine, or perhaps not so difficult to imagine but for reasons I have still yet to completely understand, they all seem to share an unrivaled love of profanity. Every other word spouted in the course of an "intellectual" verbal exchange invariably seems to start and end with an "F" word – and I don't mean fish, fireplace, fanatic or even Freud. I am talking about the good old "F bomb". At times, which would be just about anytime they are awake, I am sure they could make a sailor on shore leave or even Madonna blush. They have a knack for creating entire sentences using various derivatives of the word as if they can't formulate enough multi-syllabic expressions to add a little variety to their choice of syntax. They can and will use the word as a noun, adjective, verb and adverb all in the same sentence! It's not entirely out of the question to hear a scholarly dialogue between two of them that sounds something like this…

"F… That's f'ing f'd…"

"F, yeah! F'ing f'er, f'ing f'd the f'ing f'er…"

"F'ing really?"

"F'ing right as I'm f'ing here now!"

"F!!!"

Quite the cerebral stimulator, don't you think? Verging on the best of Steinbeck to be sure! I'll bet you still think I'm joking? I'm not. I am, actually, for perhaps the first time in this entire book, dead serious. But if you think that's funny, I've always thought it would be really quite humorous to replace the "F" word, for purposes of endorsing the hallowed halls of academia, with the much more clinical and sterile word "intercourse" since that is the literal definition. Would make for some very entertaining sentences, don't you think?

Anyway, getting back to what I so rudely got away from, the close friends I was talking about were and are, of course, the fans. I don't know how many times a fan told me I was his closest friend and then proceeded to buy me a plethora of drinks (Some even with fruit and paper umbrellas!) in an effort to prove it beyond the shadow of a doubt. I'm not complaining, at least about the drinks, though for someone who was struggling with alcohol abuse, regardless of whether or not I thought I had a problem at that point, it probably wasn't the prudent choice on my part. A cup of tea and the related temperance would have been a much more responsible option, although that would have severely tarnished the image of a Scorpion I suspect. I mean, imagine you finally meet Superman only to discover he's irregular. And in truth, by that time we were headliners, so alcohol wasn't as necessary or needed in helping us with our selection of an evening's "companion" as it had been a few years earlier. I realize such gestures were always done with the utmost sincerity (The buying of drinks, not the indiscriminate sex with groupies, though I always sincerely proclaimed my love to each...), but at times, the zealous nature of adornment by those who only know you from afar can become a bit difficult to deal with. They will have an illusion of you based on what they think they know about you from some questionable sources. In all honesty, such reputations are quite difficult, impossible, really, to live up to. I was never rude or negative toward any of them, mind you, or at least I never tried to be like many others who are notoriously aloof. I always maintained the proper perspective, and realized they (the fans) were the ones responsible for making me who I was in the first place. However, there were those select moments I'd rather forget when someone just wasn't able to comprehend that I was a person like him or her and enjoyed my privacy on occasion.

The positive result of the tour (As if the abundance of alcohol and the indiscriminate sex with countless beautiful women wasn't enough. At that point, both were more important than the money, though money and women went together as I already documented regarding my tenure with the now famous Mastermen.) was, of course, an album that, to date, at least the date of its release, was, in essence, our "greatest hits" album, *World Wide Live*.

Recording a live album is quite different from working in the studio as I'm sure you can figure out. Even a complete moron could, I think, figure this out. (I figured it out about six months into the tour. Like I said, I'm not the quickest draw in the west.) To facilitate the recording, we hired mobile studios in some of the cities within which we played (It would have been pretty stupid to hire mobile studios in cities we didn't play in... Talk about moronic...) in an effort to collect and capture not only the sound and songs, but also the feel and spirit of the tour. However, this can often be quite a task since we weren't "locals" in too many places. Like in California, for example, where Dieter hired a local outfit with a mobile unit to record whatever we did on stage in both Los Angeles and San Diego to insure we had a lot to choose from when we got back to the studio. We were always a bit leery and suspicious of any company we hired no matter how great a reputation they may have had, or whose recommendation or reference they might wave in front of us because, in all honesty, there are a lot of so-called "recording companies" that have absolutely no idea what they are doing or how to do it on as large a scale as we needed. I mean, just because a guy owns a Rolls Royce doesn't necessarily mean he knows how to drive. (Not to be patronizing, but for you ladies out there who may not be aware of such things, a Rolls Royce is a big car. I know this is another "male" analogy, but I'm sure you can equate this to something in your own way. I am certain most of you know the theory regarding men and the kind of car they drive...) There is also the "kickback" concept always in play, which cannot be ignored and has to be taken into consideration as part of the decision making process. A company will pay a percentage of the amount they earn to an individual, like an agent, to secure their "endorsement". As you may be starting to see, there is a lot of this sort of thing that goes on behind the scenes in many aspects of the music business that is completely unbeknownst to the artist. There is a lot of this kind of thing in all walks of life so why should entertainment be any different?

In America, obviously, we were foreigners. No, not like Lou Gramm and Mick Jones... I meant we were not Americans, and as such we had to put our faith and trust in others to help find us good people to work with. But still we were more than a little bit cynical and could only hope for the best. Needless to say, the production costs for such a recording are substantially higher than going into a private studio, such as we customarily did when recording in Dieter's, and the results were often less than were hoped for. Just ask Peter Frampton. He overdubbed (rerecorded) virtually his entire *"Comes Alive"* album in the studio. If the live recordings were worth a damn, he would just have mixed and used those. It really would have been more appropriate to title the album, *"Comes to the Studio"* but I suspect such honesty might have killed sales.

In Europe, it was certainly much easier since Dieter had his own mobile equipment. We had already used it when we recorded *Blackout* in France as you might well have already deduced. But unlike Peter Frampton, who, I think, still has the largest selling "Live" album ever released (I think number two might be *Tiny Tim Live from the Tulip Garden*), we did very little overdubbing after the fact. What you hear is pretty much what we played! Ultimately, it was the result of recordings made in Southern California and a couple of dates in France and Germany.

I know the question is bound to come up as to why we didn't just record everything in Europe since Dieter had his equipment there, and we could depend upon it. Right? That would be a logical question. However, the only answer I can give may not be quite so logical in most of your eyes. As perhaps you already know, fans are an interesting lot. First off, they love to be a part of the rock and roll world whether or not they have talent. (Come to think of it, this same concept may apply to many, ahem, "artists" I've encountered in my life. But that's beside the point.) Karaoke is a dead giveaway of this desire to be in the spotlight as are the endless, not to mention, mindless "reality" shows on television, if you ask me. How else can you explain supposedly mature adults getting up in front of a bunch of people happily butchering a Johnny Cash or Bob Dylan song by singing further off-key than the original artist? Everyone seems to want to make an ass of himself. He only needs the opportunity! (I will forever be thankful for having had my opportunity, and I took full advantage of it!)(I'm not sure I phrased that quite right. Oh well...) Anyway, playing off the known fact that the latest estimates at that time were that more than 23 million people claimed to have been at Woodstock, many of whom were not even old enough to have been born in 1969 but claimed they would have been there had they been born, and since the largest music market was the United States, we wanted to record there to insure that the buyers could brag to their friends that they were in the audience when we did it.

Secondly, our shows in the U.S. were often a stark contrast to those in other countries because, for one thing, we would obviously speak English and interact much more with the audience than we would in other countries. It added a different feel and dynamic to those shows. However, most importantly along that same line was perhaps the fact that we would always adjust our sets according to the audience. I know some of you may not realize this, but there were songs in each country, and even each area in each country, that were more popular there than in other places. Remember, in Japan, they loved our *Taken By Force* album as well as much of what came before I entered the band that most of the remaining balance of the world had ignored. As such, we would amend our set list there to accommodate the anticipated desires of the audience. It is all a part of being in the business, and again, the good bands, the ones that endure, pay attention to such detail to insure they give the people what they want and expect. Remember, they are paying money to see you. Though you may ostensibly be on tour to promote a new album, you have a responsibility to them, and that can and should never be ignored or taken lightly. So if you load up your set with songs from the new album in an effort to boost sales, you will often alienate fans who will be upset that you didn't play one of their all-time favorites. At any rate, our goal with the recording was to capture our whole world tour, not just a few select, convenient dates in and around our homeland. That is why the album was titled *World Wide Live* not *Just Live in Germany and France*.

What also has to be considered is the fact that we really didn't know which cuts we would ultimately use until we got back to the studio. We also weren't even sure which songs would be a part of the album as we were recording and playing. To be truthful, some of the nights I thought we sounded best were hardly the best for various reasons when we heard the playback. Drugs and alcohol can alter and impair your perspective considerably.

I will take a moment here to re-emphasize what I was exposed to early on in my music education, which is the importance of "meter" in playing drums. A consciousness in meter, an internal, mental metronome, or as I like to think, a "metronomical" train of thought, is the most vital tool a drummer can bring to a band. I admit I don't know if "metronomical" is an actual word, but it does say what I want to say. I did seem to have, or perhaps I developed an innate "click track" in my head just as any professional percussionist should. Note that I said should. I have seen and heard many pathetic excuses for drummers on stage. The sense of rhythm and meter is what separates greatness from mediocrity and a professional from an amateur. I'm not trying to brag here. It's just a fact of life. No band can play consistently without a solid backbone setting an appropriate and steady tempo. A guitar player's riffs are often more recognizable to listeners and concertgoers, but they are over and forgotten in seconds, and the majority of a live audience doesn't even know if he's played them right or wrong. But a drummer's impetus is constant and runs throughout the duration of a song. Remember, the drummer is responsible for the speed at which a song is played. If he rushes, the band sounds like they need to go to the bathroom. They will speed through a set seemingly in hopes of finishing before one of them has an accident on stage. Granted, some of us, those who are now in our "golden years" with prostates to match, may have some difficulties in that area. However, we are all still professionals and must fend off the discomfort for the sake of our art. Okay, so that is one reason the "drum solo" became a staple in many bands' set. It wasn't really meant as a showcase for the drummer so much as a break for the other members of the band to take care of that need, should it arise, during a 90 minute or longer set. Most, at least when we were younger, preferred to use the time for something they deemed as much more important like taking another shot of booze, smoking a joint or perhaps a quick rendezvous with a female (or male depending upon the artist) fan backstage. However, that changes with age.

You know I have to relate something here. Please forgive me for straying again, but a thought just came to me, which means it probably would have been clear to most others several pages ago. Anyway, as perhaps you already figured out, I'm no longer considered a young musician. I'm not saying this is a bad thing, or that I'm Methuselah. I already lived those years, and I like to think I learned from the experience to be even better as a musician and, of course, in many other ways as well. The thing I wanted to touch on here is the way my conversations with friends have changed through the years. When we were young, we would talk about how much we drank the previous night or the drugs we used or the girls we had had sex with or other silly, frivolous things like that. By contrast, today when I meet with friends, we seem invariably to go into detailed discussions about trips to the doctor, the function, or actually, the malfunction of various organs within our body, or the state of our sciatic nerve… Unless, of course, I'm talking to Pete Way.

Anyway, getting back to the original point, meter is vital for any drummer. As a player on stage in front of thousands of people, I will testify that it's difficult to reel in the emotions and control your adrenaline, and so many percussion players find themselves taking a five minute song and making it about three and a half. Of course, drugs can help curb these tendencies when used appropriately and wisely, though as I think about it now, there is little I feel that would constitute appropriate "wisdom" with regards to drug use. However, many drummers do depend on such artificial aids to keep their emotions under control. And yet, in numerous cases, drugs also give the illusion to many that they are actually playing better when in reality they are out of their freaking minds!

Dieter was very responsible for my development in this area – the goddamn prick! (Said with only the highest regard and reverence.) No, not in the development of my drug use… I meant in the area of learning how to control myself behind my kit and keep good time. Let's not forget, this is quite different from "having a good time"! Studio work is rarely fun. It's exactly that – work! He harped on me constantly to "stay with the click" emphasizing and reemphasizing the invaluable necessity in the recording process. Though I knew he was right, he demanded I play perfectly on each track in the studio, which, since I was only human, was quite difficult and stressful. One mistake and I had to start all over from the top. It was like having a wife bitching at you non-stop for several hours a day. (Not mine, of course. Just a generic wife...) What an intercoursing pain in the ass he was! But the results do show in the recordings. Some producers lack that same zeal when it comes to meter preferring a more "natural" feel for the music verging on a "live" sound. They will not stress precision so much as they do feel. Which is better? I think it depends completely on the artist. Some artists could never be the same if their songs were built on such rigid lines. Others, like the Scorpions, benefitted from the stability in meter. It gave our songs the proper feel for what we were trying to create.

Personally, I do think live albums serve a great purpose as if there needed to be one beyond that of giving the fans what they want. Promotion for the band and the reusing of the same material to enhance the group's revenue intake are also quite important. (I will talk about a different, blatantly self-serving derivative of this same concept in a little bit. Stay tuned.) A live album allows a band an oft-needed respite from writing as well, which can just as often produce even better material than they had for previous albums. It is difficult to write music continuously while you're on the road, as I have said time and again. The songs begin to take on the feel and monotony of the road, not that of a band that takes time working out songs in rehearsal spaces and studios for months and years prior to recording. Lyrically, as well, the songs become quite redundant. They tend to be about the same subjects since your schedule includes very limited variation on a daily basis. Most can't escape that reality long enough to refocus properly for the creative writing of words. (Perhaps that is another reason some turn to drugs.) It's like a virgin writing a love song compared to someone who's been around. A virgin will always have the idyllic sense of love, and it will shine through in everything he or she creates. By contrast, his or her worldlier counterpart has perhaps had some of the luster tainted from having had their share of difficult or even painful relationships. You can't recapture what you have lost. And so that which you see on the road becomes your life, your world, and it is about the only thing you can think about. Love is as synthetic and artificial, not to mention as fleeting, as the next town and the next groupie. As I said about the song "Arizona", it was written about a woman I "loved". However, I never saw her again, so I doubt it was love. It was only a lustful remembrance for a man on the road.

With regard to the music, rehearsal of new songs on the road is often piecemeal at best. You rehearse during your sound checks, or try to work out new pieces as best you can in hotel rooms, bars or on buses. (Note I said work out new pieces not work over or on new pieces… I don't want anyone to get the wrong idea. There are a lot of people who will try to misconstrue everything I write for purposes of erotic titillation.) It's hardly a conducive environment for the creation of greatness, even though we had produced some incredible music through the years in just that manner. But at that point, we were all looking forward to the time away from the limelight to get some things straightened out personally as well as professionally.

As for being on the road, it can and did take a toll on our personal lives, as well you might imagine, not only at home but within the band, too. No matter how close you may be, how much of a bond you may form, you will still begin to get on each other's nerves after endless time together. Like a woman in a constant state of PMS, the slightest things will piss you off! 18-months non-stop on the road can have that sort of effect. How could it have anything but? Okay so not exactly like a woman since none of us ever complained about cramps or someone having left the "seat" up. I have mentioned the latter a few times within this book, but, honestly, I really don't understand why the latter is such an issue with women. I mean, why is it that we have to put the seat down, but they don't have to think of us and raise it when they are finished? True equality, as women claim they want, would be to provide such courtesies equally. Anyway, the bottom line here is that we were anxious, to say the least, and happy to spend time at home while Dieter mixed our tour recordings and got them ready for release in 1985.

In the meantime, we did, indeed, begin work on our next studio album, *Savage Amusement*. Among other things, it features my favorite Scorpions song, "Passion Rules the Game". Why is it my favorite? Well, aside from the fact that I wrote it together with Klaus who wrote the lyrics, frankly, it's just a very good song in my opinion. Does there need to be any further reason or explanation?

I will say that we did take a little longer than the traditional year in between the live album and ...*Amusement*. However, it wasn't the fault of "fast" Herman on drums since I only took about three weeks in the studio to finish my parts. You see, it may well have been the availability of time, the same availability that we longed for, that led to our complacent and at times, I suspect, overly obsessive behavior. And so after completing my work, I had no choice but to bide my time and patiently wait for the others to take care of business. I honestly have no idea why it took them so long, so I should not be speaking out of turn. You will have to read their books to find out. Of course, I'm sure they'll find a way to blame me since I'm blaming them! That would only be fair. Truthfully, I don't know that it matters, really. History is hardly something one should lose sleep over or try to tamper with. You can't change the past, so what good does it do to rehash the errors or mistakes from yesterday? Though at the time it seemed like a long time, today I really couldn't care less.

I will say that when we initially played the new songs for Dieter, he was less than enthusiastic. That's putting it mildly. A prison inmate on death row is more excited about seeing a New York steak dinner being carted down the hall in his direction. He basically thought the songs were self-indulgent, decadent horse manure (Edited for family reading...I know, why start now, right?). Those were some of the nicer things he said. He then told us to go home and write some that were actually worthy of recording. I guess he figured with the time we had to write, as I mentioned before, we should have come up with a goldmine of classics! In a way, it may have been a lot like the conversation producer Paul Rothchild allegedly had with the legendary Southern California band the Doors when he reportedly referred to the material they had composed for what would eventually become the *LA Woman* album as, "cocktail jazz". The Doors proceeded with the recording without Rothchild utilizing studio engineer Bruce Botnick's experience and knowledge to help them self-produce the album, and in my opinion, they produced a true classic.

However, today as I think back about the situation as it applied to us, the material itself may actually have played a role in the elongation of the recording process. If a producer isn't too happy with the music, he will toy and tinker with it, at times even rework it over and over to get it to a point where he can feel comfortable with what he has created. Remember, his name goes on the product, and so he takes a lot of responsibility on himself for that which is released for public dissemination. (To this day I can tell you, Dieter still hates the album.)

I was amused to read Wikipedia's account of the *Savage Amusement* album as those who post the information there decided that opinion mattered more than strictly adhering to the guideline of providing unbiased, encyclopedic information. A lot like the so-called media today. Anyway, the controlling powers at that entity decided that the album didn't follow the traditional Scorpions style of rock, and that we changed direction as we produced the album. Though to some it may be certainly subject to debate (Which I will do in the next few paragraphs for sake of argument.), having been there, I can tell you it's a bunch of unmitigated malarkey. To me, it's Scorpion rock and roll – pure and simple.

All right, in an effort to be fair to those who wrote their asinine thoughts from an obviously uninformed, uneducated background and perspective, and wanting to give them the benefit of any doubt I can since I am not one who enjoys confrontational deliberation, I'll play the devils advocate. Any change in sound, if in fact there was one (The jury is still out in my mind. Okay so there are those who will say my mind is out as well. That's beside the point and not subject to debate here.), probably had a lot to do with changes in our world. I'm not admitting anything was consciously done here. Only stating that there was potentially an environment for change, given everything that was going on around us in the real world of music. But I don't think it had a lot to do with having too much time to write. However, again, having time to do something can lead to distractions that we may not even realize are there. Maybe we all, unconsciously, listened to the radio or spent too much time watching MTV and were adversely influenced by some of the crap we were exposed to. (If it smells, it sells... Never was this truer, it seems, than during the 1980's.) This rarely happened while on the road. When you're on the road, you go to bed at dawn, get up in the middle of the afternoon and head out for a sound check in some non-descript city after maybe taking time to grab a bite to eat.

Allow me to clarify something here. People often say that musicians stay skinny because of the drugs they take like cocaine. Let me tell you, in the 1980's most of us stayed skinny for one very good reason. No one wanted to see a fat guy in spandex. The thought isn't a pretty picture. So that was motivation enough to try and keep fit. But seriously, drugs have little or nothing to do with staying thin, in my opinion. It's more a matter of just not having time for big meals. Sure the promoters of concerts will have things backstage for us. But honestly, when it comes down to a choice between eating dinner or eating... Well, let me put it another way that's a bit more delicate. When it comes to a choice between eating dinner or having great sex, (Or for that matter any sex at all regardless of the quality.) when you're young, it's a no brainer. Even not so great sex takes a priority when you're young. (See?) I think that's the reason older musicians start to put on weight. Their interest in sex wanes over the years, while their interest in food increases! Just a thought, mind you...

Anyway, getting back to what I was saying about time, when you're on the road there's no time to watch television or listen to the radio. Most of your offstage time is spent resting and recuperating from the sex, booze and drugs. So having time at home might have been a negative since it did cut into most of our sex lives, and that may have adversely altered our point of view. (I am, of course, only joking. You know the one thing I know to be completely true is the fact that when you love someone, you will never talk about, or for that matter, lie about, the sex you have together. Such chivalrous propriety is the most telling sign of true love.) We had too much time to listen to what was "popular". It is possible, and I'm only saying possible here, mind you, perhaps it did sublimely influence some of us. Maybe that was what Dieter was trying to indelicately infer. (He was about as subtle as a politician expecting a bribe.) Educated perspectives from the outside do give a person a better understanding of the moment. But to us, we only saw the moment. We only saw ourselves being badgered by a producer about our labor of love!

Okay, so let's assume there was change in our sound for the sake of argument here, and to move on with the story. I mean, honestly, in what field of endeavor can you ever continue to do the same thing over and over in exactly the same way without any evolution whatsoever? Yes, I know, shoveling manure (I'm once again trying to use the most delicate of terms, but I will assume you know what I mean.) in a barn pretty much stays the same. But tell me, how many people are going to attend a shoveling? Two, maybe three, tops… "Gee Martha, what d'ya say we go out to the race track tomorrow morning and watch the groom clean the stalls?" It is, most certainly, almost impossible not to be affected by changes in technology and changes within the world. (Even then, I think improvements or at least changes in the general design and overall handling of a shovel might lead to better performance in the stables.) It would be like trying to record an old-fashioned analog tape album today when there is so much available technology with computers and digital recording that does, admittedly, change the feel of music, but still allows artists a great deal more freedom during production. I'm not saying this is better. It is just easier, and it would be foolish to go back to the days of prehistoric recording.

Along this line as well, another thing that has to be considered is the fact that there was four years between *Love at First Sting* and *Savage Amusement*. During that time, our only release was the live album. Music itself had gone through a huge series of quite significant changes during that period. In 1984, when we recorded ...*Sting*, new wave bands and a great many "one-hit wonders" like Katrina and the Waves, Ah Ha and Flock of Seagulls, as well as many "electronic" wizards sporting their limited wears, were all the rage and dominated the popular rock world during the middle parts of the decade. The list is really rather endless just as it is forgettable in many ways. Well, by 1988, they were virtually all gone but had left their mark. Also gone were the myriad of "hair bands" and "glam rockers". New wave had, unconsciously, slipped into the early stages of rap while rock had splintered a bit with a part of the genre embracing computers and keyboards as was most apparent with artists like Peter Gabriel and Steve Winwood as well as some previously hard-rockers like RUSH, while their antithesis went out of their way to openly express their disdain for that sort of music by going "grunge" with young bands like Guns and Roses, Metallica and Nirvana leading the way. We were no longer young guys. We were part of the "old guard" – one of only a handful of acts that had actually spanned the gap from disco to digital, spandex to blue jeans, LPs to CD... We really seemed to have no home. And so we were faced with the dilemma of trying to find our place and stay somewhat current in an effort to continue an expansion of our fan base as well as remaining true to ourselves in order to avoid alienation of our long time followers. It was a delicate balancing act, but if you look at the bands that sustain over a long period of time, the old school bands that stay true to themselves while keeping up with the trends appropriately are the only ones who have endured the many incarnations calling itself rock and roll. We felt we were doing this. We felt we were taking steps forward in our evolution as a band.

We never set out to try and record a progressive rock song or album, which is a ridiculous term if you ask me. What is progressive rock? I know people will say it's this or that but to me, rock and roll is just rock and roll. I know that's a line from an AC/DC song, but in truth, it's one of the greatest statements in rock history! (As you may have noticed, AC/DC always seemed to come up with a great way to express a cliché about music in their songs.) Rock and roll really is just rock and roll. When you think about it, what is different today from what Chuck Berry or Elvis did almost 60 years ago? The music is still based in blues. All that has changed is the technology. If you want to know what I think progressive rock is, I think it is everything that is a part of the rock music genre because it's all progressed from the origins in a logical, evolutionary spiral.

What I do today in my solo career is simply write rock and roll music. I don't think about the instrumentation or the way I'll play this or that song when I write it. Most songwriters write songs, not arrangements. A group does that. An artist will do that when it comes time to record, though often it is the input of the producer that decides the arrangement. But the writer writes rock and roll and then allows the players to interpret it their own way. That is what separates it from other forms of music. Most other music is well scripted with each member of the orchestra or band playing what they read on a chart or copy of sheet music. They don't play with feel but more with their eyes. They play what is put in front of them with very little emotion or expression.

Rock and roll is not like that at all. It is much more interpretive. I will tell you honestly, I could take just about any song from any era or genre and make it a rock and roll song. All it would take is simply an adjustment in instrumentation, tempo and overall feel. Why is it, do you think, that the same song can be released by several artists, sometimes simultaneously, and only one version becomes popular? There is an endless list of songs like this, especially in "pop" music. For example, in the early 1970's a British band called Hot Chocolate that had a string of hits in the U.S., wrote, recorded and released a song by the title of "Brother Louie" in 1973. Though it had some success locally in the U.K., it did little to nothing on the American charts. Several months later, a group from New York called Stories covered the song, and it shot up to #1. It's all a matter of interpretation. And so if our sound changed, getting back to the initial point of all this rhetoric, it was perhaps nothing more than Dieter's interpretation of our work and his efforts to keep us current, or, perhaps, our own mutual desire to stay current. There was never a conscious effort on our part to do something different.

The album itself, as I already mentioned, featured my favorite song "Passion Rules the Game". But that song wasn't the one that pushed us to the #5 spot on the Billboard charts, or took the album to platinum by June of 1988. It was much more than that. It was, in part, due to the touring. The more you are out there, the more you're going to become a name brand rather than just another rock and roll band from Germany. We built quite a following around the world, and that is what opened the door to our trip to the Soviet Union in the spring of '88.

The song, "Rhythm of Love" was the single that raced up the charts, and it was, in my opinion, nothing different than we had done on any of our prior albums. It was a straightforward hard rock song about sex. What could be more Scorpion-like? And so with that song leading the way, the album did very well around the world, and was a fitting studio follow up for …*Sting and World Wide Live*.

Over the years there have been many who have been curious about the huge drum sound we produced for the song "Rhythm of Love". Well, unlike many breasts in California, it was completely natural. In Dieter's studio, there is a large room with a ceiling five to six meters high. For you Americans, who have yet to learn the metric system that would be about 15-20 feet high. In other words, it is like a giant ballroom! Natural, ambient reverb is always the best as I said earlier with regard to our reasons for recording at the French chateau. And so I basically was playing in a theater that was empty! It lent itself perfectly to the sound we wanted to create! Or actually, Dieter wanted to create, but I, too, was very happy with the result.

As I think back about the album, going back to the previously rehashed menagerie regarding our alleged changes in our sound, I will admit that the song "Media Overkill" did utilize some new effects, and the guitar tones throughout the album were altered and changed to what may seem to be a bit more of an electronically developed, digital sound than the traditional sound Rudolf and Matthias had used on prior albums. But again, these are technicalities, and some of it had to do with our just growing and experimenting with some of the new stuff that was out there. It also may have had something to do with, I'm sure, Dieter's efforts to help keep our crap from stinking up the place!

Though "Passion..." is my favorite Scorpions song, I had a couple other contributions lyrically on this album with "Don't Stop at the Top" and "Love on the Run". Ultimately, regardless of what any critic or anyone else has to say, the album sold more than 1 million units worldwide within a few months of release. I think that is what matters. The fans liked what we did, and it was reflected in their purchases.

And then just as quickly as we were finished with production on the album, we were once again off and on the road! This time we were headed to some truly foreign territory, breaking through the shroud of steel to the east, and, in the words of Mr. Gorbachev, forever tainting the Soviet landscape. Russia was on the tour docket, and we were quite anxious to see what was behind that Iron Curtain.

17
PASSION RULES THE ROAD

If I had to be completely honest, and I have tried to be throughout this book, by that time the touring had become not only mandatory, but also a bit laborious, and, in some ways, monotonous. Being a married man, the lifestyle wasn't the best. It was difficult to pick up and start out on the road one more time. Yes, it's true, we were scheduled to make our first appearances in Russia, excuse me, the "Union of Soviet Socialist Republics" as they were technically designated at that time, but still the lure of the road wasn't as attractive as it was to me 10 years earlier when it was all new and novel.

As I already mentioned, living out of a suitcase can take its toll not only on non-permanent press clothing but also on even the best marriages. Very few endure because of the seductive lifestyle physically as well as mentally. You become so engrossed with travel and touring and being a "star" that you often overlook the most important things. We opened with 10 days of shows in Leningrad, though we were scheduled originally to do five in both Leningrad and Moscow. But as already noted, if you can remember back to Chapter 1, the latter five were changed and gave us a taste of what a dictatorship was all about. Then again, most of us already knew it very well since we were married, and in my case my wife, Anne Marie, was with me on that particular jaunt as well. But that's beside the point.

Here, I have to say, it was Rudolf who came up with the bright idea for us to go to Russia in the first place. The fees we were going to be paid there, however, hardly covered our expenses since we wanted to present to this new and ever-expanding market the full Scorpions stage experience. So we had to invest our own money into our first visit thinking all the while that it would be returned via exposure and the related sales after we were through. However, I was shocked to discover how large the "pirate" music industry was in Russia. I don't mean people were singing, "Yo ho ho and a bottle or rum!" I mean music sold on the black-market. The revelation of the existence of such a huge, unlicensed music sales market in the Soviet Union meant we weren't going to reap any tangible benefits from the shows since virtually no one there paid the customary and required fees. So the whole trip to Russia, our entertaining of our fans as well as our aiding in the downfall of communism, was worthless! Useless! Idiotic! What the hell was Rudolf thinking? He was simply doing the right thing for our fans, and I cannot agree more completely with the thought and gesture.

I do remember that "Still Loving You" was on the Soviet charts, whatever that meant, before our first trip, and was still on them when we got there! What was funny was watching the Russian kids singing along with our songs in English since we knew, more than likely, they didn't know what the words actually meant. But I think I already told that story, didn't I?

To continue the review (There will be a test on this book at the end…), remember we ended up playing all the dates in Leningrad because of the fact it was near the May 1 celebrations in Russia, and the government didn't think it was a good idea for us to be around the capital city. Don't forget, Russia was still communistic, and the government was everywhere. (Hell, I couldn't go to the "can" without feeling like someone was watching me. I hope I put on a good show for them!) Why they didn't think about that before making the bookings is beyond me. But I guess no one really thought about dates, or perhaps they just figured that it wasn't going to be a very big deal. Or maybe it was meant to be, at least in the minds of some more progressive members of the politburo, a wonderful gift to the people for the Labor Day celebration. I wonder if those members wound up wandering aimlessly in Eastern Siberia soon after?

After spending a few days at home following the Russian "fiasco", we were off again to another communist country, the United States. (I know I'll get letters after that line... It was meant as a joke. However, I do have many American friends who actually feel that way. They tell me they are afraid to express an honest opinion about anything that matters because of the way some will try to use it against them.) Initially, we played as part of the "Monsters of Rock" tour. I admit, looking back at pictures from that time, we were sort of scary with all that spandex and huge hair... But I still don't think we were monsters by any stretch of even the most vivid Stephen King-ish imagination. To be honest, in my opinion, there were a lot of guys out on the road who looked a lot worse than we did. For example, I don't wish to be rude, but hell, at that point in time, Keith Richards of the Rolling Stones looked like he was six months past an autopsy and had somehow manage to wander out of the morgue! Anyway, other "monsters" with us on the tour were Kingdom Come, Dokken featuring our old friend Don Dokken, and Metallica; all three at that time were really pretty much unknown entities. Headlining, rightly, was the Sammy Hagar era Van Halen. Van Halen wanted us on the bill because they knew we would attract even more people to the shows as a result of our popularity within the states. (I will say, if things were reversed and we were playing in Europe, our roles would also have been reversed.) For the majority of the next two months, June and July, we played with this line-up and finally at the end of July, started our own tour with Kingdom Come tagging along. All in all we crisscrossed the country playing not only stadiums like Candlestick Park in San Francisco with the Monsters but also "smaller" venues like the 16,000 seat Cow Palace (By that time we were so popular in California that the demand brought us back for an "encore" in San Francisco.), and the similarly sized Summit in Houston among others, before heading back across the Atlantic and home to Germany to start the European wing of our tour in December. Why someone thought it was better to play in Europe in the freezing months of winter rather than allowing us to enjoy the sunshine in the "sun belt" within the United States is way beyond me. I mean, does it make sense to route us through Phoenix, Arizona, El Paso, Texas and Las Vegas, Nevada in August when it's six thousand degrees and Scandinavia (Oslo, Norway, Stockholm, Sweden, Copenhagen, Denmark and Helsinki, Finland) in January when there is sixteen centimeters (About six inches for those of you in the U.S.) of snow? I know, sixteen centimeters of snow doesn't sound so bad. But I'm not talking about outside. Outside there was five meters of snow. I meant in my room! It was so damned cold I couldn't even see my own breath because it had the good sense to stay inside! It seems like we were always playing in Europe in the winter.

Our path, such as it was, took us through Saarbrucken of all places, which, of course, was "home", though at that point, I don't really know if I knew where home was any longer. On such dates, however, I would get all the guest passes from everyone else since I had more than 200 leec…, I mean, "friends" wanting to come to the show. It always was amazing how many friends I had the minute we were coming to town to play! Even people who hated me were all of sudden my best, long-time pals! The promoters, on the other hand, weren't too happy that I gave out so many free passes. I can understand their point because each freebie was one less ticket they might sell. (Though knowing my "friends", I have to wonder if they actually would have paid if they had to.) And yet, if you think about it, what difference did it make? If a few tickets one way or the other were going to make or break the show financially, then maybe it wasn't such a good idea to have the show. I kind of doubt they were saying in a back room someplace, "Gee, we were hoping to make a 100 bucks on this show tonight, but damn it, that Herman took that away from us by giving out all those tickets!"

We were on the road for just about an entire year for the album as we concluded near the end of March and picked up again with the shows in Moscow in August. It was tiring, but it was my life, or at least what my life had become. I thought of the old adage, "Be careful what you wish for because you just might get it." Yet, I wasn't really complaining. I was just tired. Real life was now fully at home as far as I was concerned. The attraction of the road was never less significant or more mundane, as just prior to my departure for Moscow the Lord blessed Anne Marie and myself with the birth of our daughter. This one event truly changed my life as I began to sincerely reassess my priorities, at least to a point. And so rather than wasting time buying frivolous things like kimonos, I began to spend my free time looking for toys for the new love of my life, Leah.

18
A CRAZY WORLD TO BE SURE

W e sensed as we were finishing our tour that perhaps it was time for a change. No, not just a wind of change was blowing throughout the world – a wind of change within the Scorpions, as well.

As a result of what the band perceived to be difficulties in getting the previous album recorded and completed, and perhaps, in part, Dieter's less than enthusiastic reception of our writing, before we began work on our *Crazy World* album, we decided to make a change in the production team replacing the "sixth Scorpion", Dieter Dierks. To put it as simply as possible, Dieter's contract with the band expired, and after many very animated and heated discussions, we simply were not willing to, or interested in, renewing it. Maybe that was a mistake. Maybe it wasn't. Can't really tell what might have been after the fact. I have my own opinion, of course, and I can say that it is quite contrary to that of the others in the band. But we were a team, at least I thought we were at the time, and so I went along with the others. Though Dieter had done a lot for us as a band, and we were quite grateful to say the least, at least I was, we had just reached a point where we felt we needed some fresh blood and ears to keep us moving in a good direction. Sometimes a band can stagnate, and we felt this was the case. (This was the team position, and as I said, I was a member of the "team".)

Our first choice to take the helm was Bruce Fairbairn who, you may remember if you are learned in the annals of rock and roll, produced Loverboy, Blue Öyster Cult, Bon Jovi, Poison, Aerosmith, AC/DC, Van Halen, Chicago, The Cranberries, INXS, KISS and Yes.

We, ourselves, had a brief history in the studio with Fairbairn as some of you may know. In 1989, wanting to capitalize on our successes to that point, we decided to release a greatest hits package titled *Best of Rockers and Ballads*. Though almost all of the songs were glommed from previous albums, we did record one new track, a cover of the Who's "I Can't Explain". Being very big fans of the band (Rudolf and Francis were both about 184 centimeters tall. For you American's, that's a shade over six foot. I know that's not so big, but it was the best we could do...), we all loved the song, and felt it was one we could do justice to. Personally, I had always wanted to record the song, because, as I have already documented, Keith Moon was one of my earliest influences on drums. Well, as you know, we had already given Dieter his walking papers by that time, and so Fairbairn was engaged to handle the production of the song and, of course, it was added to the compilation album. Also on that album, by the way, is the only Scorpions song not sung by Klaus. "Hey You", an early Scorpions song featuring Rudolf on vocals, was also included though it had never appeared on a previous album. (It was included as a "bonus track" on some versions of the Animal Magnetism CD a few years later.) Anyway, the single itself (I Can't Explain) had some decent sales and chart success, which, of course, kept our momentum going. It honestly seemed like we could do no wrong, which actually may have been what prompted the release of Dieter from our employ. As I have said many times, ego can destroy from within.

Anyway, upon making contact with Fairbairn as we prepared to begin production of the new album, we were a little dismayed to discover he wasn't immediately available as he was busy producing an AC/DC album (Razor's Edge). Not being the most patient guys on the planet, we decided not to wait, and turned to Keith Olsen who we all liked at least from the standpoint of his previous work with Whitesnake and Foreigner to name but a few.

The change behind the scenes is probably quite obvious to those who know our albums. Most people don't recognize changes like producers because they aren't really so focused on the liner notes or sound. Audiences tend to accept changes in behind the scenes personnel more easily than they do replacing any member of a band. Fans become attached to individual members (No pun intended... Unless, of course, you laughed. Then it is completely said with purpose.), and as such any change in the line-up can lead to not only an alteration in the sound of the band, but also to an attitude adjustment by fans. A lot does depend upon the way such things are handled. If you force someone out, there can be a backlash. But in all honesty, in all my years in music, I've yet to hear anyone say, "I'm not interested in that band anymore because they changed producers!"

The resulting album not only marked a shift back toward our original sound, but, as you know, brought forth the worldwide smash "Wind of Change". It was the first song Klaus had ever written completely by himself, and there is a little anecdote that goes with it. When he originally presented it to me, he whistled the melody. The words were not yet written. Just a melody... I told him right then and there, "This is a smash hit! Keep it just as it is." The whistling was so compelling that we decided to make it a part when we finally recorded it. After all, a whistle is a wind of sorts. I know that's a very esoteric metaphor, but we hoped our fans would understand it. Anyway, when the record label and the then president of Polygram Records, Allen Levy, got "wind" of it, metaphoric or not, he basically thought the song as we had recorded it "broke wind". He said, "What the hell is this, the Andy Griffith Show?" But we didn't care, nor did we know who the hell Andy Griffith was. (Levy actually didn't say the part about Andy Griffith. He wasn't that funny...) We liked it! That was what mattered. And I think you liked it as well since the song propelled the album and the Scorpions to even greater acceptance and recognition in markets around the world!

One thing that can't be overlooked or ignored is the fact that at that point, the basic core of the group, Klaus, Rudolf, Matthias, Francis and myself had been together through thick and thin for more than a decade. And in truth, there are positives and negatives with such longevity. One negative is that everything begins to get a little stale. As a result, we had, with this album, a collaborator on the writing side in Jim Vallance. Vallance, a Canadian music legend as some of you may know, was the writing partner of Bryan Adams for many years as well as being part of bands like Bachman-Turner-Overdrive. Bruce Fairbairn recommended him to us originally and, in fact, Klaus and I went to Vancouver and started writing with him there. He contributed to several of the songs on the album.

I liked him a lot, and I have to say he was probably the most diligent and regimented songwriter I've ever known. He would start at around 11:00 each morning and work until he took a break for teatime in the afternoon, and then work straight through until 7:00 at night. He kept this up for the entire three weeks we spent there writing songs with him. Most people who write songs can only write when an inspiration strikes them. Vallance could write anytime, anyplace and provide his own inspiration.

Crazy World is one of my favorite albums, and Keith Olsen had a lot to do with it. He did a tremendous job bringing out the best of what we had left. It was really the most fun I had ever had working in the studio, and the contrast between Olsen and Dierks was like night and day. Again, this is not meant to belittle or slight the work Dieter did with or for us, or that the album would not have been just as good had he been the man in charge of production. In truth, I don't think we could ever have reached the level of success we did if it were not for him. The lessons we learned and the techniques he taught us sort of "paper-trained" us for those who followed. The recording of

206

the album was completed in about three months, and the rigidity of structure that was so much a previous trademark of the band was replaced by feel and soul. If you listen to the album, you can't help but get caught up in the groove. In that way, it was unlike anything we had ever done, and yet, the overall sound was perfectly in line with what I knew our fans expected and wanted. That is what mattered the most.

19

THE LONG AND WINDY ROAD (YAWN...)

I cannot say in all specificity when I began to think about a future beyond the Scorpions. Traveling, touring and seeing the world as we were was, of course, an incredible gift I was given by the music gods. Yet within me, as there is I suspect with most artists in the world, there was always an itch. (Especially those who... I can't say it. But it's a funny thought. You're on your own to try and decipher my train of thought.) At that point in time, the early 1990's, I had been with the Scorpions following the same basic routine for more than 15 years. Sure there were breaks in the status quo (Another British band that never called me during my time in England...). In fact, for a man who had never spent more than 5 years doing any one thing, contemplation of the future was an inevitable reality.

However, as we toured in support of our *Crazy World* album in 1991, the only thoughts I had were those of a man who was content. That's what I kept telling myself. But the endless days that now seem to run together of life on the road have made it in some ways seem very anti-climactic, as it was hardly the way people portray it or want to believe it is. Today, as I look back at my life, I see only albums and tours, and relate the events within my own personal life to where I was and what I was working on, not the people I met or the places I visited. I know I was in Zagreb, Yugoslavia (At least it was then... I think.), during that tour, for example and can remember events not only taking place there, but also taking place in my life while I was there. But there are many other events, events outside of music, that in all candor, I couldn't tell you the exact year it happened because for me there were no months, years or days in the week. Maybe I did something during 1983? Or perhaps it was 1993? It's only those events that were tied directly to our music that I can date more specifically because there is a timeline to follow.

We toured in 1991 with an assortment of young stallions like Trixter and Winger who would both come and go while we continued atop the mount. Many groups were in support of us through the years, and most came and went with every shift of the winds of change. Artists and groups can have the door opened for them. However, it takes much more than an open door to help boost an act from being one of support to one in the lead. I have watched some outstanding musicians die a slow death not because they weren't talented, but because they had limitations in their presentation. Magnetism can't be taught. It is inherent. Certain artists clearly have it. Elvis. The Beatles. Mick Jagger. Tom Jones. Other artists earn respect through their musicianship. I don't mean this as a negative thing in the least. Some of the greatest talents in rock history fall into this category, if you ask me. Jeff Beck, Eric Clapton, Jimmy Paige and Robin Trower as well as bands like Steely Dan, Pink Floyd and Emerson, Lake and Palmer are all part of this eclectic group. And then added to these lists are the ones who learn to play the publicity and promotion game but don't necessarily have the musical credentials to be called legendary. This is not meant as a criticism. There are many ways to reach the top and more ways to entertain the masses. KISS comes immediately to mind, for example. I personally like what they do and have done musically, but I don't know if it really can be attributed to the music more than it can be to the presentation and promotion that originally propelled them. That is one problem a group or artist can face by being too dramatic or dynamic when it comes to performance. It can overshadow the music. The perception might be that they are all show and no go. I think in some ways, great bands like Alice Cooper, The Tubes and, yes, KISS have had their reputations tarnished and tainted because they were putting on tremendous shows for the public. Media types love to find fault with artists in hopes of attracting attention to themselves.

Today in music, as a result of those earlier pioneers of the genre, there are countless artists who have promotion teams pushing them so hard they can't possibly fail, even though their talent is, in fact, marginal at best. Do you really believe the best music available is that which you know about? If you search the Internet, I'm sure you can find all kinds of hidden treasures that no one has taken the time to uncover. I know several myself, and I really don't spend much time searching. Being in the right place at the right time means much more than actually having talent. That's why, when I look back at the Scorpions, I find it hard to fathom how we were ever able to get discovered considering our genesis. There was just little to nothing happening when it came to original rock and roll in West Germany. We simply defied the odds.

Just as it isn't always the best looking guy who gets the girl, it isn't the best group or artist that reaches the pinnacle of rock and roll. I can site some wonderful examples here. Rory Gallagher is one who I think never received his due. Though respected within the industry as one of the greatest blues guitarists ever to come down the pike, on a par definitely with Clapton and Beck to be sure, he just never found the right support to give him the needed push. (Dieter, in fact, produced an album for him in the early 1980's, *Jinx*.) Without that, no one can ever hope to rise above the status of "cult" hero, especially today, when there is so much out there competing for the limited amount of attention available. That is what many don't realize. You can be the greatest guitar player the world has ever known, but that doesn't mean anyone will notice or care. Presence and presentation is just as much a part of performance as talent, and don't let anyone tell you differently. Herman Ze German is hardly the world's greatest drummer. Frankly, there are many much better. But the reason you are reading this book is as much a tribute to the presentation of my work as any talent I might otherwise actually have. Oh sure, I do think I have some talent. (I can walk and chew gum simultaneously!) One has to have a little arrogance to become famous. But I'm not going to sit here (Or anywhere else for that matter...) and tell you I'm Buddy Rich or Gene Krupa. (I would really have to be stupid to do that since both of them are dead...) I really just think, as I said before, it's sometimes a matter of fate – being in the right place at the right time. I was that night in England when I crossed paths with Michael Schenker.

Of course, there are other reasons groups and artists fail to catch on with the public. Labels lose interest. Groups fail to capture the imagination of the audiences on the road. Inner ego clashes. The list is truly endless. To sustain as we did for so many years is a tribute to our ability to work together, and yet, as I mentioned, there was a slight twinge of curiosity beginning to show itself within my music and my life. Perhaps there was more for Herman than just playing drums in the Scorpions. I was content but curious – sort of like a Bill Clinton at a beauty pageant. It was during this tour that I did begin to wonder as my mind began to wander.

Our tour lasted throughout most of 1991, again seeing much of the world (Yawn...) along the way. The fans seemed really to notice very little with regard to the new album as compared to the predecessor. We were still the Scorpions, and that was what mattered to most of them, though in truth our sets began resting on our past laurels and accolades more than they did on our present album excluding, of course, "Wind of Change". When you have a catalog of popular songs as we had amassed and accumulated through the years, there is only so much that can be presented on stage during the time we had allotted to us between sexual interludes. (But even the sex got old, believe it or not. No, I don't mean that we only attracted a bunch of geriatrics in iron lungs and wheelchairs now that we were a bit older... I meant the act and routine itself got old.) And so even though technically we were touring in "support of" our *Crazy World* album, the bulk of our 90 minutes on stage was dedicated to our history. We had no other choice. If we didn't play someone's favorite, we'd surely be tagged with the label of being insensitive or uncaring regarding our fans' wishes or egocentric asses by critics hoping to topple us from atop the apple cart.

One very notable appearance we made during this tour of "change" was a performance in our native country. We had the honor of opening a concert at the Berlin Wall called, appropriately, "The Wall", at the exact spot where the separation of east and west was such a predominant part of the Cold War. Roger Waters of Pink Floyd put together an all-star extravaganza of artists to take part in that event, which made us initially wonder why the hell we were invited. Bryan Adams, Cyndi Lauper, Jeri Hall (Mick Jagger's wife) took part as well. (After seeing the line up, we figured we must have been the drawing card...) Each performer played one of the songs from the classic Floyd album. Our contribution was that of playing the song "In the Flesh".

Though it is often said, it's most difficult to be appreciated at home, if you can imagine this, we were treated like royalty by the promoter of the event. For example, as a part of the show, we rode on to the stage in a big, decadent, white, stretch limousine, which, in some ways, was the epitome of what the Cold War was all about. I don't know if that was a point they were trying to make, but we weren't, as I said, a political band, so we did what we were told to do without too much concern for our placement on the world's stage. What has to be mentioned about the procession or motorcade is that local Hell's Angels on motorcycles (As if they would have been on foot...) escorted the limo – six or ten in front and the same number at the back – on to the stage. (By the way, the difference between European Hell's Angels and those in America is quite stark to say the least. Those of you in America remember only "Altamont", whereas we in Europe know why the Rolling Stones chose members of that group to do security for their concert. In Europe, they are completely different.) I recommend highly that you watch "The Wall" concert on DVD because it was a spectacular event not just for those of us who grew up in postwar West Germany but also for everyone everywhere who just enjoys the grandeur of a great spectacle.

20
IF YOU CAN'T STAND THE HEAT...
GET OUT OF THE SCORPIONS!

A s the tour wound down, Herman Ze German did as well, as we began work on what would be my final studio album with the Scorpions, *Face the Heat*. In fact, gone, already, was Francis. I think it's important to at least touch upon the circumstances surrounding his departure. I can say, it is hardly as innocent as he portrays it on his website. Simply put, we fired him as well as our accountant Dieter Winkler. Francis was the CEO of the Scorpions, a company we had created for tax benefits and purposes. We basically had lost confidence in what he and Winkler, with whom he worked closely, had been doing. That's as inoffensively as I can put it. You fill in the blanks however you wish. We had a lot of suspicions, and we really were not comfortable about the entire situation. I will keep this brief, but I will say there was a lot more to it. I just don't wish to go into it at this point in time. Incessant whining and belly-aching about the past will never lead to anything more than just more whining and belly-aching. This book is written to entertain, amuse and celebrate a great band, not become a kiss and tell piece garbage that is meant to provide innuendo, speculation and scuttlebutt for those who enjoy hearing about the problems of others. However, I think I have left enough of a trail in my wake here to give you a pretty good idea as to what happened.

As for myself, I really began to feel as if my own time was growing short with the band as well. Some of that was the result of the treatment I was receiving from the remaining members. For the first time, I was completely locked out from the songwriting on an album. My replacement in the writing was a fellow from Los Angeles named Mark Hudson. He worked with Klaus and Rudolf through the recommendation of someone, though, in truth, I don't know exactly who.

Face the Heat, itself, was a well-produced album. I will say that. However, I really didn't like the songs on it if I am going to be completely honest. Some will surely say that my opinion was simply "sour grapes". So be it. But if you want the truth, I just didn't think they were up to the standard we had previously set with the remainder of our catalog.

At that point, for me playing in the band seemed much more like the band had evolved into Klaus and Rudolf's supporting cast, not so much a band of five equals, six or even seven or eight if you wish to count Dieter and go back to Michael and Uli. Throughout all the prior years and the previous successes, we worked together. We were a "team". I think that is really what made me start to assess and consider all my options quite seriously. I had written numerous songs through the years, and needed an outlet. It was apparent the outlet wasn't going to be within the band's context. So that meant I needed to really do some inner soul searching.

There were other elements adding to the confusion, as well. There was yet another change in producers, as we had committed to Bruce Fairbairn before making *Crazy World* and honored that commitment, even though we were so very pleased with the work Keith Olsen did. One thing in this world that should never be compromised is a man's word, and in that case, we remained steadfast in honoring that which we had verbally put in place. No formal contract had been signed, and I suspect most bands in our position would have simply kept

215

dancing with the same date. But as I said, we weren't like that, and so Olsen was sent packing and Fairbairn came aboard to give us his version of our music. But with each change came an added wedge between the members, as the band was more than simply growing apart. It was verging on an estrangement. Every change added to the division and separation. From six we were now down to only 3 of the "original" members. As I said, a quick look around at all that was happening gave me a very real sense that I was next and my days were numbered, and I didn't really question it. It was only a matter of time, and the clock was clearly ticking.

I remember when we met with Fairbairn for a preproduction meeting for the *Face the Heat* album, we were all sitting around in one room listening as he played the demos, and he told us he liked what he heard. However, I wasn't so sure of his sincerity. He sounded a great deal more like a politician than a producer. I'm sure if I had told him the world was flat he would have found some way to agree with me. I was used to Dieter who always told us straight out what he liked or didn't like, and I think in some ways that may have ultimately spelled his demise. Some people want to hear the truth while others will say they do while expecting the truth to mean what they want to hear. Ego can often destroy as I've alluded throughout this book, and the deterioration of the Scorpions might well be attributed to that. I'm not without sin in this area at all, so please don't think I'm trying to point fingers at others. I was just as much a product of my own ego as the rest of the guys.

Anyway, during that initial meeting with Fairbairn, he asked if we wanted to continue on the lighter side of rock, or if we wanted to go heavier. We were a bit confused by the comment and wondered if Fairbairn really knew what we did. We all felt that the previous album was quite in line with all that we had built our reputation on over the previous 15 years. However, with little choice being given, Rudolf, Matthias and myself, said we'd prefer to go heavier because we felt that would be more in line with what our fans expected, and we preferred, even though, as I said, we felt the previous album was very good. It appeared we had only two options, and we didn't want him to turn us into the next ABBA, which it sounded as if he may have had in mind. Remember, Led Zeppelin influenced us initially, and just as had happened when they released their third album which was a dramatic contrast to their first two, some of our fans after *Crazy World* may have been a little disappointed in the direction we were headed. Can't imagine why or how but not everyone likes soulful, boogie rock and roll – at least that was the bread that Fairbairn was buttering. And so we bought the loaf and thought maybe it would be best to go back in the direction of our roots.

Also contributing to what was quickly deteriorating into a full-blown cluster-intercourse, was the addition of our new bass player, Ralph Riekermann. I knew Ralph from some production work I had done for my friend Dave Cooper. As you may recall, he (Cooper) played on my first solo album, *Herman Ze German and Friends*. Laypeople often overlook or even disregard a bass player not really knowing why he's there in the first place. But for us, or more appropriately, for any drummer worth a damn, the bass player was and is vital. Together we make up the "rhythm section". It is our responsibility to provide the foundation for all the virtuosity out front. This is what is called in the industry the "pocket", and in this case, it wasn't there. Though Riekermann was a very good player, perhaps even better than Francis in many ways, there just wasn't the same feel to anything we were doing.

When the album was finally released, the "politically incorrect" "Alien Nation" was the first single. Keep in mind, the lyrically upbeat ballad "Wind of Change" was the previous single, and so when we sent out the very hard driving, heavy rock song "Alien Nation" with it's extremely pessimistic and dark lyric laced with racist overtones, most radio stations didn't know what to do with it, though I suspect many simply filed it in the circular filing cabinet. They were waiting for another "innocent" power ballad filled with optimism and hope, and we gave them only the power without the ballad serving a message they probably didn't appreciate. We were disappointed in their behavior to say the least, and yet, they were rightfully disappointed in us as well.

After the negative response, the label decided it would be best to release another ballad to appease the radio stations, and so we released "Under The Same Sun" which was written by Hudson, Fairbairn and Klaus. But as is always the case when you try to kiss-ass, they, the radio stations, didn't care for the song, and, as such, didn't play it because they said it wasn't Scorpions music. I can't say that I disagree because a look at the writers pretty much tells the story. When you have too many cooks, you can't help but stray from the original recipe. Our stew had simmered too long, and we had begun to get too many chefs with their spatulas in the pot.

I know I have been a bit harsh with my criticism of this album, but in fairness, there were some high points like the third single we released, "Woman". Written by Klaus and Rudolf, I felt that it was true Scorpion rock and roll, and the video for the song was fantastic. However, the fans had a different tale to tell because the sales continued to slump and were hardly what we expected or had become accustomed to with our previous offerings. All the touring in the world couldn't and wouldn't help.

The label, as they always did, started pointing fingers at everyone except themselves for perhaps their own errors in marketing the product. We pointed a finger at them, though I won't bother to mention which one. But the truth was, in my opinion, there was plenty of blame to go around. As for me, I had been reduced to being just a member of the band. Dieter wasn't there to kick me or the others in the ass, and perhaps I personally may have not played as well as I could have because my heart wasn't into it 100%. Though I truly think I played as well as I ever had or at least as well as the material required, it still may not have been my best. I did enjoy the way Fairbairn handled me, yet it wasn't the same as recording with Dieter. Again, in stark contrast to Dieter's hard-line approach, which at times had me playing the same damned thing 100 times in an effort to get it perfect, and much more like Olsen on the previous album, Fairbairn only asked me play each song about three times before telling me he'd fix any of the mistakes in the mix. If it were to come to a debate, personally I don't think it had any adverse affect on the music, but it was different.

As for the label's failures, they were the ones behind the choice of singles, and they were trying to push us toward what they thought the market was. We weren't kids in a grunge band, but that is what they wanted us to be. We were old-timers for rock and roll, and there is nothing more disgusting than people who try to be something they aren't. We were not self-conscious of our age or anything of that kind. We were proud of who we were, and we didn't think we needed to change our image. As I said, the fans didn't buy any of it. Our true fans didn't need us to be 25 again!

In the fall of 1993, we began a tour of the world yet again that would run most of the next year. I really didn't have my heart in the tour, even though we journeyed to four continents playing for very excited fans. I guess I had just had enough of it all. I don't know if the others knew how I was feeling, but I felt much more reclusive, and in a way, excluded – like an employee rather than a partner. It was nothing against Klaus or Rudolf or Matthias. I love them like brothers. They had their vision, however, and they carried the ball throughout most of our time together. But for me, it was like I was on the outside looking in. I kind of felt like the kid stuck inside having to take a violin lesson while they were the kids out in the street in front of my house playing football.

21
THE LAST DANCE

As the tour closed and my role within the band seemed fated to diminish ever further as Klaus and Rudolf continued to take more control of the music and direction, I began to think about and remember my past. I could not be angry or even remotely disappointed because, as I thought about it, I realized, honestly, that even though we all worked together to make the Scorpions, without Klaus and Rudolf we probably would not have gotten where we did. And further, they were the ones who opened the door for me. When I was banging on the pots and pans in the kitchen I could not have imagined I would travel the world several times over, make a small fortune financially, meet heads of state and even see Fresno.

There was one more Scorpion album to be released prior to my final bow with the band, and that was another live album, *Live Bites,* which we recorded in Mexico City, Leningrad, San Francisco, Berlin and Munich from the period 1988 through the *Face the Heat* Tour in 1994. I felt the album itself was very good. Was it better than *World Wide Live?* Well, that can be debated, of course, but to me each has its own merits, and I don't like to spend time comparing one to the other. If you like something, it's good. It really doesn't matter what I think. I admit that I tend to be considered a biased critic, but I think the cuts included on the album show exactly how good we were during those five or six years. However, unlike a lot of groups that will record a live album every few years, it wasn't a rehash of the old since the bulk of the album consisted of songs that had been on the albums after *World Wide Live*. That was something that some found difficult to swallow I am sure, yet it was meant as a continuation of the prior album not for purposes of supplanting. Sure some wondered where was "Rock You Like a Hurricane" and "Still Loving You" but again, the idea wasn't to try and better our prior work, but simply to give the audience some new cuts to basically extend our first album from 80 minutes to 160. So our later hits, "Tease Me, Please Me", "Rhythm of Love" and, of course, "Wind of Change" are the centerpieces on the album. So, honestly, comparing the two live albums would be the same as comparing both of them to the Tokyo Tapes from the late 1970's. Yet, when all three are combined, you have one of the most complete, chronological histories of live performances any band has ever had!

As we returned to Germany and began to consider the next step, which would eventually be the group's album *Pure Instinct*, I was, in truth, not all that enamored with the demos I heard for the album, to put it quite mildly. I better understood how Dieter felt when listening to what we had proudly assembled as our song list for *Savage Amusement,* or how Uli must have felt after *Taken By Force*. To me the songs sounded like prefabricated, boilerplate rubbish without any trace of personality, identity or soul. There wasn't anything that was along the lines of what I knew our fans would want, expect or, most importantly, deserve. They were definitely spiraling in a negative direction. In my opinion, they were getting away from the Scorpion entree – straight ahead, hard-driving rock and roll – digressing to foreign territory that seemed completely out of synch with who they had worked over 20 years to become. As they were excitedly playing the demos for me, bragging about their creations along the way (Dr. Frankenstein probably had a similar sense of glee until his monster was released on the world…), at no time did they even remotely ask me for any input.

Note, I'm saying "they" rather than "we" throughout this discussion because, honestly, that was the way I was feeling. After having been snubbed on the previous album as a writer, I was more than a little bit disappointed in the whole situation. I thought at some point clearer heads would prevail, and they might recognize that maybe the missing ingredient in our music was the open forum that invited input from all of us in all aspects of the music making process. I suspect they just felt that it really was the record company's fault that the prior album didn't sell so well. Or maybe they recognized that there were too many "outsiders" involved in the writing and recording. They felt I was no longer part of the inner circle and made it quite clear to me, especially Klaus. After his success with "Wind of Change", which, keep in mind, was at that point several years in the rear view mirror, they had every intention of making not only the new album but all future albums featuring songs exclusively from he and Rudolf. Again, in my opinion, the end result, at least with *Pure Instinct* (I don't recall if I've even heard anything by them after that.) was more a Klaus Meine solo album than a Scorpions album.

A group will forever be a group regardless of what any smaller faction within that body may want to believe. The idea of the "stars aligning" is not mythical in the least. It is real. Those in music often learn harsh lessons when they try to create "magic". Magic isn't created. It's inspired. Whether it is realized or not, I am sure everyone has, at one time or another, been in a situation that inspires them to a higher level. You may be innocuously going about your daily routine, but then, suddenly, perhaps out of nowhere, a twist of fate occurs, and you are surrounded by a group of individuals or events that just seem to raise your performance a notch or two. It doesn't take much to go from mediocrity to greatness. However, the moment that that combination of elements is altered, even if only slightly, the magic seems to disappear and it is almost impossible to recapture once it is gone. I am sure there are those of you reading this who perhaps have never even considered this concept. And yet, in my mind, it is as genuine as the beauty of a young Sophia Loren. (Actually, she's even more beautiful today…) It is the epitome of synergetic logic. The strength of the many always overcomes the strength of the few. Or in simpler and more generic terms, two heads are better than one.

There was no animosity whatsoever. There still isn't. That is an important point I hope I've made. As I said, I was grateful for the opportunity that was given to me. It was just time to go, and so amicably and diplomatically I related my feelings to them at that time. "I'm really not into playing on this album," I began. "I'm a bit burned out, and honestly the music just doesn't do anything for me. Why don't you get Curt Cress?" Cress was a very well-known session player in Germany. If they wanted a session player on drums, which was the role I felt I was now "asked" to assume, then I thought they might as well bring in a real session player because they didn't want me. There was no doubt now that my role in the Scorpions, if I stayed, was going to be limited and redefined in a manner I was particularly comfortable with.

As I look back from a more learned and worldly perspective today, I suspect they may have had an ulterior motive behind their headstrong and aggressive behavior toward me, which was an obvious attempt to deceive and manipulate the fans. By "giving me the gate" outright, they would have risked the alienation of fans who would not like or agree with their behavior. It was a political move to be sure. They wanted to find a way to simply nudge me out the door, and make it look like it was my own choice to move on.

I think what it really came down to was very simple, really. They didn't want to share the wealth any longer. As such, they committed the cardinal sin when it comes to the music industry. They allowed a Deutche Mark symbol to fill their thoughts rather than the production of great music and even better albums, or actually at that point, CD's. I don't know the structure of the band after I left, so I cannot say with all certainty, but I suspect what ultimately happened is they decided they could hire a drummer and simply put him on a salary rather than share percentages on album sales, concert performances, merchandise and everything else related to the band. Such individuals are called

"Hired Guns" in the music industry. In the end, it would mean a split of the big pie fewer ways.

In some ways, the motives are becoming much more obvious now some 15 years after the fact. The remaining members of the group are seemingly in the process of trying to rewrite history in a conscious effort to erase whatever true legacy of the band may exist. At least that is what appears to be happening from the outside. Having been unable to produce a "hit" over the past decade and a half, I understand the current line up, whatever it may be, is rerecording some of our songs as I write this book. Some may ask why they would need to do this? It does seem rather silly. I mean they could easily record a live album featuring all the songs rather than doing it in the studio. If you ask me, it is actually rather transparent to be honest. The original songs are still played on the radio, and fans still buy the original albums. By rereleasing the old songs with the new line up they can hope radio stations will start playing the new versions, which would mean Dieter, Francis, Uli, Michael and myself as well as anyone else who may be able to claim a piece of the action each time a song is played will no longer get anything more than perhaps the writer's share we may be legally due since we are not part of the new performances. I really don't understand this sort of thing, and I suspect the fans will not be fooled. Putting out a newly recorded "greatest hits" CD is purely a blatant attempt to capitalize on the past by changing it to better suit the needs and desires of the individuals in the present.

So as has been the demise of so many groups, it all comes back to money, and that's a shame. The fans are the ones who lose out in such situations. As for the *Pure Instinct* album, it fell flat on its face. I'm not saying this out of spite. The proof is in the pudding. From the millions in sales, as had been the norm for our prior albums, to a pedestrian number somewhere in the range of a few hundred thousand copies, the Scorpions had finally been toppled from atop the Mount Olympus of rock royalty we had worked so hard to climb. They had been transformed into just another classic rock band on the "senior circuit" that had perhaps stayed just a little too long and seemed destined to rest on their laurels. Even though the album had a fairly successful top 20 single, "You and I", the fans just weren't interested any longer. Now maybe it was because they (the fans) read between the lines and were disenchanted with what the band was doing. Or, more likely, they, too, just didn't feel the music was Scorpion music. Who is to say? I only know that the desire for money, and the new contract we had for publishing that gave more to the writers was ultimately the final straw that broke the camel's back. The golden goose was now only able to lay eggs of fool's gold.

In the subsequent years, I do not believe the group, in any incarnation, has produced a single million-selling album or hit single. Somehow, I think this leaves the argument open as to my real place in the history of the band. But, of course, there were others who were vital as well, like Dieter. However, in the simplest timeline of history one can look and say, as Dieter has already done in his foreword, before Herman Ze German arrived on drums, there were lyrics like "Steamrock Fever" and little to nothing in the offing... After he left, once again the cupboard was bare. But in between, the Scorpions made more than music... We made history.

22
A NEW DAWN

So there I was, for the first time in 20 years, without a job. Perhaps I was in the midst of a midlife crisis of some sort, or maybe it was just the right time. But regardless of the situation, my time as a Scorpion was up, and so I packed my snare, kick and hi-hat and prepared to move on. I felt there was more out there for Herman Ze German, and a cordial adieu, adios, sayonara, dasvidania, farewell and auf wiedersehen was in order. I was far from walking away from music all together. I was simply saying goodbye to two decades of history, and embarking on the next phase of my life. (If one can simply say goodbye to almost half of his life…)

I understand there are those within this world who think a drummer is only a drummer. They thought Ringo would disappear after the Beatles, for example. (Some probably think it would have been for the best… However, I'm not among that group.) And truthfully, if I were only a drummer that might easily have become the case. Thankfully, the training at the Saarbrucken Music Academy, for all the fun I have had at their expense throughout this book, afforded me more than a few options. Remember, there is reverence and respect in all humor. Imitation (And I will personally add mockery…) will forever be the sincerest form of flattery.

Having been around the music industry for more than 30 years at that point, I had seen so much that I felt could have been done differently and better. For example, I had always thought about the mistakes made by record companies in their handling of artists and music, some of which I have alluded to within this book. (Such things are almost a certainty given the fact that you have overly rigid businessmen interacting with overtly laid-back musicians.) I felt there was a place for a real musician on the other side of the bargaining table and probably a place for someone like me as well... I had heard so many talented artists tell their tales of woe that I thought surely there had to be options other than the obviously political ones that existed in most record companies.

It is easy to say here that many of the bands we worked with on the road were a little bit more than simply disenchanted with the labels with which they had signed. (I suspect most would have been happier with an inflamed case of hemorrhoids since both are pains in the butt.) I don't recall hearing too much praise coming from artists about their label. Okay, so a great many should realistically have been counting their lucky stars that anyone even noticed them because, frankly, they sucked. But for those with more than a shred of talent, I understood how they felt. I could relate it to the way I felt when we were with RCA. It was clear they didn't know what to do with us, and as a result, it led to frustration. It wasn't really their fault. RCA was hardly considered a "rock" label, and so the A and R department (Artists and Repertoire) was probably ill-equipped to handle one. I suspect, now as I look back, they just really had no real interest in us since our songs didn't include the steady drone of a bass drum and a lyric about someone shaking their booty. Those who originally signed the band to the label had, more than likely, departed to pursue other options (Like renting "tandem" bikes on Malibu Beach...). The turnover at labels is always quite high. I had seen some great bands that seemed destined for big things fall by the wayside because they just didn't have the support they deserved. So many "should have beens" that wound up "never weres" because they simply signed on the bottom line with the wrong pen.

Well, I felt my opportunity was there to try to make a difference at least to the extent and degree that my name and financial wherewithal could. I was hardly capable of raising the dead (That was better left to the people who created Viagra.), but I felt that I could bring integrity to the music industry I thought it might have lacked. (Hell, at times there was more honesty in the Nixon White House than at many record labels. Many. Not all. As it is with agents and managers and just about everything else in the world, there are some outstanding labels as well. I have been blessed to work with some of these within my career.) With the concept somewhat developed in my head, I immediately contacted my friend Prince Albert of Monaco who not only is a great music lover, but also one of the truly wonderful people I've ever had the opportunity to meet. He was a big fan of the Scorpions and a drummer himself as well. (Being the Prince, he was by far the best percussionist in all of Monaco, hands down! Who the hell was going to argue?) As a result, we had met and gotten to know each other while I was living in Monte Carlo. However, initially, when I mentioned my idea to him, that of starting our own record label, he was a bit skeptical. (Columbus, I'm sure, probably received a similar reaction from Queen Isabella initially.) But as I detailed and discussed it further with him, he began to recognize that we could do something very special. And so together we broke the proverbial bottle of champagne on the bow of the ship we christened Monaco Records in 1996 with the production and release of our first album by a German artist I loved named Thomas Perry. Shortly thereafter, we also signed a great artist from America named Gregory Darling who had previously been working for Polygram with his band Darling Cruel. Darling and his band had already achieved a gold album for their only release for Polygram, so we thought a lot of him and his chances to pull even bigger numbers for our much more specialized and personal label. We also signed a world music group named Neapolies from Italy that I felt had a sound that was destined to catch on and surely was deserving of a forum for release. For the next several years we brought forth talent that we believed was worthy of our name and, honestly, we did have some very talented artists in our fold.

But with all things, of course, there was an end in sight to this venture. To be quite honest, the music industry changed drastically with the advent of the Internet. Downloads replaced CD's, and so the need for labels decreased significantly as the big distribution companies like Sony wouldn't buy our product and help get it out there to the masses. And so I decided to close down the company and go on to other adventures in life.

Even though I was technically "at home" during that period of time in Monte Carlo with my family, honestly, there was very little time for me there as I was seemingly attending to countless other things I sometimes wrongly deemed as more important than Anne Marie and Leah. Not really more important. That's not the right way to put it being completely honest. At no time was there anything more important than my family. It was my priorities that were screwed up. I was, myself, motivated by money rather than doing that which I should have done. Okay, so some of the separation was caused by the passing of my parents in Germany, my father in August of 1996 and my mother in June of 1998. This left me on the road going back and forth from Monaco to Germany handling their affairs and other related responsibilities during most of those years. Remember, I was an only child. And then add to that the time I had to spend trying to promote and build my new record company, and I think you can see my life was not one spent on the golf course. However, in retrospect, I now realize how much I missed in not being there for my daughter or my wife, both of whom I know loved me and needed me as part of their everyday life. They both deserved better. I said all of this before, but it's worthy of reiteration. I was not a model father, nor hardly the perfect husband. It is only in recent years that I have finally come to understand all of that. And so, as I mentioned previously, in 1998 Anne Marie filed for divorce, and our life "together", such as it was, was over.

As I mentioned earlier, it was about a year after Monaco folded (The record label, not the Principality. We closed the door on the label in 2002, and as far as I know, the monarchy is still going strong.) that I met Claudia. I really didn't know professionally where I was headed or what exactly I wanted to do. But with her musical talents, which were and are enormous, I thought it would be fun to do something together. By the beginning of 2004, we did our first project together called "Art Meets Music". The basic idea was to introduce paintings from known music artists supported by live music. Ronnie Wood of Rolling Stones took part in the first show. The second featured the work of a painter named Roland Muri from Switzerland. Though he isn't a music artist, he is an incredible talent. As part of the shows, the paintings, themselves, were posted all about the room, while we projected images of the artwork above the stage where our band that featured Claudia and myself, played. Along with our band on the stage was a bevy of beautiful dancing girls to enhance the presentation. But even though the artists sold a lot of pictures, we only did two shows as the production costs became quite prohibitive. But that doesn't diminish the success we achieved for the artists in terms of sales, or the quality of the music we released on the *Art Meets Music* CD.

In 2005, Pete York, a long time friend and the original drummer with the Spencer Davis Group, and I decided to form a band called Drum Legends. We added another great Swiss drummer named Charly Antolini. Claudia took part as well playing sax in the back-up band that was made up of other outstanding musicians from Munich. We were together for more than a year playing all over Germany in town halls that were sold out. The set up for the shows was quite unique. Pete, Charly and I had our drums out front at the foot of the stage with the remainder of the band playing behind in support. As you can imagine, we played at least 36 different version of "Wipeout", and had some wonderful drum wars, as we competed constantly in a cordial competition for attention! For me, this was heaven. Playing with good friends who were also outstanding musicians, I couldn't have been happier. In my opinion, though many may not know his name, Charly Antolini is one of the greatest technical drummers I have ever seen or had the pleasure of working with. The same goes for Pete. I have to say

Pete is also by far the most jovial and light-hearted guy I've ever met in music. I believe if he had not become a drummer, he surely would have been a comedian. At our concerts, he would do a monologue between the songs that would have the audience in stitches. He quite well could have been the next Benny Hill. We worked together, a bit later, on my audio book, *My Life As A Scorpion*. He played the part of a magazine writer who was interviewing me, and together we had about as much fun as two old bastards can legally have.

In the summer of 2006, we, the Drum Legends, had an offer to play in Spain. However, a little dispute broke out between Charly and the rest of the group. As a result, it pretty much brought the Drum Legends to an end. But it doesn't change the fact that for me it was a wonderful experience. The mere fact that I was playing with such incredible percussionists forced me to rethink my own work habits and spend much more time working on my chops in practice sessions.

After taking a little, and I think given all that I had done in my life, well-deserved break, I again assessed and weighed my options. I decided perhaps it was the right time to revive a version of Herman Ze German. And so I began to write songs with the aid of not only Thomas Perry but my wife Claudia as well, and in 2007 I released my latest solo album in Germany, which initially was titled *I'm Back*. After local success within the fatherland, I decided to release it worldwide and in 2010 it was re-titled and repackaged as *Take It As It Comes*, which is the single on the album, not to mention my philosophy of life as I enter this stage of my career. (The video for the song can be seen on my website. It features not only myself, but also Claudia playing sax.) I think for those who have heard the album they now realize what Herman Rarebell is all about – hard-driving rock and roll meant for all to enjoy.

EPILOGUE

Have you ever taken time to ponder the odds against your being exactly where you are today? I know that sounds rather cryptic, and yet if you were to take time to think about how truly ambiguous everything around you can be, it might stagger you to consider the odds you have defied just to be where you are today. If you look back at your life and see the road upon which you have traversed, you might find it was filled with crossroads and junctions that could have led you to a completely different destiny. And yet you are where you are right now because of the choices you made en route.

When I think back about my own life, I realize that I have had an interesting ride. That's putting it mildly. I have had what I am sure many would refer to as a fantasy life, though I am not one who will ever use such highfalutin verbiage. I will only say that my life has been what it has been. I understand that's quite profound, but I can only speak from my heart. There was a time not so long ago, actually, when I would have said I have lived a life filled with regret, and the entirety of this book would have dwelled on what should have been. I was misled, and my allegiance misaligned. Yet I made my own choices, and so I cannot and should not point fingers at others. However, people are often tricked by the lies they tell themselves. I was no different. I could lie with the best of them! A part of that was the greatest lie of all, drugs. When added to the mix, you can see how easily I led myself astray.

In truth, we all have the potential to have a fantasy life if we accept the fates as they come to us. However, as I look back, I think how fortunate I am to be alive. I still have countless regrets, but not in areas that most might believe. They have changed quite significantly as the years have passed. My perspectives have been altered through strides I've made in personal growth. I now find myself regretting many of the choices I made within my life. I regret the mistakes I made with regard to the setting of my priorities. I see this book as a cleansing of the soul in many ways as I have tried to express myself as openly and honestly as any man could. As perhaps you recognized, I am a long way from canonization.

I have learned a great many lessons within my journey through this life. For example, I have discovered that we all have our purpose and place. Some find it, and they wisely realize they have found it for the betterment of others. Many more search for their entire life without even an inkling as to why they were put in this place and time. And yet, sadly, there are some who don't seem to care. You have to believe in a higher being, or you cannot possibly find peace. That much I am sure of. I know this is a bold and perhaps alienating opinion given the times within which we live, but I do have strong feelings about this. There has to be a reason why we are all here. If you ask me, finding that answer is finding utopia. To endlessly argue and debate the question is to live a life in turmoil and confusion.

I am not trying to be Aristotle or Plato here. There's nothing within these words that is unique or unilateral. I am so very thankful to all of you who are reading this book. You are the ones who have given me a life. Life is not about me. It's all about that which I can bring to the lives of others to enhance or brighten their existence here in some way. Each person I meet, I wish to have a relationship with. It doesn't matter how deep the relationship might be. It may be little more than a simple hello as we pass each other at an airport. We may never see each other again, and yet, we shared a relationship for that instance in time. The world is filled with teachers; we only need to be open to their lessons. Each person offers something different and can teach me that which I may never have had the chance to learn had we not met. I'm quite grateful because I have been blessed to have the opportunity to make people happy and to see that happiness etched on their faces and in the glow within their eyes as we played our music for them time and again. And yet, on a much smaller stage, I am just as proud of the happiness I may bring to those I meet while having lunch or afternoon tea just by saying please or thank you. You see it's not the size of the stage that matters but what you do with it. Yes, the world is truly a stage where each of us plays a part. There are no small parts, only diminutive actors.

I know there will be arguments contrary to the opinions I have expressed within these pages, but in truth, I don't think it really matters. What matters is that we have had the chance to share some time together. The time you have given me is the most precious of all gifts. And so to you I say thank you.

There are those who will attempt to cast a cynical pall over all of this by saying that I can spout such things because I am on top of the mountain. But guess again. I am nothing more than another human with all the same qualities, good and bad, as everyone else. That is the message I've tried to relate throughout the preceding text. I don't pretend to be better. I don't arrogantly try to impress others with who I am or expect them to bow down to my résumé of accolades and accomplishments. Today I live a quiet life where many of my acquaintances only know me as Herman. I prefer it this way. I will forever be Herman "Ze German" Rarebell. No one can take that away from me, nor can they forever ignore my legacy, whatever it may have been or ultimately will become. And yet, I am no different than the rest of you. We all have a legacy whether it comes from having raised children properly who contribute to our world in a positive manner or simply being the best person we can be. I know that I wasn't the greatest father in the history of parenthood, and yet, I am proud of my daughter Leah, and today we share a very close relationship. I visit her as often as possible in Scotland where she currently attends school. I am thankful for that and to Anne Marie for her work in raising her to be so very special.

I am certain there are those who will wonder if writing a book like this and sharing so many intimate details about my life will perhaps taint the image I have painted of myself for my family and friends. For example, there is my daughter to consider. What will she think? What will her friends think? I do not know what she knows about my life beyond the stories I have related to her through the years, but in truth, I hope she will take the time to read this book. As a parent, I want her to see me as human, learn from my mistakes, and know that I will love her no matter what choices she makes just as I hope she will love me regardless of how tarnished my image may become. Showing your child you are human is perhaps the most important step a father can take. Within this book I think I've been quite frank with regard to the number of poor decisions I have rendered throughout my life. When presented with similar situations, I do hope Leah will use the information to help make wiser choices than her father made.

If you really want to cut to the chase about life, the one thing that I think is most important is really quite elementary. Treat everyone as you wish to be treated. That has been, and will forever be, my mantra. Yes, it is a derivative of the "Golden Rule", and yet it goes much deeper than simple verbiage. It is what life is all about. Imagine if everyone thought this way. John Lennon wrote a song about that, and, in my opinion, his views on life may well have contributed to his assassination. He was a threat to the status quo, because he represented a vision that was not welcome. No, I am not offering some sort of conspiracy theory here. However, because he was so outspoken about peace and love of all people he probably seemed much more accessible and approachable than other celebrities, and that may have left the door open to his assailant. But the message cannot be ignored and may be the most important aspect of his vast legacy. Peace and love is really what life is about. So imagine, if you can, a world within which you are last in your life but first in the lives of everyone else.

Do you not truly believe that this would be a better place for not only yourself but for everyone?

Of course, as perhaps you have found within my story, it wasn't always this way for me. The ego can alter our best intentions and our perspective as it did my own at various times in my life. It is only now, in recent years, that I have discovered the secrets to happiness. It isn't about what you do or what you can do but simply that which brings you peace. You cannot put a number on that, nor is there a proper measuring stick to weigh and balance your efforts and achievements. It isn't selfishly motivated in the least. Too many people parade around yelling and screaming about their "rights". Well, just because I may have the "right" to do something it doesn't mean that it's necessarily "right". As I said previously, that is what my friend Michael has always believed, and I agree 100%. I think there are those who seek inner peace with all the wrong guidance. They start with the self. From the get-go they are doomed to failure since it doesn't start with the self. It is always about everyone else. Once you can willingly subjugate yourself to all that is around you, you have reached the point of nirvana. I don't know that I am at rest, but I do know the most joyous feelings, as I have said, come from what I do to make others happy. Ultimately, those efforts bring me joy and make me happy. Life is truly one long chain! So maybe there is selfishness involved, and yet I always want to focus on what makes others happy because the world is about them, not me.

On my new album, *Take It As It Comes*, the title song says it all. It is just about this one thing – inner peace. There are those who live in a constant state of fear. They are worried about what will happen tomorrow. They are worried about what happened today. They are worried about what happened yesterday. All the worrying in the world won't change anything. And yet there are those who will spend every minute of everyday trying to fix things in the past that cannot be fixed. Like a neutered dog, there's no point to looking back there. You can only control the moment, and that which is ahead will be regardless of whether we are a part of tomorrow or not. Thus we have the idea of taking life as it comes.

My life has been filled with so much that I could not have begun to fathom when I was a young boy in West Germany. However, you may ask, given the relative obscurity I fell into after leaving the Scorpions, if I regret my decision. I don't. Not in the least. I have everything I need. For example, after having spent so many years wandering aimlessly and confusing the terms lust and love or at least convincing myself that they were interchangeable, at last I found true love with my wife Claudia. After so many disappointments in that area of my life (And there were substantially more than documented within these pages…), you cannot even begin to imagine the joy that such a stable and loving relationship has brought to me.

One thing that is important to remember, God brings us here naked, and we are assured of leaving naked. I know that's cliché, but it is also a reality you cannot deny even if you deny the existence of God. We enter with nothing and leave with even less unless, of course, we have done right by others. Then we will forever leave that lasting impression for the world to remember. I have been told that the American author William Saroyan has a beautiful thought inscribed on the headstone of his resting place. The basic thought is, to paraphrase it a bit since it's out in California and I'm in Europe, if you can live your life knowing you have never brought any sorrow or pain to the lives of others or even the life of another, then you have had a good life. What could be more perfectly said or thought?

In case you are interested, I am not affiliated with any particular denomination or religion, but one thing is clear, I do believe in God and love. You can call God whatever you wish. But love and God will forever remain the driving force within all that is good with the world. I believe something created all that is here, and I don't think we evolved from monkeys. Even though there have been times when I, myself, partook in some "monkey business", I hardly think it is enough to draw metaphoric lines of symmetry for the sake of trying to prove a point.

The greatest gift we have is life itself. It is an opportunity to spend whatever time we are given doing what is right. What is all the money in the world worth if you don't use it to benefit others? Or tell me, what is money worth if you are not healthy? Perhaps that brings the thought even closer to home for many. Gifts from God are taken for granted until they are no longer ours. We are helpless within this world. We are all one-step from disaster at any point. Everything and everyone here is transient. We can't take it with us. Wait till next year... (Just threw that one in to see if you were paying attention.) Yes, these are more clichés, and yet how true are the thoughts? That is what you have to ask yourself. Though the phrases may be trite, the thoughts behind them are not.

At my age today, I realize as I think about it, how many of my friends have already left this world. So many who shared the road with me are now only a remembrance in the pages of rock history, as they have exited this stage for that which is beyond here. All they had is still here, while they are no longer with us. And in some cases, what they left behind is a legacy for all to behold. It still brings joy and happiness to many whom they will never have the chance to meet. That is what life is all about.

Believe in yourself. Be happy. Make others happy. Give to other people because you will find that others will give back. Love begets love. There is no place for anger or hate. Yes, these are more clichés. But again, tell me where there is something so bad within any of these thoughts. A good example of this is this book. No, not the physical book, but the fact that I'm writing it. I had a thought about writing a book (Who doesn't?), and yet I had no way to even address the undertaking of such an overwhelming project. I had met my co-writer several years ago through his work with the Rock and Roll Remembers Foundation. About two years ago, he approached me with the idea, and even though, in truth, I knew him only fleetingly at the time through some telephone conversations and emails we had exchanged, I trusted my instincts and his sincerity. I believe I have been rewarded for my faith. Or perhaps it is you who has been rewarded, because you're the ones who are reading this book, and as I said in the dedication, it is written for you. He has helped capture the spirit of my life and my true inner being in a way no one else ever could have. I could never have written this book in English, or even in German to be honest – not like we have together. And so God sent to me just the person who could help me bring to the written page my thoughts in a manner that at times made me shake my head and marvel. And, I'll admit here, he even brought tears to my eyes on a couple of occasions. He got inside of my head, and helped me bring forth all that was bound up inside. I know I have shattered completely the traditional stealth-like protocol for books of this nature. But unlike many others who have "written" an "autobiography", I am not going to try to hide the truth even though Michael is not happy with the inclusion of this admission, nor is he comfortable with the praise. But I wanted it here. This has been a joint effort of two people working together. Michael took my stories, and he gave them literary legs for you. He inspired me to greater creativity through his efforts. He is a genius in my eyes, as I have said time and again within these pages, and he is now a great friend. I will forever believe he was a Godsend. I know, given the sordid details about my past that have come up at various points in this book, there may be those who'll view this statement as blasphemous. So be it. But for me, it is nothing more than simply a statement of the truth.

Several years ago, Claudia introduced me to a book written by a man I regard now as my "teacher", Paramahansa Yogananda. His book, "Autobiography of a Yogi" forever changed my life in ways that I am only now starting to comprehend. I see today as I have never seen before and understand so much more about why things happen the way they do within this world. It has truly changed my life, as I said. I highly recommend it to all of you, as it will surely help you find that which you may not even realize you are seeking. I have since joined his organization, *Self-Realization Fellowship* or *SFR* in Los Angeles (*www.yogananda-srf.org/*). He clearly seems to echo my thoughts, or perhaps I echo his when it comes to life. Though he, of course, comes from India, and I know my first impression of that country was not all that spectacular, given the incident after the ice cream I ate, but I do believe his thoughts and impressions of the world around us seem as concise and accurate today as they were the day they were first written. You don't have to be lost to seek the truth. You only have to be open to it when you see it. That is what stops most people. The message is the problem as most don't like what they find.

And so, this is the life of Herman "Ze German" Rarebell. I don't know if you think differently about me now that you have read these words, but as I've said from the outset, my life isn't about me. It is about you. If, as you were reading you were brought to laughter or pleasant remembrances of times now passed, then I think I have accomplished my goal. At no time did I write anything with the intent of offending anyone. I simply am one who tries to find the humor in all parts of life, and I hope you found it with me as you read. As I hope you could tell, in my opinion life is more about smiles than tears, and so I chose to write a book with my tongue firmly planted in my cheek to insure that ultimately everyone would have fun and understand the spirit of my life as a Scorpion.

Cheers to you all…

Herman

RELATED LINKS

Herman Rarebell
www.hermanrarebell.com

Dieter Dierks
www.dierks-studios.de

The Scorpions
www.the-scorpions.com

Self-realization Fellowship
www.yogananda-srf.org

Rock and Roll Remembers
www.rockandrollremembers.org

Michael Krikorian
krikorianmichael@yahoo.com or krikorianmichael@aol.com

Special Thanks

The following deserve special thanks for helping make this book a reality.

The owner and staff of the Lane's Hotel in Brighton, England.

The hours we spent in the lounge of the hotel putting the basics of this book together cannot be ignored, nor can the hospitality we encountered from everyone there.

Irina Rausch

Tirelessly tolerating our endless changes as she designed the cover artwork for this book.

Svetlana Krikorian

Her help in reeling in the incredible imagination and creativity of her husband as well as providing a grammatical conscience throughout the writing cannot go without mention.

Michael Schenker

Without Michael, this book would not have been possible... Actually, it would have been possible, but it would not have been about my life as a Scorpion. (In other words, blame him!) (Actually, if you think about this, then I should thank his mom and dad... But then I'd be on a track that would lead all the way back to Adam and Eve. Clearly there would be too many people to thank then. So I'll stop with just Michael, but hopefully you'll get the picture.)

And last but not least and perhaps most importantly, Pete Way

For just being Pete Way... And for being a good sport and friend....

CPSIA information can be obtained at www.ICGtesting.com
Printed in the USA
LVOW032133201011

251467LV00008B/128/P